THE BARBOUR COLLECTION
OF CONNECTICUT TOWN
VITAL RECORDS

QUI TRANSTULIT SUSTINET

THE BARBOUR
COLLECTION
OF CONNECTICUT TOWN
VITAL RECORDS

EAST WINDSOR 1768–1860

ELLINGTON PART I —
Vital Records 1786–1850

ELLINGTON PART II —
Marriage Records 1820–1853

Compiled by

Lorraine Cook White

INTRODUCTION

As early as 1640 the Connecticut Court of Election ordered all magistrates to keep a record of the marriages they performed. In 1644 the registration of births and marriages became the official responsibility of town clerks and registrars, with deaths added to their duties in 1650. From 1660 until the close of the Revolutionary War these vital records of birth, marriage, and death were generally well kept, but then for a period of about two generations until the mid-nineteenth century, the faithful recording of vital records declined in some towns.

General Lucius Barnes Barbour was the Connecticut Examiner of Public Records from 1911 to 1934 and in that capacity directed a project in which the vital records kept by the towns up to about 1850 were copied and abstracted. Barbour previously had directed the publication of the Bolton and Vernon vital records for the Connecticut Historical Society. For this new project he hired several individuals who were experienced in copying old records and familiar with the old script.

Barbour presented the completed transcriptions of town vital records to the Connecticut State Library where the information was typed onto printed forms. The form sheets were then cut, producing twelve small slips from each sheet. The slips for most towns were then alphabetized and the information was then typed a second time on large sheets of rag paper, which were subsequently bound into separate volumes for each town. The slips for all towns were then interfiled, forming a statewide alphabetized slip index for most surviving town vital records.

The dates of coverage vary from town to town, and of course the records of some towns are more complete than others. There are many cases in which an entry may appear two or three times, apparently because that entry was entered by one or more persons. Altogether the entire Barbour Collection--one of the great genealogical manuscript collections and one of the last to be published--covers 137 towns and comprises 14,333 typed pages.

TABLE OF CONTENTS

ABBREVIATIONS

ae.------------age
b. ------------born, both
bd.------------buried
B. G.---------Burying Ground
d. ------------died, day, or daughter
decd.---------deceased
f.--------------father
h.--------------hour
J. P.-----------Justice of Peace
m.-------------married or month
res.------------resident
s.--------------son
st.-------------stillborn
w. -----------wife
wid.----------widow
wk.-----------week
y. ------------year

THE BARBOUR
COLLECTION
OF CONNECTICUT TOWN
VITAL RECORDS

EAST WINDSOR VITAL RECORDS
1768 - 1860

Page

ADAMS, (cont.)

Nov. 3, 1842, by Rev. Joseph Scott, of St. John's Ch. ("Margin
gives name "Stephen **BROOME**") 113

Thomas, of Hartford, m. Huldah H. **WELLS**, of East Windsor, Dec.
8, 1841, by Shubael Bartlett 111

ALBE(?), Rufus Strong, see under Rufus Strong **ABBE**

ALCORNE, Mary Ann, m. Alexander **McMASTERS**, b. of Thompsonville,
Mar. 30, 1838, by Rev. Francis J. Clerc, of Grace Ch. 121

ALDERMAN, Charlotte E., m. Judson **HERICK**, Oct. 21, 1846, by Rev.
Henry H. Bates, of St. John's Ch. 120

Julia E., m. Elizur **BATES**, Oct. 21, 1846, by Rev. Henry H.
Bates, of St. John's Ch. 120

ALDRICH, Jacob T., of Colebrook, N. H., m. Elizabeth **PEASE**, of East
Windsor, Aug. 5, 1833, by Rev. Shubael Bartlett 96

Pliny M., of Woonsocket, R. I., m. Celestia **JOHNSON**, of East
Windsor, Nov. 9, 1852, by Rev. James Mather 135

ALEXANDER, Harriet Maria, m. James M. **NEWBERRY**, Dec. 22, 1841,
by Levi Smith 112

Mary, m. William **HERRIDEN**, [Aug.] 12, [1821], by Rev. Thomas
Robbins 84

Mehitabel, of East Windsor, m. Thomas **BURNHAM**, of East Hartford,
May 6, [1829], by Rev. Thomas Robbins, East Hartford 91

Robert, m. Abigail **BANCROFT**, Nov. 28, 1833, by Rev. William
Bently 97

ALLEN, [see also **ALLING & ALLYN**], Alfred, m. Henrietta
THOMPSON, Apr. 17, 1834, by Rev. Shubael Bartlett 97

Alvira L., of East Windsor, m. John **CADWELL**, of Westfield, Mass.,
July 3, 1836, by Rev. P. T. Kenney 100

Amanda P., m. Elizur **RISLEY**, Jan. 4, 1847, by Shubael Bartlett 119

Amilia, m. Alanson **HORTON**, Jan. 10, 1822, by Rev. Shubael
Bartlett, of 2nd church 84

Annah, d. Nathaniel & Annah, b. Oct. 11, 1782 1

Azuba G., of East Windsor, m. Nathaniel P. **HEATH**, of North Troy,
N. Y., Apr. 29, 1840, by Rev. Benjamin C. Phelps, Warehouse
Point 109

Benjamin, of Warren, N. Y., m. Charlotte **PHELPS**, of East Windsor,
May 11, 1828, by Rev. Shubael Bartlett 90

Betsey M., of Ellington, m. James **HAYNES**, of Manchester, Oct.
18, 1835, by Rev. Pardon T. Kenney, of M. E. Ch. 99

Caroline Jane, m. Ralph **BLODGETT**, Sept. 1, 1846, by Shubael
Bartlett 118

Charlotte A., of East Windsor, m. Henry P. **GOWDY**, of Enfield,
Apr. 18, 1833, by Rev. Shubael Bartlett 96

Charlotte R., m. Charles **STEPHENS**, Apr. 14, 1858, by Rev.
W[illia]m M. Birchard 149

Chester, Jr., of Ellington, m. Sophia E. **CARPENTER**, of East
Windsor, Nov. 7, 1847, by Rev. Franklin Fisk 120

Clarissa S., of East Windsor, m. Tho[ma]s I. **HUBBARD**, of

Page

ALLEN, (cont.)
    Jan. 11, 1831, by Rev. Gurdon Robins, of Bapt. Ch.   94
Julia A., m. Jason WELLS, b. of East Windsor, Dec. 23, 1828,
    by Rev. Shubael Bartlett   90
Julia A., m. James U. TERRY, Nov. 28, 1844, by Shubael Bartlett   117
Julia Ann, m. Marcus C. FARNHAM, b. of Broad-Brook, Nov. 7,
    1837, by Rev. John H. Willis   102
Julia R., of East Windsor, m. Elam GOWDY, of Enfield, Oct. 6,
    1831, by Rev. Shubael Bartlett   94
Laura, of East Windsor, m. Horace PHELPS, of Enfield, May 10,
    1827, by Rev. Shubael Bartlett   89
Loretta, m. Henry BARTLETT, b. of East Windsor, Feb. 21, 1839, by
    Shubael Bartlett   106
Lucina, m. Elijah MEACHAM, of Tolland, Apr. 19, 1840, by
    Shubael Bartlett   107
Lucy Ann, m. Phenehas LaFayette BLODGET, June 30, 1844, by
    Shubael Bartlett   114
Luke D., m. Caroline E. PATCHEN, b. of East Windsor, Apr. 10,
    1853, by Rev. James Mather   136
Marietta, of East Windsor, m. John C. ROBERTSON, of South
    Windsor, Apr. 12, 1853, by Rev. Samuel J. Andrews, of Cong.
    Ch.   137
Martha A., m. Sylvester RISLEY, Dec. 31, 1841, by Shubael Bartlett.
    (Perhaps 1840?)   109
Martha C., m. Titus OLCOTT, June 20, 1839, by Shubael Bartlett   106
Mary, d. Nathaniel & Annah, b. July 3, 1780   1
Mary, m. Jabez PHELPS, Dec. 27, 1821, by Rev. Shubael Bartlett
    of 2nd Church   84
Mary M., m. William H. WEEKS, Nov. 24, 1858, at the home of
    Luke Allen, by Rev. E. J. Avery   150
Melissa J., m. Henry SKINNER, b. of East Windsor, Mar. 10,
    1834, by Rev. Shubael Bartlett   97
Miranda, of East Windsor, m. Simeon OLMSTED, Jr., of Enfield,
    Sept. 28, 1831, by Rev. Shubael Bartlett   94
Nancy P., of East Windsor, m. Samuel B. PINNEY, of Ellington,
    this day, [Mar. 17, 1842], by Rev. Edwin C. Brown   111
Noah, Dea., m. Mary POTWINE, Apr. 2, 1822, by Rev. Shubael
    Bartlett of 2nd Church   84
Rhoda E., of East Windsor, m. Samson DUNN, of Albany, N. Y.,
    Dec. 31, 1838, by Rev. Marvin Root   104
Rossanna E., m. Nathaniel C. STRONG, b. of East Windsor, May
    30, 1850, by Rev. John Cadwell   128
Samantha D., m. Otis BARTLETT, b. of East Windsor, Jan. 27, 1841,
    by E. Marsh   109
Samuel, m. Azubah MOODY, b. of East Windsor, this day, [Jan.
    12, 1824], by Asher Allen, J. P.   86
Samuel, of East Windsor, m. Hannah GLEASON, of Enfield, July
    15, 1841, by William Barnes, J. P.   110

Page

AMES, Lydia, of East Windsor, m. William Vine SESSIONS, of
 Wilbraham, Mass., Nov. 26, 1829, by Rev. Shubael Bartlett   92
Stephen, of Lunenburg, Vt., m. Emily B. KINGSBURY, of East
 Windsor, Oct. 3, 1827, by Rev. Shubael Bartlett   89
AMIDON, AMADON, Ebenezer, m. wid. Minerva FOWLER, June 22,
 1845, by Shubael Fowler   117
Ruth Harmoni, m. Rufus Strong ABBE*, July 3, 1842, by Shubel
 Bartlett *(ALBE?)   112
Sanford, m. Elisabeth Ann NICHOLS, Apr. 4, 1847, by Shubael
 Bartlett   119
ANDEREAU, Joseph, m. Albertine NESSBAUMER, Nov. 20, 1856, at
 Warehouse Point, by Rev. Henry McClory of St. John's Ch.   146
ANDERSON, Chester, s. George & Aurelia, b. Dec. 8, 1791   1
Henry, m. Dulcinea ELMER, b. of East Windsor, this day [Nov.
 26, 1840], by Rev. Samuel Spring, of Cong. Ch. East Hartford   109
Stephen Stedman, s. George & Aurelia, b. Feb. 27, 1796   1
Theodosha, d. George & Aurelia, b. May 1, 1798   1
Violette, d. George & Aurelia, b. May 14, 1790   1
ANDRUS, Emeline, m. Hardin STOUGHTON, b. of East Windsor, June 9,
 [1836], by Rev. Marvin Root   100
Roswell S., of Hartford, m. Elizabeth HAYDEN, d. of the late
 Daniel, of East Windsor, Dec. 12, 1838, by Rev. O. E. Daggett, of
 2nd Ch. Hartford   104
APSTEIN, Albert, m. Barbara GEIER, Sept. 3, 1859, at Warehouse Point,
 by Rev. Henry McClory, of St. John's Ch.   152
ARCHER, John, m. Maria A. BUCKLAND, Dec. 12, 1859, by Rev. J. F.
 Sheffield   152
Luther L., of Suffield, m. Pamelia P. PRIOR, of East Windsor, Nov.
 29, 1852, by Rev. C. S. Putnam, of St. John's Ch.   135
Sarah F., m. Stephen W. SPERRY, b. of Suffield, Mar. 4, 1852,
 by Rev. Henry H. Bates, of St. John's Ch., at Warehouse, Pt.   133
ARMSTRONG, Jane E., of Philadelphia, Pa., m. Edward M. JENCKS, of
 Canterbury, Sept. 27, 1850, by Henry H. Bates   129
Richard, of Willington, m. Elizabeth PEARL, of East Windsor,
 Nov. 26, 1829, by Rev. Shubael Bartlett   92
ASPINWALL, George, of Providence, R. I., m. Mary D. PALMER, of East
 Windsor, June 27, 1849, by Rev. Samuel J. Andrews   125
ATCHISON, ATCHINSON, John, m. Olive W. CHAPIN, June 23, 1856,
 by Rev. F. Munson   145
Laura, d. Silvester & Submit, b. Sept. 3, 1794   1
ATHERTON, Newton C., m. Harriet E. HALL, b. of Hartford, Oct. 2,
 1839, by Shubael Bartlett   106
ATKINS, Isaac, m. Mary Ann PARKER, b. of Enfield, July 6, 1850, by
 Rev. Henry H. Bates, of St. John's Ch., Warehouse Pt.   128
ATWOOD, Elizabeth, of East Windsor, m. George SANDERSON, of
 Rockville, Oct. 14, 1849, by Rev. Samuel J. Andrews, of Cong.
 Ch.   126
Timothy, of Rockville, m. Elizabeth GLYNN, of East Windsor, Nov.

Page

BALLARD, John, s. Daniel & Freelove, b. Nov. 19, 1784   4
   William C., of Maine, m. Mary A. NEEDHAM, of Warehouse Pt.,
     Mar. 3, 1850, by Rev. Henry H. Bates, of St. John's Ch.,
     Warehouse Pt.   128
BARBER, BARBAR, Allen P., m. Susan E. THOMPSON, Feb. 12, 1846,
   by Shubael Bartlett   117
   Alonzo R., m. Nancy M. BARBER, Dec. 11, 1844, by O. F. Parker.
     Int. Pub.   115
   Alpheus Harris, m. Lucinda SEXTON, b. of East Windsor, July 2,
     1851, by Rev. Henry H. Bates, of St. John's Ch.   131
   Anne, d. Oliver & Anne, b. Mar. 22, 1778   3
   Anson E., of East Windsor, m. Sarah M. COLTON, of Enfield, May
     16, 1850, by Rev. W[illia]m S. Simmons   128
   Ashbel, m. Elizabeth PHELPS, Sept. 4, 1823, by Rev. Shubael
     Bartlett of 2nd Church   85
   Aurelius B., m. Lucy FULLER, b. of East Windsor, Dec. 26, 1852,
     by Rev. Samuel J. Andrews, of 1st Cong. Ch.   136
   Caroline L., m. Junius M. WILLEY, May 29, 1845, by T. C.
     Brownell, Bishop of Conn.   116
   Cynthia, d. Simeon & Lois, b. Oct. 20, 1772   3
   Delia E., of East Windsor, m. William VINTON, of South Windsor,
     Nov. 29, 1849, by Rev. Samuel J. Andrews, of Cong. Ch.   127
   Edwin, m. Sophia ADAMS, b. of East Windsor, June 7, 1854, by
     Rev. Samuel J. Andrews, of 1st Cong. Ch.   139
   Eldad, Rev. of Milan, O., m. Mrs. Hannah E. CROSBY, of East
     Windsor, Apr. 24, 1834, by Rev. Shubael Bartlett   97
   Elisabeth O., of East Windsor, m. Alfred B. REDFIELD, of Hartford,
     July 5, 1854, by Rev. Julius Marshall Willey, in St. John's Ch.,
     Warehouse Point   142
   Ellen M., m. Lemuel R. LORD, Oct. 15, 1857, by Rev. Frederick
     Munson of 1st Cong. Ch.   147
   Eunice, d. Oliver & Anne, b. July 6, 1772   3
   George W., m. Aurelia ST. CLAIR, Sept. 22, 1844, by Shubael Bartlett 117
   Grove, s. Oliver & Ann, b. July 19, 1769   3
   Hadassah, d. Simeon & Lois, b. Dec. 22, 1784   4
   Henry, s. Oliver, Jr. & Sarah, b. July 2, 1796   4
   Henry, m. Mary PEASE, b. of East Windsor, May 10, 1827, by Rev.
     Shubael Bartlett   89
   Henry, 2nd, m. Emily Terry OSBORN, b. of East Windsor, Jan. 27,
     1829, by Rev. Shubael Bartlett   91
   Jairus, m. Abigail O. THOMPSON, June 16, 1842, by Shubael Bartlett 112
   John, of Palmer, Mass., m. Sarah GRISWOLD, of Wilbraham, Mass.,
     Sept. 15, 1839, by Rev. Benjamin C. Phelps, of Warehouse Point 106
   Joseph A., [m.] Cecelia B. BANCROFT, d. William & Caroline B.,
     Nov. 23, 1852   5
   Joseph A., m. Cecelia B. BANCROFT, b. of East Windsor, Nov. 23,
     1852, by Rev. James Mather   136
   Leete, d. Oliver & Anne, b. Apr. 25, 1782   4

Page

BARBER, BARBAR, (cont.)

Lois, d. Simeon & Lois, b. Oct. 16, 1775   3

Lucy, m. Noah PHELPS, Dec. 5, 1820, by Rev. Shubael Bartlett   59

Margaret, of East Windsor, m. William S. KELLOGG, of Hartford,
Oct. 8, 1833, by Rev. Shubael Bartlett   97

Maria, m. James A. THOMPSON, b. of East Windsor, Jan. 8, 1829,
by Rev. Shubael Bartlett   91

Mary A., m. Samuel W. THOMPSON, Dec. 25, 1834, by Rev. Shubael
Bartlett   98

Nancy M., m. Alonzo R. BARBER, Dec. 11, 1844, by O. F. Parker.
Int. Pub.   115

Nath[anie]ll, m. Peggy SAUNDERS, Nov. 4, [1821], by Rev. Shubael
Bartlett of 2nd Church   59

Oliver, of Windsor, now of East Windsor, m. Ann ROOT, of
Westfield, Jan. 30, 1766   32

Oliver, s. Oliver & Ann, b. Mar. 3, 1767   3

Orriss, s. Oliver & Anne, b. Oct. 2, 1775   3

Phebe, m. Henry JOHNSON, Nov. 5, 1840, by Shubael Bartlett   108

Rachel, d. Simeon & Lois, b. Sept. 25, 1781   3

Sarah, m. John MANLY, b. of East Windsor, June 19, 1828, by
Rev. Shubael Bartlett   90

Shadrack, m. Elizabeth S. PEASE, Sept. 28, 1842, by Shubael Bartlett   112

Simeon, m. Lois ALLYN, b. of East Windsor, Sept. 26, 1771   32

Simeon, s. Simeon & Lois, b. Mar. 17, 1774   3

BANCROFT, BANCRAFT, BANDCRAFT, Abigail, m. Robert
ALEXANDER, Nov. 28, 1833, by Rev. William Bently   97

Alfred, m. Minerva CLARK, Mar. 3, 1824, by Rev. Shubael
Bartlett of 2nd Church   86

Alona, of East Windsor, m. Valorus HALL, of Manchester, this day
[Apr. 16, 1829], by Rev. Thomas Robbins   91

Benjamin, m. Docia GOODALE, [Mar.] 14, [1822], by Rev. Thomas
Robbins   85

Betsey, m. Leicester KING, of Suffield, July 19, 1835, by Rev.
Shubael Bartlett, of 2nd Church   100

Bissell, s. [Isaac & Lovice], b. June 2, 1801, m. Joanna MORTON,
Nov. 24, 1824; d. Dec. 18, 1865, ae 64   5

Bissell, m. Joanna MORTON, b. of East Windsor, Nov. 24, 1824,
by Rev. Shubael Bartlett of 2nd Church   87

Caleb Jones, of Enfield, m. Chloe WOLCOTT, of East Windsor,
Oct. 5, 1831, by Rev. Shubael Bartlett   94

Cecelia B., d. William & Caroline B., b. Mar. 2, 1833;
[m.] Joseph A. BARBER, Nov. 23, 1852   5

Cecelia B., m. Joseph A. BARBER, b. of East Windsor, Nov. 23,
1852, by Rev. James Mather   136

Charlotte, of West Windsor, m. Hiram PIERCE, of Plymouth, Nov.
6, 1828, by Rev. Samuel W. Whelpley of 1st Church   91

Chauncey, s. Isaac & Lovice, b. [   ], 1795; m. Julia R.
WOLCOTT, Jan. 5, 1860; d. Jan. 22, 1867, ae 72   5

Page

BANCROFT, BANCRAFT, BANDCRAFT, (cont.)
Chauncey, m. Julia R. **WOLCOTT**, Jan. 5, 1860, by Rev. Silas P.
    Babcock   153
Chloe, d. John & Anna, b. June 19, 1773   3
Chloe, d. Edward & Sarah, b. Sept. 13, 1781   3
Chloe, of East Windsor, m. Richard S. **HAMILTON**, of Ellington,
    Oct. 13, 1835, by Rev. Pardon T. Kenney, of M. E. Ch.   99
Clarissa, of East Windsor, m. Randall **HARRINGTON**, of Springfield,
    Mass., Aug. 31, [1841], by Rev. Marvin Root   110
David, of Grafton, Vt., m. Sarah Roselle **PERRIN**, of East Windsor,
    this day [Jan. 15, 1839], by Bennet Tyler   105
Editha, d. Edward & Sarah, b. Feb. 20, 1778   3
Elisabeth, of East Windsor, m. James M. **ELLIS**, of Long Meadow,
    Mass., June 8, 1837, by Rev. Shubael Bartlett   102
Eunice, m. Bevil H. **ALLING**, b. of East Windsor, Apr. 9, 1834,
    by Rev. Shubael Bartlett   97
Francis, m. Julia **PINNEY**, b. of East Windsor, Apr. 11, 1844, by Levi
    Smith   114
Francis, of South Windsor, m. Ann Jane **WAITE**, of East Windsor,
    Nov. 24, 1853, by Rev. Shubael Bartlett, of 1st Cong. Ch.   138
Harriette N., of East Windsor, m. Henry H. **WILDMAN**, of Hartford,
    Jan. 15, 1843, by Levi Smith   112
Hattie Heath, [d. Mahlon H. & Mary S.], b. May 25, 1869;
    d. Dec. 27, 1881   5
Horace, m. Cynthia **SLATER**, b. of East Windsor, Nov. 1, 1835,
    by Rev. William Bentley   99
Isaac, b. [   ], 1775; m. Lovice **BISSELL**, d. of W[illia]m,
    [   ]   5
Joanna, d. Jan. 8, 1773, in the 97th y. of her age   61
John H., m. Persis Ann **SPERRY**, Feb. 28, 1858, at Warehouse Pt.,
    by Josiah Ellsworth, J. P.   149
Lorinda, of East Windsor, m. Jerome **GRISWOLD**, of Windsor, Mar.
    16, 1831, by Rev. Shubael Bartlett   94
Lottie Bliss, [d. Mahlon H. & Mary S.], b. Aug. 10, 1870   5
Louisa, m. Harvey **PRIOR**, Jr., Sept. 10, 1835, by Rev. Shubael
    Bartlett   100
Lovice, d. [Isaac & Lovice], b. [   ], 1798; d. Apr. 8, 1864, ae 66   5
Lucinda, m. John F. **BUCKLAND**, May 19, 1824, by Rev. Shubael
    Bartlett of 2nd Church   86
Mahlon H., s. [William & Caroline B.], b. Oct. 17, 1837; [m.] Mary
    S. **RICHARDS**, June 27, 1862   5
Marcia, m. Rev. Alling **HOUGH**, Sept. 2, 1822, by Elisha Cushman   85
Maria, m. Buckley P. **HEATH**, b. of East Windsor, Dec. 8, 1829, by
    Rev. Sam[ue]l W. Whelpley   93
May Louise, d. Mahlon H. & Mary S., b. Aug. 26, 1867   5
Nathaniel, s. Edward & Sarah, b. Oct. 28, 1783   4
Sarah, d. Edward & Sarah, b. Jan. 5, 1770   3
Sarah S., of East Windsor, m. Alonzo **WETHERBY**, of Hollis, N. H.,

Page

BANCROFT, BANCRAFT, BANDCRAFT, (cont.
Apr. 12, 1846, by Shubael Bartlett — 118
Tamar, see under Tamar THOMPSON — 93
Thomas, s. Edward & Sarah, b. Aug. 3, 1771 — 3
Willard Hall, [s. Isaac & Lovice], b. [ ], 1810; m. Eliza Ann
MORTON, [ ]; d. Jan. 7, 1882, ae 72 — 5
William, [s. Isaac & Lovice], b. Nov. 8, 1805; m. Caroline B.
HEATH, Feb. 7, 1832; d. Oct. 31, 1887, ae 82 — 5
BANGHAN*, Nancy J., m. Lucius F. BABCOCK, Oct. 4, 1858, at
Warehouse Pt., by Rev. Henry McClory, of St. John's Ch.
*(Perhaps "BAUGHN"?] — 150
BANKS, John, m. Mary A. STORMS, Aug. 5, 1858, by Rev. John F.
Sheffield — 149
John, m. Mary A. STORMS, Aug. 5, 1858, by Rev. John F. Sheffield
(Entry crossed out) — 150
BARKER, James, of Somers, m. Mary PIERCE, of Somers, Sept. 28, 1851,
by Rev. Henry H. Bates, of St. John's Ch. — 131
Lamira Amelia, m. William RHONER, b. of East Windsor, Dec. 15,
1851, by Rev. Henry H. Bates, of St. John's Ch., at Warehouse
Point (Written in margin "Lamira A. BARNES") — 132
BARNES, George B., m. Nancy J. KINGSBURY, Apr. 10, 1855, by Rev.
W[illia]m K. Douglass, in St. John's Ch. — 142
Henry A., m. Mary Theresa WOODWARD, Sept. 29, 1858, at
Warehouse Pt., by Rev. Henry McClory, of St. John's Ch. — 150
Lamira A., see Lamira Amelia BARKER — 132
Sarah M., m. Joseph OLMSTED, Jr., June 2, 1852, by Rev. C. S.
Putnam, of St. John's Ch., at Warehouse Pt. Int. Pub. — 133
William, m. Maria HOLKINS, b. of East Windsor, Apr. 26, 1827,
by Rev. Shubael Bartlett — 89
BARR, Eliza, m. Samuel COOK, b. of Thompsonville, Nov. 24, 1850, by
Henry H. Bates — 129
Margaret, m. John COOK, Nov. 7, 1847, by Rev. Henry H. Bates,
of St. John's Ch., Warehouse Point — 122
BARRETT, Francis, m. Ellen WHARING, b. of Enfield, Nov. 24, 1849,
by Rev. Henry H. Bates, of St. John's Ch., Warehouse Pt. — 127
Thomas, m. Fanny ELCOTT, b. of Enfield, Nov. 24, 1849, by Rev.
Henry H. Bates, of St. John's Ch., Warehouse Pt. — 127
BARROW, John, m. Mary CLAGG, b. of Broad Brook, Sept. 9, 1847, by
Rev. Francis J. Clerc, of Grace Ch., Broad Brook, at Grace
Church — 121
BARTLETT, BARTLET, Abigail, of Stafford, m. Hezekiah ALLYN, of
East Windsor, Dec. 13, 1768 — 31
Abigail, d. Samuel & Ann, b. June 25, 1772 — 3
Alce, d. Hannah BARTLETT & reputed d. Eliphalet CHAPEN, b.
Mar. 20, 1767 — 3
Algernon Sidney, of Granby, Mass., m. Sylvia OSBORN, Nov. 23,
1843, by Shubael Bartlett — 113
Anne, d. John & Elisabeth, b. June 25, 1773 — 3

Page

BARTLETT, BARTLET, (cont.)

Page

BARTLETT, BARTLET, (cont.)

W. Conant, of M. E. Ch.   146

Samuel W., m. Octavia C. **TARBOX,** Sept. 14, 1843, by Shubael
Bartlett   113

Sam[ue]l W[illia]m, m. Elizabeth Bartlett **NOBLE,** Sept. 29, 1830,
by Rev. Shubael Bartlett   93

BASCOM, Flavel, Rev. of Chicago, Ill., m. Elizabeth B. **SPARHAWK,** of
Warehouse Point, Aug. 16, 1841, by Rev. Zebulon Crocker, of
2nd Cong. Ch. Middletown   110

BATES, Elizur, m. Julia E. **ALDERMAN,** Oct. 21, 1846, by Rev. Henry
H. Bates, of St. John's Ch.   120

BAYER, Mary, m. Michael **KEHLER,** Aug. 8, 1848, by Rev. Francis J.
Clerc, of Grace Ch., Broad Brook   124

BECKER, Franceska, m. Sebastion **HORIG,** May 23, 1859, at Broad Brook,
by Rev. John F. Mines, of Grace Ch.   151

BEEBE, BEEBEE, Elizabeth, Mrs. of East Windsor, m. Gurdon **SMITH,** of
Ellington, June 2, 1851, by Rev. Charles N. Seymour   131

George, of West Springfield, Mass., m. Elizabeth **THOMSON,** of
East Windsor, Jan. 13, 1825, by Rev. Shubael Bartlett   87

BELCHER, Abigail, of East Windsor, m. Henry **TREAT,** Jr., of East
Hartford, Aug. 28, 1822, by Rev. Elisha B. Cook, of East Hartford   85

Bathsheba, m. Lucius **PARKER,** Jan. 1, 1829, by V. R. Osborn,
V.D.M.   91

Elizabeth, of East Windsor, m. Chauncey B. **MILLER,** of West
Windsor, Apr. 1, 1822, by Rev. Elisha B. Cook, of East Hartford   84

Emily, m. Willys **GRANT,** b. of East Windsor, July 6, [1820], by Rev.
Thomas Robbins of 1st Eccl. Soc.   59

Frances, m. Thaddeus **HORSMER,** [Dec.] 5, [1821], by Rev. Thomas
Robbins   84

Jonathan W., m. Jerusha **ROCKWELL,** b. of East Windsor, Nov. 13,
1833, by Rev. Salmon Hull   97

Matilda, m. Herman **HALL,** b. of East Windsor, Jan. 2, 1828,
by Rev. Shubael Bartlett   89

BELDEN, George F.*, of Hartford, m. Mary A. **ROCKWELL,** of East
Windsor, Feb. 12, 1843, by Levi Smith   *(Written in margin
"George S.")   113

BELKNAP, BELNAP, Amelia E., m. Roderick **CLARK,** b. of East
Windsor, Apr. 10, 1836, by Rev. Shubael Bartlett   101

Amy, m. Reuben **WOOD,** Sept. 17, 1821, by Rev. Shubael Bartlett
of 2nd Church   59

Diadema, Mrs. of East Windsor, m. Asahel **THOMPSON,** of Ellington,
Aug. 26, 1832, by Rev. Edmund M. Beebe   95

Eliza I., m. Asahel C. **STILES,** b. of East Windsor, Jan. 31,
1832, by Rev. Shubael Bartlett   94

Francis, m. Hannah **PRIOR,** b. of East Windsor, June 7, 1824, by Rev.
Shubael Bartlett of 2nd Church   86

Lavinia A., of East Windsor, m. William H. **TREMAIN,** M. D., of
New Mareboroug*, Mass., Mar. 15, 1842, by Shubael Bartlett

Page

BIRGE, (cont.)

[Apr.] 17, [1834], by Rev. Chauncey G. Lee   97

Julius, m. Maria Ann **STOUGHTON**, b. of East Windsor, [Nov.] 25,

[1824], by Rev. Thomas Robbins of 1st Church   87

Julius, m. Emeline **BOW**, b. of East Windsor, this day, [Nov. 5,

1839], by Bennet Tyler   106

Mary B., m. Willis **STOUGHTON**, b. of East Windsor, Nov. 23, 1824,

by Rev. Francis L. Robbins of Enfield   86

Priscilla, wid., m. Amasa **LOOMIS**, Feb. 1, 1783   44

Priscilla **BIRGE***, m. Amasa **LOOMIS**, Dec. 30, 1784 *(Perhaps

PAGE")   44

BISSELL, Aaron, s. Aaron & Dorothy, b. July 27, 1761   3

Adelia, m. Francis W. **SHEPHERD**, of Northampton, Mass., Apr. 29,

1844, by Shubael Bartlett   114

Alfred, s. Aaron & Naomi, b. Dec. 13, 1804   4

Betsey, Mrs., m. James **PELTON**, [Feb.] 23, [1834], by Rev.

Chauncey G. Lee   97

Chester, s. Dan & Lydia, b. Dec. 6, 1780   3

Chloe, d. Aaron & Dorothy, b. Aug. 30, 1758   3

Chloe, m. Capt. Erastus **WOLCOTT**, Jr., b. of East Windsor, Dec.

27, 1783   56

Clarine, d. David & Elisabeth, b. Sept. 14, 1771   3

Clarissa, d. Jonathan & Prudence, b. May 21, 1783   4

Cornelia M., of East Windsor, m. Charles H. **TALCOTT**,of

Glastenbury, Jan. 8, 1851, by Rev. Samuel J. Andrews,of Cong.

Ch.   130

Dan, m. Lydia **MUNSEL**, b. of East Windsor, Dec. 27, 1768   32

David, of East Windsor, s. Ens. David & Sarah, of Windsor,

b. Apr. 27, 1732   3

David, m. Elisabeth **BACKUS**, b. of East Windsor, Feb. 25, 1761   32

David, s. David & Elisabeth, b. June 6, 1764   3

David, m. Fanny **LATTIMORE**, b. of East Windsor, Oct. 15, 1827,

by Dan[ie]l Hayden, J. P.   90

Dolly S., of East Windsor, m. Rufus **RUSSELL**, of Sunderland,

Mass., Dec. 8, 1833, by Ebenezer Pinney, J. P.   97

Dorothy, [twin with Epaphras], d. Aaron & Dorothy, b. July 24, 1765   3

Edgar, s. Aaron & Naomi, b. June 30, 1800   4

Edward, of Rochester, N. Y., m. Jane Ann Maria **REED**, of East

Windsor, [Sept.] 15, [1823], by Rev. Thomas Robbins of 1st Ch.

Eleanor P., of East Windsor, m. Josiah S. **RICE**, of Hartford,   86

Apr. 24, 1832, by Rev. Shubael Bartlett

Elisha, s. Elisha & Roxy, b. Feb. 14, 1787   95

Elisabeth, w. David, b. May 19, 1734   4

Elizabeth Backus, d. Noadiah & Sybbel, b. Apr. 26, 1795   3

Elisabeth E., m. Monroe **HIBBARD**, Jan. 21, 1845, by Shubael Bartlett   4

Epaphras, [twin with Dorothy], s. Aaron & Dorothy, b. July 24, 1765   117

Esther, d. Dan & Lydia, b. Apr. 21, 1777   3

Esther, d. William & Jemima, d. Mar. 18, 1786   3

Page

BISSELL, (cont.)

Olive, d. Jonathan & Prudence, b. Nov. 4, 1771   4

Ozias, m. Irene **WARD**, b. of East Windsor, May 14, 1833, by Rev.
David L. Hunn   98

Prudence, d. Jonathan & Prudence, b. Sept. 13, 1773   4

Reuba, d. Jonathan & Prudence, b. Aug. 18, 1775   4

Rhoda A., m. Solomon G. **PARSONS**, Mar. 28, 1858, by Rev. W. M.
Birchard   149

Roxy, d. Elisha & Roxy, b. Sept. 10, 1788   4

Silee Burt, d. Elisha & Roxy, b. Mar. 17, 1793   4

Simon Backus, s. David & Elisabeth, b. Jan. 16, 1769   3

Sophia, d. Aaron & Naomi, b. May 17, 1785   4

Sukey, d. Aaron & Naomi, b. Nov. 14, 1787   4

Sukey, d. Aaron & Naomi, d. Jan. 31, 1789   61

Sukey, d. Aaron & Naomi, b. Mar. 18, 1790   4

Sybbel, w. Noadiah, d. June 19, 1796   61

Sybbel Enos, d. Noadiah & Betsy, b. Dec. 12, 1797   4

Thankfull Annah, d. Sylvester & Mahittabel, b. Nov. 20, 1800   4

Triphena, had s. Roswel **COLSON**, b. Feb. 24, 1781   6

Wareham, s. Jonathan & Prudence, b. Apr. 2, 1778   4

BIVINS, Chauncey, m. Abigail **CAHOON**, Apr. 16, 1827, by Rev. Shubael
Bartlett   89

BIXBEE, Jared, m. Lydia **CADEY**, b. of East Windsor, Jan. 7, 1821, by
Rev. Shubael Bartlett of 2nd Church   59

BLACK, Albert, Jr., s. Albert & Lodema, b. Jan. 14, 1807   4

BLANCHARD, Levi, m. Melissa C. **PASCO**, Mar. 18, 1851, by Rev.
Sanford Benton   130

BLINN, Minerva, of East Windsor, m. William **RICH**, of Manchester,
this day [Jan. 31, 1825], by Rev. Thomas Robbins, of 1st Church   88

BLISS, Achsah, d. Rev. John & Betty, b. May 3, 1772   3

Anne, d. John & Alice, b. Dec. 19, 1773   4

Betty, d. Rev. John & Betty, b. Nov. 30, 1766   3

Betty, d. Rev. John & Betty, d. Sept. 9, 1769   61

Betty, d. Rev. John & Betty, b. Apr. 9, 1770   3

Daniel, s. Rev. John & Betty, b. Feb. 5, 1780   3

Elisabeth, wid. Pelatiah, d. Feb. 23, 1781   61

Hosea, s. Rev. John & Betty, b. Feb. 26, 1776   3

Joel White, s. Rev. John & Betty, b. Mar. 31, 1774   3

John, Rev. of East Windsor, m. Mrs. Betty **WHITE**, of Bolton,
Jan. 15, 1766   32

John, s. Rev. John & Betty, b. June 16, 1768   3

Pelitiah, m. Lucina **GRANT**, [June] 6, [1821], by Rev. Thomas
Robbins   84

W[illia]m, s. John & Betty, b. May 11, 1783   4

BLODGETT, BLODGET, Abigail R., of East Windsor, m. Stedman **NASH,**
of Quincy, Ill., Apr. 14, 1840, by Shubael Bartlett   106

Abner, of East Windsor, m. Rachel **PHELPS**, of Enfield, Mar. 23, 1768   32

Abner, s. Abner & Rachel, b. Oct. 1, 1771   3

Page

BLODGETT, BLODGET, (cont.)

Abner, d. Dec. 2, 1834   61

Alva R., m. Laura A. **CHAPIN,** Apr. 15, 1846, by Shubael Bartlett   118

Benoni, s. Abner & Rachel, b. Jan. 9, 1778   4

Cephas, [twin with Rufus], s. Abner & Rachel, b. July 2, 1784   4

David, m. Maryann **SKINNER,** b. of East Windsor, this day, [Apr.
      29, 1832], by Erastus Doty   95

Elizabeth, m. Rollin C. **CRANE,** b. of East Windsor, Feb. 28, 1839, by
      Rev. Ebenezer Blake, of Warehouse Point   105

Elizabeth M., m. Edward **BRIDGMAN,** of Amherst, Mass., Nov. 5,
      1840, by Shubael Bartlett   108

Emeline, of East Windsor, m. Charles **PACKARD,** of Springfield,
      Mass., Apr. 19, 1827, by Rev. Shubael Bartlett   89

Emeline D., m. George R. **BILL,** June 4, 1857, by Rev. W[illia]m
      M. Birchard   147

Hannah, d. Abner & Hannah, b. July 10, 1815   4

Hannah, m. Lemuel **STOUGHTON,** Dec. 29, 1841, by Shubael Bartlett   111

Harriet G., of Amherst, Mass., m. Charles **MONTAGUE,** of Lenox,
      Mass., Nov. 19, 1840, by Shubael Bartlett   108

Henry S., of South Windsor, m. Rebecca **OSBORN,** of East Windsor,
      Apr. 9, 1848, by Shubael Bartlett   122

Job, s. Abner & Rachel, b. June 18, 1782   4

Martha, d. Abner & Rachel, b. Oct. 18, 1775   3

Mary Bartlett, of East Windsor, m. Alvah **MORELL,** of Hartford,
      Feb. 8, 1832, by Rev. Shubael Bartlett   95

Phinehas LaFayette, m. Lucy Ann **ALLEN,** June 30, 1844, by Shubael
      Bartlett   114

Rachel, d. Abner & Rachel, b. Aug. 2, 1773   3

Ralph, s. Abner, Jr. & Hannah, b. Oct. 30, 1811   4

Ralph, m. Caroline Jane **ALLEN,** Sept. 1, 1846, by Shubael Bartlett   118

Rhoda Maria, of East Windsor, m. Austin **PEMBER,** of Ellington,
      Aug. 3, 1825, by Rev. Shubael Bartlett   87

Rufus, [twin with Cephas], s. Abner & Rachel, b. June 2, 1784   4

Sarah Maria, m. John Terry **THOMPSON,** b. of East Windsor, Jan.
      6, 1831, by Rev. Shubael Bartlett   93

BODFISH, Elizabeth H., m. Levi G. **FOX,** May 1, 1839, by Shubael Bartlett   106

Silas B., m. Lucretia G. **CHAFFEE,** Oct. 9, 1836, by Rev. Shubael
      Bartlett   101

BOING, Amanda, m. Charles **MORGANVECK,** Nov. 11, 1856, at
      Warehouse Point, by Rev. Henry M. Clory of St. John's Ch.   146

BOLLES, Lorenzo, Jr., Rev. of Hartford, m. Ann A. **ELLSWORTH,** of
      East Windsor, Oct. 26, 1845, by Rev. Sewall Lamberton   117

BOLTE, Christian H. F., m. Christine M. E. **SCHMAHLFELDT,** May 28,
      1848, in Grace Church, Broad Brook, by Rev. Frances J. Clerc   128

BOLYEN, Cordelia L., of Enfield, m. Joel M. **PORTER,** of Glastenbury,
      Apr. 24, 1850, by Rev. Shubael Bartlett   128

BOND, Sarah A., m. George P. **CALE,** b. of Springfield, Mass., this day
      [Oct. 6, 1840], by Bennet Tyler   108

Page

BONE, Joseph, m. Anna KELLENBERGER, b. of Thompsonville, Apr. 8,
    1848, by Rev. Francis J. Clerc, of Grace Ch. Broad Brook   121
BONINVILLE, Julia E., m. Harvey SIKES, b. of Springfield, Mass.,
    Sept. 5, 1844, by Rev. Henry H. Bates of St. John's Ch.   116
BOOTH, Aaron, s. Aaron & Desire, b. Sept. 29, 1790   4
Aaron, s. Aaron & Desire, b. Mar. 1, 1797   4
Abigail, [twin with Eunice], d. Jsaiah & Eunice, b. Aug. 19, 1777   3
Anne, d. Ephraim & Elizabeth, b. Jan. 17, 1775   4
Anne, d. Caleb, Jr., & Ann, b. July 10, 1775   3
Ashbel, s. Simeon & Elisabeth, b. Sept. 28, 1766   3
Betsey, d. Ephraim & Elisabeth, b. Feb. 7, 1767   3
Betsey, m. Joel W. SMITH, Nov. 13, [1821], by Rev. Shubael
    Bartlett of 2nd Church   59
Betty, d. Capt. Caleb & Anne, b. May 28, 1788   4
Caleb, Jr., m. Anne BARTLETT, b. of East Windsor, May 1, 1775   32
Caleb, s. Caleb, Jr. & Ann, b. Jan. 27, 1777   3
Caroline, of East Windsor, m. Albert S. WELLS, of Enfield, Jan. 8,
    1851, by Rev. Samuel J. Andrews, of Cong. Ch.   130
Celinda, d. Ephraim & Elizabeth, b. July 30, 1788   4
Chauncey, s. Caleb & Anne, b. Mar. 15, 1783   4
Chloe, d. Ephraim & Elizabeth, b. Aug. 23, 1780   4
Chloe, d. Aaron & Desire, b. Sept. 15, 1788   4
Clara, d. Ephraim & Elizabeth, b. Oct. 9, 1776   4
Clarissa Miranda, d. Gaius & Clarissa, b. Oct. 11, 1807   4
Clarissa Miranda, of East Windsor, m. Peter CHAPIN, of Enfield,
    Oct. 22, 1828, by Rev. Shubael Bartlett   90
David, of Oxford, N. Y., m. Lovicy Turner BOYNTON, of East
    Windsor, Oct. 29, 1832, by Rev. Shubael Bartlett   95
Desire, d. Aaron & Desire, b. May 6, 1793   4
Elisabeth, d. Simeon & Elisabeth, d. Feb. 2, 1772   61
Elon, s. Simeon & Elisabeth, b. Sept. 11, 1769   3
Ephraim, s. Ephraim & Elizabeth, b. Aug. 2, 1778   4
Eunice, [twin with Abigail], d. Jsaiah & Eunice, b. Aug. 19, 1777   3
Gaius, s. Caleb, Jr. & Ann, b. May 30, 1779   3
Gaius, of East Windsor, m. Clarissa DEWEY, of Suffield, Dec. 1, 1806   32
Hannah, d. Caleb & Ann, b. Dec. 21, 1780   3
Hannah, m. Rev. John McFRASER, Sept. 20, 1842, by Shubael
    Bartlett   112
Henry, s. Capt. Caleb & Anne, b. Feb. 28, 1784 *(Perhaps 1785)   4
John Ruggles, of Enfield, m. Julia Theresa HEATH, of East Windsor,
    Jan. 5, 1853, in St. John's Church, Warehouse Point, by Rev. C. S.
    Putnam   136
Jsaiah, s. Jsaiah & Eunice, b. May 16, 1779   3
Levi, s. Ephraim & Elizabeth, b. Feb. 22, 1786   4
Lucretia, d. Ephraim & Elizabeth, b. Jan. 8, 1771   4
Margaret, m. Thomas BALDWIN, b. of Springfield, Mass., Aug. 10,
    1851, by Rev. Henry H. Bates, of St. John's Ch.   131
Polly, d. Ephraim & Elizabeth, b. June 29, 1793   4

Page

BOOTH, (cont.)

Sabra, d. Capt. Caleb & Anne, b. Sept. 16, 1790   4

Sarah, of East Windsor, m. George S. **MARJORUM,** of Trenton, N. J.,
Apr. 9, 1835, by Rev. Shubael Bartlett   99

Seth, s. Ephraim & Elisabeth, b. Apr. 16, 1769   3

Seth, Jr., m. Sally **WATSON,** [Oct.] 29, [1820], by Rev. Thomas
Robbins of 1st Eccl. Soc.   59

Seth, m. Parmelia **SPENCER,** Mar. 26, 1860, by Harvey Pease, J. P.   153

Silvia, d. Ephraim & Elizabeth, b. June 19, 1773   4

Simeon, s. Simeon & Elisabeth, b. Sept. 30, 1763   3

Stephen, of Charlton, m. Electa **WARNER,** of West Springfield, Mass.,
Feb. 23, 1832, by William Barnes, J. P.   95

Walter, of Meriden, m. Sarah H. **LATHROP,** of East Windsor, May
17, 1842, by Shubael Bartlett   112

BOSCH, Charles, m. Johane **LEIBER,** Nov. [ ], 1850, by W[illia]m S.
Simmons   129

BOTTOM, Jacob, late of Norwich now of East Windsor, m. Prudence
HEBARD, of Windham, Dec. 2, 1773. "Entered from certificate
on Mar. 7, 1775"   32

Lydia, d. Jacob & Prudence, b. Sept. 15, 1774   3

BOUCHER, John, m. Mary **O'HALLARAN,** Apr. 24, 1858, at South
Windsor, by Rev. James Smyth   150

BOWE, BOW, Emeline, m. Julius **BIRGE,** b. of East Windsor, this day,
[Nov. 5, 1839], by Bennet Tyler   106

Wealthy, m. Eleazer **FENTON,** b. of East Windsor, this day,
[Jan. 22, 1835], by Chauncey G. Lee   98

BOWER, BOWERS, Abigail, d. John & Catharine, b. Oct. 31, 1793   4

Abner, s. John & Catharine, b. Apr. 26, 1795   4

Ann, m. Samuel **STILES,** Dec. 10, 1843, by Shubael Bartlett   113

Azel, s. Azel & Susanna, b. Aug. 15, 1768; dec.   3

Azel, s. Azel & Susanna, b. Aug. 24, 1771   3

Azel, s. John & Catherine, b. June 22, 1797   4

Azel, m. Mary **CRAW,** b. of East Windsor, Nov. 5, [1820], by Rev.
Shubael Bartlett   59

Chester A., m. Hannah **ELLSWORTH,** Sept. 27, 1839, by Shubael
Bartlett   106

Cyrus, s. John & Catherine, b. Mar. 28, 1785   4

Erastus W., s. John & Catharine, b. Aug. 28, 1787   4

Erastus W., m. [ ] wid. of Enos **MUNSELL,** Nov. 25, 1830,
by Rev. Shubael Bartlett   93

LeRoy R., m. Sarah E. **DARLING,** Oct. 17, 1842, by Shubael Bartlett   112

Lodema, d. John & Catherine, b. Sept. 6, 1783   4

Rhoda, d. John & Catherine, b. Nov. 22, 1789   4

Sidney, of Windsor, m. Sarah **BUCKLAND,** of East Windsor, Nov.
24, 1830, by Rev. Shubael Bartlett   93

BOYNTON, Lovicy Turner, of East Windsor, m. David **BOOTH,** of Oxford,
N. Y., Oct. 29, 1832, by Rev. Shubael Bartlett   95

Mary H., m. Ezra H. **WATERMAN,** Nov. 17, 1842, by Shubael

Page

BUCKLAND, BUCKLIN, (cont.)

Mary, m. John **HUNN,** b. of East Windsor, June 5, 1844, by Rev.
B. M. Walker   114

Mary L., of East Windsor, m. John Quincey **ADAMS,** of Milford,
Mass., Nov. 24, 1852, by Rev. Samuel J. Andrews of Cong. Ch.   136

Oliver C., m. Sarah E. **ELLSWORTH,** b. of East Windsor, this day,
[Apr. 9, 1840], by Rev. Moses Stoddard, of M. E. Ch.   107

Sarah, of East Windsor, m. Sidney **BOWER,** of Windsor, Nov. 24,
1830, by Rev. Shubael Bartlett   93

Sophronia, of East Windsor, m. Timothy **KEENY,** of Manchester,
Apr. 4, 1836, by V. R. Osborn, V. D. M.   100

Walter, of Springfield, Mass., m. Mary W. **HEATH,** of Enfield, Conn.,
Jan. 1, 1840, by Rev. Benjamin C. Phelps, of Warehouse Point   107

BUGBEY, George H., m. Mary E. **PIKE,** May 24, 1857, at Warehouse
Point, by Rev. Henry McClory of St. John's Ch.   147

BULKLEY, Mary, m. John **PELTON,** Jan. 24, 1847, by Shubael Bartlett   119

BUNCE, Charles, of New York, m. Julia **BIDWELL,** of East Windsor,
[Aug.] 12, [1822], by Rev. Thomas Robbins   85

BURBANK, Marietta L., m. Shadrach L. **FISH,** July 28, 1859, by Rev.
John F. Sheffield   151

BURGESS, Clarissa, d. Julius & Charlottee, b. May 18, 1811   4

Philetus M., m. Hannah C. **ELLSWORTH,** Jan. 1, 1846, by Shubael
Bartlett   117

BURLINGAME, Richard A., m. Margaret B. **WILLIAMS,** b. of East
Windsor, Aug. 25, 1840, by Benjamin C. Phelps   109

BURNHAM, Austin, of East Hartford, m. Sophia **COLE,** of East Windsor,
Nov. 10, 1831, by Rev. Gurdon Robins of Bap. Ch.   94

Clarissa, of East Hartford, m. Harvey **ELMER,** Apr. 19, 1830, by
Rev. Sam[ue]l W. Whelpley   93

George, m. Maria **SEDGEWICK,** b. of East Windsor, Mar. 18, 1832,
by Rev. George Goodyear   95

Hannah, m. Merrow **MARBLE,** b. of East Hartford, this day, [May
30, 1822], by Rev. T. Robbins of 1st Church   85

Julia I., m. Orrin **BRAGG,** Mar. 22, 1830, in Gurdon Robbins   92

Louisa, of East Windsor, m. Lorenzo D. **RICHARDSON,** of Hartford,
this day [Oct. 13, 1840], by Rev. Samuel Spring of Cong. Ch.
East Hartford   108

Mary, of East Windsor, m. William **WILLIAMS,** of Willington,
Mar. 12, 1832, by Rev. Geo[rge] Goodyear   95

Roger, of East Hartford, m. Roxey **KILBOURN,** of East Windsor,
[Mar.] 30, [1825], by Rev. Thomas Robbins   88

Roxey L., of East Windsor, m. John **CRAMER,** of Woodbury, Jan.
11, 1835, by Cha[rle]s Remington, Elder   98

Spencer, of East Windsor, m. Mary W. **JONES*,** of Ellington, Oct.
2, 1842, by Levi Smith *(Written in margin "Mrs. Mary W.
JONES")   112

Thomas, of East Hartford, m. Mehitabel **ALEXANDER,** of East
Windsor, May 6, [1829], by Rev. Thomas Robbins, East Hartford   91

Page

BURNHAM, (cont.)

William C., of East Haddam, m. Hester R. **RISLEY,** of East Windsor,
Aug. 6, 1834, by Rev. Salmon Hull — 98

BURROUGHS, Abel, s. Abner, Jr. & Eunice, b. July 18, 1775 — 3

Alfred, s. Abner, Jr. & Eunice, b. Aug. 19, 1777 — 3

BURT, Roxana H., m. James M. **LEARNED,** b. of Warren, Mass., [Nov. 24,
1839], by Rev. Benjamin C. Phelps, of Warehouse Point — 106

BUSH, Amris, m. Henry A. **WELTON,** Nov. 7, 1847, by Rev. Henry H.
Bates, of St. John's Ch., Warehouse Point — 122

Caroline N., m. Daniel M. **FOSS,** Oct. 7, 1856, at Warehouse Point,
by Rev. H. W. Conant, of M. E. Ch. — 145

BUSKIRK, George V., m. Ruth **MERRIMAN,** Oct. 16, 1854, by Rev.
W[illia]m K. Douglass, of St. John's Ch. — 152

BUTLER, Harriet A., of St. Lawrence Co., N. Y., m. Henry **SEXTON,** of
East Windsor, Sept. 30, 1851, by Rev. Henry H. Bates, of St.
John's Ch. — 131

Julia A., of East Windsor, m. John **CLARK,** of Suffield, Nov. 1,
1830, by Rev. Shubael Bartlett — 93

BUTTON, Henrietta, of East Windsor, m. Ransom **SPERRY,** of New
Haven, Apr. 2, 1829, by Rev. Shubael Bartlett — 91

Hulday, d. Jonathan & Naomi, b. Mar. 25, 1789 — 4

Jesse, s. Jonathan & Naomi, b. July 25, 1791 — 4

Josen*, s. Jonathan & Naomi, b. June 22, 1778 *(Perhaps "Josep[h]") — 3

Levi, s. Jonathan & Naomi, b. Mar. 24, 1776 — 3

Naomi, d. Jonathan & Naomi, b. July 12, 1780 — 3

Rhoda, d. Jonathn & Naomi, b. May 14, 1785 — 4

CADWELL, George W., m. Fanny W. **ROBINSON,** b. of East Windsor,
May 9, 1853, by Charles Bartlett, J. P. — 137

John, of Westfield, Mass., m. Alvira L. **ALLEN,** of East Windsor,
July 3, 1836, by Rev. P. T. Kenney — 100

CADY, CADEY, Lydia, m. Jared **BIXBEE,** b. of East Windsor, Jan. 7,
1821, by Rev. Shubael Bartlett of 2nd Church — 59

Sabra, m. Eli **FITCH,** b. of East Windsor, Sept. 23, 1821, by
Rev. Isaac Dwinel of Bap. Ch. East Hartford — 59

Sophronia, of East Windsor, m. Aden **KENEY,** of Manchester, Oct.
17, 1832, by Rev. Hezekiah S. Ramsdell — 96

Stephen, m. Harriet **MAY,** of Ellington, Sept. 21, 1851, by Rev.
John W. Case — 131

CAESAR, Anna, of East Windsor, m. Ambrose **WAY,** of Windsor,
(colored), [May] 8, [1823], by Rev. Thomas Robbins — 86

CAHOON, Abigail, m. Chauncey **BIVINS,** Apr. 16, 1827, by Rev. Shubael
Bartlett (See also **COHOON**) — 89

Lucinda, m. Ephraim **WARFIELD,** b. of East Windsor, Aug. 28,
1831, by Rev. Gurdon Robins of Bap. Ch. — 94

Mary, of East Windsor, m. Levi **ABBE,** Jr., of Enfield, last
evening, [Nov. 28, 1833], by Rev. Francis L. Robbins, at
Warehouse Point — 97

Reuben, m. Jerusha **WATSON,** Apr. 16, 1842, by Shubael Bartlett — 111

Page

CHAMBERLIN, CHAMBERLING, (cont.)

Page

CHAPIN, (cont.)

Peter, of Enfield, m. Clarissa Miranda **BOOTH**, of East Windsor,
Oct. 22, 1828, by Rev. Shubael Bartlett   90

Sophia, d. Eliphalet & Mary, b. Aug. 17, 1776   6

Sylvester, of Springfield, Mass., m. Lucy **NEWBERRY**, of East
Windsor, Dec. 2, 1827, by Rev. Shubael Bartlett   89

Wight, s. Eliphalet & Anne, b. Mar. 26, 1779   6

CHAPMAN, [see also **CHIPMAN**], Clarissa, m. Ephraim **WYLLYS**, [Apr.]
16, [1835], by Bennet Tyler   99

Edwin, m. Susan **SHUMWAY**, Mar. 15, 1848, by Rev. Henry H.
Bates, of St. John's Ch., Warehouse Point   122

John, of Westerly, R. I., m. Sarah **FENTON**, 2nd, of East Windsor,
Nov. 26, 1833, by Rev. Shubael Bartlett   96

John B., m. Lydia **HOLKINS**, b. of East Windsor, June 11, 1827,
by Rev. Shubael Bartlett   89

Justus D., of Hartford, m. Mary Ann **STRICKLAND**, June 15, 1842,
by Shubael Bartlett   112

L. Louisa, m. Zina K. **PEASE**, Sept. 29, 1858, at Warehouse Pt.,
by Rev. Henry McClory, of St. John's Ch.   150

Lois, of Bolton, m. Ephraim **LADD**, of East Windsor, July 14, 1774   44

CHARLTON, Edward T., d. Feb. 3, 1816   63

Edward Thomas, s. [Jesse & Rebecca M.], b. June 21, 1813   6

Elizabeth*, of East Windsor, m. Charles F. **GLEASON**, (Rev.), of
Worcester, Mass., May 14, 1845, by Bennet Tyler *(Written in
margin "Elizabeth H.")   115

Elizabeth H., d. Jesse & Rebecca M., b. Apr. 29, 1811   6

Harriet I., d. Aug. 19, 1841   63

James Henry, s. [Jesse & Rebecca M.], b. Nov. 22, 1814   6

Jesse, m. Rebecca M. **THOMAS**, Nov. 2, 1809   34

Jesse, m. Harriet **JONES**, Mar. 24, 1830   34

Jesse, m. Harriet **JONES**, b. of East Windsor, Mar. 24, 1830, by Rev.
Sam[ue]l W. Whelpley   93

Rebecca M., d. Feb. 13, 1829   63

CHARTER, Laura Ann, of Ellington, m. Albert **STEBBINS**, of Springfield,
Mar. 22, 1830, by Horace Barber, J. P.   93

Louisa E., m. Ebenezer J. **ALLEN**, Aug. 19, 1848, by H. C. Atwater,
in Broad Brook   123

CHASE, Betsey, of East Windsor, m. Elisha **KINGSBURY**, of Coventry,
this day, [June 25, 1820], by Rev. T. C. Brownell   59

Harriet A., m. Francis **TALCOTT**, b. of East Windsor, Mar. 21,
1838, by Shubael Bartlett   103

Joann F., m. Alphonso C. **CROSBY**, b. of East Windsor, Nov. 29,
1838, by Rev. Freeman Nutting   105

Lucinda, of Warehouse Point, m. Andrew **RIGGS**, of Wilmington,
Del., Apr. 2, 1843, by Rev. Joseph Scott, of St. John's Ch.   113

Porter, of Vernon, m. Maria **FLETCHER**, of East Windsor, June
25, 1841, by Shubael Bartlett   110

CHILD, CHILDS, Esther, of Manchester, m. Morgan **STEDDMAN***,

Page

CHILD, CHILDS, (cont.)
Nov. 12, 1833, by Rev. Hezekiah S. Ramsdell *(Morgan
STEADMAN, in margin) 97
Gardner, of Green Bay, Wis., m. Elmina **ROBERTSON,** July 29,
1840, by Shubael Bartlett 108
CHIPMAN, [see also **CHAPMAN**], Horace, m. Mary B. **PORTER,** Oct. 7,
1832, by Rev. Chauncey G. Lee, of 1st Church 95
CHUBBUCK, Hollis S., of Orwell, Penn., m. Elizabeth Ann **HEATH,** Oct.
10, 1831, by Rev. Shubael Bartlett 94
John, Dr. m. Mary **ABBY,** b. of East Windsor, Feb. 28, [1822], by
Francis L. Robbins, Enfield, at Warehouse Point 84
CHURCH, Mary A., ae 22, b. Wales, res. Broad Brook, m. Needham A.
THOMPSON, Manufacturer, ae 21, b. Wales, res. Monson,
Mass., Nov. 17, 1853, by Rev. James H. Soule 141
CLAGG, Mary, m. John **BARROW,** b. of Broad Brook, Sept. 9, 1847, by
Rev. Francis J. Clerc, of Grace Ch., Broad Brook, at Grace Church 121
CLAPP, Ebenezer S., m. Sophia R. **PINNEY,** b. of East Windsor, Apr.
17, 1832, by Rev. John W. Case 95
CLARK, CLARKE, Asahel, of Granby, m. Lydia Barber **GRAVES,** of
Belchertown, both Mass., Feb. 5, 1823, by Rev. William Josephus
Buckley of Warehouse Point 85
Charlotte, of East Windsor, m. Daniel **AUSTIN,** of Long Meadow,
Mass., Sept. 8, 1833, by Rev. Shubael Bartlett 96
Edward C., of Middletown, m. Emeline **LORD,** of East Windsor,
Nov. 4, 1849, by Rev. W[illia]m S. Simmons 126
Emeline, m. John **SADD,** b. of East Windsor, Nov. 28, 1826, by Rev.
Shubael Bartlett 88
Esten P., of Ellington, m. Clarissa **CRAW,** of East Windsor, Apr. 1,
1832, by Rev. John W. Case 94
Henry, m. Cynthia **WELLS,** July 27, 1837, by Shubael Bartlett 102
John, of Suffield, m. Julia A. **BUTLER,** of East Windsor, Nov.
1, 1830, by Rev. Shubael Bartlett 93
John, m. Mary Ann **GARGILE,** Aug. 6, 1849, by Rev. Henry H. Bates,
of St. John's Ch., Warehouse Point 125
Jonathan C., of Haverhill, N. H., m. Laura **HAMILTON,** of East
Windsor, Sept. 11, 1839, by Rev. Benjamin C. Phelps, of
Warehouse Point 106
Leonard, of Somerset, Vt., m. Agnes **FRENCH,** of East Windsor,
Jan. 14, 1822, by Rev. Shubael Bartlett of 2nd Soc. 84
Maria, m. Edson J. **INGALLS,** Aug. 11, 1844, by Shubael Bartlett 114
Maria C., m. Norman H. **COOK,** Nov. 7, 1854, by Rev. Sam[ue]l J.
Andrews of 1st Cong. Ch. 139
Minerva, m. Alfred **BANCROFT,** Mar. 3, 1824, by Rev. Shubael
Bartlett of 2nd Church 86
Orrin, of Utica, N. Y., m. Ann **POTWINE,** of East Windsor, Sept.
2, 1833, by Rev. Shubael Bartlett 96
Rachel, of East Windsor, m. Warren **FITCH,** of Tolland, Feb. 12,
1835, by Rev. Shubael Bartlett 98

Page

CLARK, CLARKE, (cont.)

Ralph E., of Haddam, m. Eunice **ABBE**, of East Windsor, Jan. 2, 1854, by Rev. Abel Gardner ... 139

Reuben B., m. Cornelia P. **ALLEN**, b. of East Windsor, Oct. 10, 1850, by W[illia]m S. Simmons ... 129

Roderick, m. Amelia E. **BELKNAP**, b. of East Windsor, Apr. 10, 1836, by Rev. Shubael Bartlett ... 101

Sarah L., m. Frank E. **STOUGHTON**, Apr. 21, 1859, by Rev. John F. Sheffield ... 151

Sophia M., m. Nathaniel **POTWINE**, [Oct.] 16, [1821], by Rev. Shubael Bartlett of 2nd Church ... 59

Stephen, m. Lavinia H. **LORD**, b. of East Windsor, Feb. 10, 1850, by W[illia]m S. Simmons ... 127

Sibyl*, m. Horatio **THRALL**, [Oct.] 17, [1821], by Rev. Shubael Bartlett of 2nd Church   *(Sybil) ... 59

CLOUGH, Sarah, of Manchester, m. Naaman **GRANT**, of East Windsor, Nov. 20, 1838, by Rev. Freeman Nutting, at Manchester ... 104

COE, Loring E., of Granvill, Mass., m. Mary **STANLEY**, of East Windsor, [May] 11, [1824], by Rev. Thomas Robbins ... 87

COGAN, M. Ann, m. Patrick **DWYER**, May 19, 1858, at Windsor Locks, by Rev. James Smyth ... 150

COGSWELL, Eliza, m. Col. John **WOOD**, of Greenfield, N. Y., Nov. 14, 1836, by J. Cogswell ... 101

Elizabeth L., of East Windsor, m. James **DIXON**, of Hartford, [Oct.] 1, [1840], by Rev. J. Cogswell ... 108

COHOON, Abigail L., d. [Josiah & Abigail], b. Oct. 2, 1805 (See **CAHOON**] ... 6

Candace, m. Erastus **WOODRUFF**, Sept. 29, 1824, by Rev. Shubael Bartlett ... 86

Caroline P., of Granby, Conn., m. Cornelius R. **STEVENS**, of Martinsburg, N. Y., Nov. 24, 1847, by Rev. J. H. Farnsworth, of Somersville ... 121

Frederick, m. Rosannah A. **DUNN**, Sept. 25, 1856, by Rev. F. Munson ... 145

George, m. Mary Ann **COTTER**, Nov. 28, 1858, at Warehouse Point, by Rev. Henry McClory, of St. John's Ch. ... 152

Harry, [twin with Horace], s. Josiah & Abigail], b. Sept. 2, 1795 ... 6

Horace, [twin with Harry], s. [Josiah & Abigail], b. Sept. 2, 1795 ... 6

Josiah, s. [Josiah & Abigail], b. Dec. 19, 1800 ... 6

Samuel, s. Josiah & Abigail, b. July 22, 1793 ... 6

COLE, Sophia, of East Windsor, m. Austin **BURNHAM**, of East Hartford, Nov. 10, 1831, by Rev. Gurdon Robins of Bap. Ch. ... 94

COLEMAN, Daniel, of Vernon, m. Arminda S. **HAYS**, Dec. 1, 1844, by Shubael Bartlett ... 117

COLLINS, Daniel, [twin with Levi], s. Levi & Hannah, b. Mar. 13, 1792 ... 6

Elizabeth, m. William **VINTON**, May 5, 1819 ... 56

Hannah, d. Levi & Hannah, b. Oct. 19, 1797 ... 6

Hannah, m. Frederick H. **SADD**, b. of East Windsor, May 6, 1840, by W[illia]m Thompson, at Wapping ... 107

Page

COLLINS, (cont.)
 Levi, [twin with Daniel], s. Levi & Hannah, b. Mar. 13, 1792 6
 Simon, s. Levi & Hannah, b. May 5, 1794 6
 Simon, s. Levi & Hannah, d. Oct. 15, 1795, ae 17 m. 10 d. 63
COLLUM, Henry M., of Vernon, m. Emily WEBSTER, of East Windsor,
 May 29, 1842, by Levi Smith, at his house 112
COLSON, Eliza, m. Benjamin SKINNER, b. of East Windsor, Dec. 15,
 1822, by Joseph Russell, J. P. 85
 Evelina, m. William P. STEBBINS, b. of East Windsor, Mar. 31, 1833,
  by Rev. Chauncey G. Lee 96
 Roswel, s. Triphena BISSELL, b. Feb. 24, 1781 6
COLTON, Calvin, m. Mary Ann FROST, Aug. 16, 1840, by Shubael
 Bartlett 108
 Caroline P., m. Samuel I. BARTLETT, Dec. 10, 1856, by Rev.
  Henry W. Conant, of M. E. Ch. 146
 Sarah M., of Enfield, m. Anson E. BARBER, of East Windsor, May
  16, 1850, by Rev. W[illia]m S. Simmons 128
COMSTOCK, Lucinda, m. Sleuman NILES, Sept. 10, 1846, by Rev. Henry
 H. Bates, of St. John's Ch 120
CONE, Carson K., of South Wilbraham, Mass., m. Mary C. ADAMS, of
 Ellington, May 24, 1838, by Rev. Deodate Brockway, of Ellington 103
 Daniel N., of Linklaen, N. Y., m. Emily C. SADD, of East Windsor,
  Aug. 25, 1831, by Rev. Shubael Bartlett 94
 Ogden Childs, of Haddam, m. Dorcas ALLEN, of East Windsor, Nov.
  14, 1822, by Rev. Shubael Bartlett, of 2nd Church 85
COOK, Bernard, m. Catharine JURKINS, b. of Broad Brook, Apr. 8,
 1849, by Rev. Francis J. Clerc 126
 Elihu, m. Sophronia M. PARSONS, b. of East Windsor, May 31,
  1837, by B. Tyler 103
 James, m. Harriet PERKINS, b. of East Windsor, Nov. 26, 1837,
  by Rev. J. Cogswell 103
 John, m. Margaret BARR, Nov. 7, 1847, by Rev. Henry H. Bates,
  of St. John's Ch., Warehouse Point 122
 Mabel, w. Benjamin & d. Amasa & Hannah LOOMIS, d. May 27,
  1800 72
 Mary, of East Windsor, m. George REYNOLDS, of Long Meadow,
  Mass., May 16, 1838, by Asahel Nettleton 103
 Mary, m. Anson F. TALCOTT, June 10, 1841, by Shubael Bartlett 109
 Norman H., m. Maria C. CLARK, Nov. 7, 1854, by Rev. Sam[ue]l
  J. Andrews, of 1st Cong. Ch. 139
 Oliver, s. Benjamin & Abigail, b. June 14, 1769 6
 Robert, m. Sarah Ann WALTON, Dec. 6, 1846, by Rev. Henry H.
  Bates, of St. John's Ch. 120
 Samuel, of Thompsonville, m. Eliza BARR, of Thompsonville,
  Nov. 24, 1850, by Henry H. Bates 129
 Sarah, Mrs., m. Jabez PHELPS, b. of East Windsor, May 25, 1842,
  by Rev. W[illia]m H. Richards, Warehouse Point 112
COOLEY, Carmaralzaman, s. Charles & Eunice, b. June 1, 1809 6

Page

COOLEY, (cont.)

Charles, s. Charles & Eunice, b. Nov. 20, 1804   6

Emily F., m. William M. WHITE, of Otis, Mass., May 23, 1844,

by Shubael Bartlett   114

Henry B., of Springfield, Mass., m. Mariah FARNUM, of East

Windsor, Sept. 6, 1835, by Rev. Pardon T. Keney   99

Juliann, d. Charles & Eunice, b. Aug. 22, 1807   6

Selina, d. Charles & Eunice, b. Apr. 12, 1806   6

Titus, of Springfield, m. Fanny ALLEN, of Westfield, [Nov.] 8, [1821],

by Rev. Thomas Robbins   84

COMMES, COOMS, Nathaniel E., m. Ann LOWRY, Nov. 25, 1847, by

Rev. Henry H. Bates, of St. John's Ch., Warehouse Point   122

William, of Enfield, Conn., m. Clarissa ROCKWELL, of East

Windsor, Mar. 8, 1826, by Horace Barber, J. P.   88

William N., m. Sarah D. SWAN, Aug. 28, 1855, by Rev. L. D.

Bentley, of M. E. Ch.   143

COON, John W., of East Windsor, m. Mary Ann GRANT, of Hebron, Jan.

20, 1830, by Rev. Samuel W. Whelpley   93

Mary Ann, of Palmer, Mass., m. Lemuel F. PEASE, of East Windsor,

July 9, 1848, by Rev. C. W. Stearns   123

CORBIN, David W., of Buffalo, N. Y., m. Cornelia R. HENDRICK, of

East Windsor, Dec. 13, 1846, by Rev. Robert Allyn, at Warehouse

Point   119

CORCORAN, Hannah, of East Windsor, m. Daniel TUCKER, of Vernon,

July 21, 1833, by Rev. David L. Hunn   98

CORKINS, Ann, m. John TIRNEY, June 30, 1852, by Rev. C. S. Putnam,

of St. John's Ch., at Warehouse Pt. Int. Pub.   133

CORNISH, Horace, of Avon, m. Lydia H. ROCKWELL, [May] 12, [1836],

by J. Cogswell   100

COSTELO, Michael, m. Jane FELTON, Oct. 13, 1857, by Rev. Henry

McClory, of St. John's Ch., at Warehouse Point   147

COTTER, Mary Ann, m. George COHOON, Nov. 28, 1858, at Warehouse

Point, by Rev. Henry McClory, of St. John's Ch.   152

COTTON, Abigail, m. Nathan GOODRICH, b. of East Windsor, Jan. 8,

1829, by Rev. S. W. Whelpley   92

George, m. Esther KILBOURN, Oct. 22, 1822, by Rev. Joy H.

Fairchild of East Hartford   85

COVELL, William C., m. Emily L. WOLCOTT, Nov. 26, 1857, by Rev.

Henry W. Conant, of M. E. Ch.   153

COWLES, Sarah, of Farmington, m. Amos S. BRAMAN, of Hartford, Feb.

17, 1830, by Rev. Sam[ue]l W. Whelpley   93

Timothy S., m. Catherine J. HOSMER, b. of East Windsor, [Apr.]

27, [1833], by Rev. Chauncey G. Lee   96

CRACE, Agnes, m. James PATTERSON, Apr. 4, 1851, by Rev. Shubael

Bartlett   130

CRAMER, James, m. Sarah Ann MONGER, b. of East Windsor, July 8,

1834, by Rev. Chauncey G. Lee   97

John, of Woodbury, m. Roxey L. BURNHAM, of East Windsor,

CRAMER, (cont.)

Jan. 11, 1835, by Cha[rle]s Remington, Elder   98

CRANDALL, CRANDAL, Esther, m. William **VINTON,** Apr. 11, 1822   56

  Esther, m. William **VINTON,** b. of East Windsor, Apr. 11, 1822,

    by Rev. Shubael Bartlett of 2nd Church   84

CRANE, Aaron, s. Aaron & Mary, b. Mar. 24, 1781   6

  Achsah, m. Abram **TENANT,** Nov. 27, 1823, by Rev. Shubael Bartlett   86

  Amanda, m. Alexander **THOMPSON,** May 1, 1832, by Rev. Shubael

    Bartlett   95

  Bemas, m. Elizabeth **GIBBS,** Apr. 15, [1821], by Rev. Shubael

    Bartlett of 2nd Church   59

  Betseyann, m. Joshua **RISLEY,** b. of East Windsor, Aug. 30, 1829,

    by Rev. George Sutherland   92

  Curtis, s. David & Jerusha, b. Nov. 9, 1781   6

  David, s. David & Theodotia, b. Oct. 5, 1775   6

  Eli, s. Aaron & Mary, b. Aug. 3, 1787   6

  Henrietta, of East Windsor, m. Merrit **DOANE,** of Tolland, Nov.

    30, 1837, by Joshua Risley, J. P.   102

  Hosea, of Somersfield, N. H., m. Laura Ann **HUBBARD,** of East

    Windsor, Nov. 15, 1827, by Rev. Shubael Bartlett   89

  Jenne, d. Aaron & Mary, b. Dec. 24, 1789   6

  Julia Amanda, m. Warren Green **CARRIER*,** b. of East Windsor, Aug.

    28, 1838, by Rev. Ebenezer Blake, of Warehouse Point *(Perhaps

    CURRIER")   105

  Lucina, d. Aaron & Mary, b. Aug. 19, 1792   6

  Polly, d. Aaron & Mary, b. May 16, 1779   6

  Rollin C., m. Elizabeth **BLODGET,** b. of East Windsor, Feb. 28,

    1839, by Rev. Ebenezer Blake, of Warehouse Point   105

  Russell Wyllys, of East Windsor, m. Lydia **PARMELEE,** of Suffield,

    July 3, 1828, by Rev. Shubael Bartlett   90

  Samuel Pitkin, s. David & Jerusha, b. Jan. 15, 1780   6

  Sophronia, m. Hiram **WOLCOTT,** b. of East Windsor, [Sept.] 23,

    [1824], by Rev. Thomas Robbins   87

  Timothy, s. Aaron & Mary, b. Jan. 28, 1783   6

  Ziba, s. Aaron & Mary, b. Apr. 16, 1785   6

CRAW, Abigail, of East Windsor, m. William **WOOD,** of East Hartford,

    Oct. 22, 1843, by Josiah Ellsworth, J. P.   113

  Austin, of East Windsor, m. Almira **FULLER,** of Glastenbury,

    [Oct.] 19, [1820], by Rev. Shubael Bartlett   59

  Chaunc[e]y, m. Florinda **FULLER,** Mar. 25, [1821], by Rev.

    Shubael Bartlett, of 2nd Church   59

  Clarissa, of East Windsor, m. Esten P. **CLARK,** of Ellington, Apr. 1,

    1832, by Rev. John W. Case   94

  Mary, m. Azel **BOWER,** b. of East Windsor, Nov. 5, [1820], by Rev.

    Shubael Bartlett   59

  Rachel, m. Jonathan **WOOD,** b. of East Windsor, Apr. 13, 1767   56

CRAWFORD, John, m. Lyllia Ann **JOHNS,** July 5, 1849, by Rev. Henry H.

    Bates, of St. John's Ch., Warehouse Point   125

Page

CROCKER, Zebulon, of Ellington, m. Elizabeth PORTER, of East
    Windsor, Oct. 11, 1830, by Rev. Shubael Bartlett   93
CROSBY, Alphonso C., m. Joann F. CHASE, b. of East Windsor, Nov. 29,
    1838, by Rev. Freeman Nutting   105
Hannah E., Mrs. of East Windsor, m. Rev. Eldad BARBER, of
    Milan, O., Apr. 24, 1834, by Rev. Shubael Bartlett   97
Harriet, d. [Elisha & Prudence], b. Nov. 21, 1819   6
Henry, m. Hannah E. OSBORN, Feb. 11, 1824, by Rev. Shubael
    Bartlett of 2nd Church   86
William Bunce, s. Elisha & Prudence, b. Dec. 9, 1814   6
CROSS, Jason, of Perry, N. Y., m. Malinda GRANT, of East Windsor,
    Jan. 20, 1822, by Rev. Oliver B. Cook, of East Hartford   84
CROSSETT, John, Jr., of East Windsor, m. Lucy WILLIAMS, of East
    Hartford, Dec. 16, 1834, by Rev. Shubael Bartlett   98
CULVER, Jerusha, m. Nathaniel BABCOCK, May 12, 1842, by Shubael
    Bartlett   111
CUMING, Alison, d. George & Mary, b. Aug. 16, 1776   6
Mary, d. George & Mary, b. May 22, 1775   6
Rhoda, d. George & Mary, b. Mar. 13, 1781   6
CUNNINGHAM, Benjamin F., of Norwalk, O., m. Susan M. SEXTON, of
    Warehouse Point, Mar. 15, 1854, by Abel Gardner   139
CURTIS, Joseph, of Hampton, m. Julia MAY, of East Windsor, Nov. 9,
    1831, by Rev. Augustus Bolles   94
DABNEY, Elizabeth, of Salem, Mass., m. Dr. Edward TUDOR, of East
    Windsor, [June] 23, [1822], by Rev. Tho[ma]s Robbins   85
DANFORTH, Frances B., of Cabotville, Mass., m. Albert B. POWERS, of
    Westfield, Mass., Aug. 11, 1844, by Rev. Henry H. Bates, of St.
    John's Ch.   116
DANIELS, Amos, of Ludlow, Mass., m. Mary BISSELL, of East Windsor,
    [   ] 10, [1823], by Rev. Thomas Robbins of 1st Soc.   86
Eli W., m. Ann MINER, Dec. 30, 1838, by Rev. John W. Handy,
    Wilbraham   105
James P., of East Windsor, m. Harriet E. GOODALE, of East Hartford,
    Apr. 5, 1844, by Levi Smith   114
Mary Ann, of East Windsor, m. Austin GOODALE, of East Hartford,
    Jan. 19, 1845, by Levi Smith   115
Nehemiah, of Vernon, m. Lucy McNALL, of Ellington, Oct. 31,
    1839, by Rev. Ebenezer Blake, of Wapping   106
DARLING, Mary, m. Eliphalet CHAPIN, b. of East Windsor, Nov. 25, 1773   34
Sarah E., m. LeRoy R. BOWER, Oct. 17, 1842, by Shubael Bartlett   112
DART, William, d. Jan. 12, 1799   64
William, m. Rhoda C. HOLLISTER, b. of East Windsor, this day,
    June 6, 1837, by Rev. Marvin Root   102
DAVENPORT, Charles W., m. Sarah J. ABEL, May 12, 1856, at New
    Haven, by Rev. Enoch Huntington, of Grace Ch. Broad Brook   144
DAVIDSON, Joseph, m. Elizabeth McCLELLEN, b. of Enfield, Jan. 21,
    1852, by Rev. Henry H. Bates, of St. John's Ch., at Warehouse
    Point   132

Page

DAVIS, Charles, of Bristoll, m. Charlotte Elizabeth **POST**, of East
    Windsor, July 31, 1853, by Rev. Charles S. Putnam, of St. John's
    Ch.   137
    David, m. Lucy **PARKER**, b. of East Windsor, Jan. 1, 1777   35
    Esther, d. Abel & Mary, b. Oct. 22, 1776   8
    Phebe, d. Abel & Mary, b. Sept. 9, 1779   8
    William W., of New York, m. Maria S. **RISLEY**, of East Windsor,
    Apr. 2, 1840, by Rev. Ebenezer Blake, of Wapping   107
DAWLEY, Andrew H., m. Helena A. **MATSON**, Apr. 5, 1860, at
    Windsorville, by A. Booth   153
DAWSON, Elisabeth, m. Horatio N. **ADAMS**, Jan. 17, 1860, at Broad
    Brook, by F. A. Hazen   153
    Juliette, m. Henry W. **BISSELL**, b. of East Windsor, Oct. 14,
    1840, by Subael Bartlett   108
    Mary, m. Isaac **BENJAMIN**, b. of East Windsor, June 30, 1853, by
    Rev. Shubael Bartlett   137
    Mary Ann, of New Hartford, m. Norton C. **PARSONS**, of East
    Windsor, Sept. 3, 1837, by Rev. Windsor Ward   102
DAY, Elisha, m. Elsy **WOODWORTH**, Mar. 12, 1848, by Rev. Henry H.
    Bates, of St. John's Ch., Warehouse Point   122
DEMING, Dudley, of Glastenbury, m. Julia Ann **OSBORN**, Nov. 27, 1834,
    by Rev. Shubael Bartlett   98
DENISON, Lorenzo J., m. Frances A. **TURPIN**, Apr. 14, 1859, by D. Ives,
    M. G.   151
    Mary Ellen, m. Nelson K. **BENTON**, Oct. 24, 1854, by Rev. W[illia]m
    K. Douglass, of St. John's Ch.   152
DEWEY, Clarissa, of Suffield, m. Gaius **BOOTH**, of East Windsor, Dec.
    1, 1806   32
    Henry, m. Charlotte **WARD**, b. of Windsor, Nov. 1, 1844, or about
    that date, by Rev. Henry H. Bates, of St. John's Ch.   116
    Lester, m. Rosannah **LORD**, Mar. 19, 1848, by Rev. Henry H. Bates,
    of St. John's Ch., Warehouse Point   122
DEXTER, Charlotte M., m. Frederick E. **BISSELL**, Nov. 18, 1857, by Rev.
    W[illia]m M. Birchard   147
DHEAER, John, m. Margaret **RECH**, b. of Rockville, June 11, 1854, by
    Enoch Huntington   139
DICKINSON, Anson, s. Obadiah & Elizabeth, b. Mar. 28, 1782   8
    Elizabeth, d. Obadiah & Elizabeth, b. Feb. 10, 1774   8
    Ethan, s. Obadiah & Eliz[abeth], b. Sept. 28, 1784   8
    Hannah, d. Obadiah & Elizabeth, b. Mar. 12, 1776   8
    Horris, s. Obadiah & Elizabeth, b. Feb. 6, 1788   8
    Lois, d. Obadiah & Elizabeth, b. June 14, 1787   8
    Mary, d. Obadiah & Elizabeth, b. Jan, 28, 1780   8
    Obadiah, s. Obadiah & Elizabeth, b. Mar. 25, 1770   8
    Seth, s. Obadiah & Elizabeth, b. Jan. 9, 1772   8
DIGGINS, Olive, m. Elijah **PORTER**, Sept. 2, [1821], by Rev. Thomas
    Robbins   84
DINKLER, Josepha, m. Heinrich **SIEGLER**, Oct. 21, 1855, by Rev.

Page

DINKLER, (cont.)

W[illia]m K. Douglass of St. John's Ch. Warehouse Pt.   143

DIXON, James, of Hartford, m. Elizabeth L. **COGSWELL,** of East
Windsor, East Windsor, [Oct.] 1, [1840], by Rev. J. Cogswell   108

DOANE, Eunitia, m. Cyrus T. **LOOMIS,** May 18, 1848, by Shubael Bartlett   122
Merrit, of Tolland, m. Henrietta **CRANE,** of East Windsor, Nov.
30, 1837, by Joshua Risley, J. P.   102

DOBSON, William, m. Maria **STOUGHTON,** b. of Vernon, this day, Nov.
3, 1837, by Rev. Marvin Root   102

DODGE, Anna, of Colchester, m. Nathaniel **DRAKE,** Jr., of East Windsor,
Nov. 27, 1768   35

DOLE, Charles C., of Hartford, m. Charlotte A. **MORGAN,** of Springfield,
Mass., Mar. 13, 1842, by Rev. W[illia]m H. Richards   111

DORCHESTER, Jane C., of Mansfield, m. Charles **CHAMBERLIN,** of
Pittsfield, Mass., Aug. 29, 1847, by Levi Daggett, Jr.   120

DOUGLASS, DOUGLAS, George A., m. Caroline **ABBE,** Nov. 25, 1847,
by Rev. Henry H. Bates, of St. Johnn's Ch. Warehouse Point   122

Hosea, Jr., of New York, m. Jerusha **McKINNEY,** of East Windsor,
Jan. 1, 1845, by Levi Smith   115

DRAKE, Alice, of East Windsor, m. Joseph **HOITT,** of Tolland, Mar. 17,
1833, by Rev. Edmund M. Beebe   96

Alvin, s. Nathaniel, Jr. & Hopefull, b. Oct. [ ], 1784   8

Anna, d. Nathaniel, Jr. & Anna, b. July 17, 1769   8

Anna, w. Nathaniel, Jr., d. Sept. 9, 1769   64

Anna, d. Nath[anie]ll, Jr., d. Nov. 22, 1769   64

Anna, d. Nathaniel, Jr. & Hopefull, b. Nov. 30, 1787   8

Anne, d. Silas & Hannah, b. May 25, 1783   8

Caleb, [twin with Joshua], s. Silas & Hannah, b. Aug. 21, 1787   8

Chauncey, s. Ebenezer & Martha, b. Feb. 10, 1773   8

Chestor, s. Silas & Hannah, b. Apr. 15, 1781   8

Elihu, s. Nathaniel, Jr. & Hopefull, b. Oct. 1, 1779   8

Elihu, m. Susan **PELTON,** b. of East Windsor, Apr. 9, 1829, by Rev.
S. W. Whelpley   92

Elizer, s. Silas & Hannah, b. Mar. 29, 1785   8

Elizur W., m. Eveline **ROLLO,** b. of East Windsor, Apr. 14, 1830,
by Rev. Sam[ue]l W. Whelpley   93

Eunice, of Windsor, m. Joseph **SMITH,** of East Windsor, Dec. 14,
1768   53

Eunice, d. Amasa & Lydia, b. Dec. 2, 1775   8

Francis, s. Amasa & Lydia, b. June 13, 1781   8

Frances Catharine, m. Charles **GRIGGS,** of Tolland, Nov. 10, 1830,
by Gurdon Robbins   93

Gideon, d. Aug. 20, 1771   64

Hannah, of Windsor, m. Zaccheus **MUNSEL,** of East Windsor, May
4, 1768   46

Hannah, d. Silas & Hannah, b. Sept. 8, 1776   8

Ira, s. Silas & Hannah, b. Oct. 8, 1772   8

Joshua, [twin with Caleb], s. Silas & Hannah, b. Aug. 21, 1787   8

Page

DRAKE, (cont.)

Lucina, d. Eben[eze]r & Martha, b. Sept. 4, 1781 — 8

Nathaniel, Jr., of East Windsor, m. Anna **DODGE,** of Colchester, Nov. 27, 1768 — 35

Nathaniel, Jr., of East Windsor, m. Hopefull **WOLCOTT,** Apr. 4, 1774 — 35

Nathaniel, s. Nathaniel, Jr. & Hopefull, b. Feb. 5, 1776 — 8

Owen, m. Hannah **FISH,** b. of East Windsor, Nov. 25, 1829, by Rev. Shubael Bartlett — 92

Polly, d. Amasa & Waistel, b. Oct. 30, 1790 — 8

Rumah, d. Eben[eze]r & Martha, b. May 12, 1775 — 8

Sarah, d. Amasa & Lydia, b. Sept. 10, 1778 — 8

Silas, of East Windsor, m. Hannah **WEST,** of Tolland, Nov. 12, 1771 — 35

Silas, s. Silas & Hannah, b. July 4, 1779 — 8

Silas, Jr., of Hartford, m. Eliza **WARBURTON,** of East Windsor, Sept. 25, [1821], by Rev. Thomas Robbins — 84

Simeon, s. Silas & Hannah, b. Oct. 30, 1790 — 8

Theodotia, d. Eben[eze]r & Martha, b. May 11, 1777 — 8

Thomas, s. Amasa & Waistel, b. June 30, 1799 — 8

Warner, s. Ebenezer & Martha, b. Jan. 13, 1771 — 8

Wolcott, s. Nathaniel, Jr. & Hopefull, b. Nov. 22, 1777 — 8

DRISKELL, John O., m. Susan M. **CARRAGAIN,** b. of Ireland, Dec. 10, 1843, by Levi Smith — 113

DUFFON, Nancy Anne, of East Windsor, m. William **MORROW,** of Suffield, Feb. 6, 1853, by Rev. Charles N. Seymour — 136

DUNHAM, Dwight P., m. Helen* H. **PRIOR,** Jan. 1, 1857, by Rev. Henry McClory of St. John's Ch. *(In margin "Ellen") — 146

Helen M., m. Andrew **HAMILTON,** b. of East Windsor, Nov. 1, 1849, by Rev. W[illia]m S. Simmons — 126

DUNN, Mary, m. George **MARSDEN,** b. of East Windsor, Nov. 25, 1852, by Rev. S. S. Putnam, of St. John's Ch. — 135

Nancy, of Cabotville, Mass., m. James **SIMPSON,** of Enfield, Oct. 24, 1852, by Rev. C. S. Putnam, of St. John's Ch., Warehouse Pt. — 134

Rosannah A., m. Frederick **COHOON,** Sept. 25, 1856, by Rev. F. Munson — 145

Samson, of Albany, N. Y., m. Rhoda E. **ALLEN,** of East Windsor, Dec. 31, 1838, by Rev. Marvin Root — 104

DWIGHT, Daniel, of Detroit, Mich., m. Sarah W. **ALLEN,** of East Windsor, Oct. 31, 1826, by Rev. Shubael Bartlett — 88

DWYER, Patrick, m. M. Ann **COGAN,** May 19, 1858, at Windsor Locks, by Rev. James Smyth — 150

EASEY, Josiah, of New York, m. Mary Ann **GERRISH,** of Broad Brook, Dec. 3, 1848, by Rev. Francis J. Clerc, of Grace Ch., Broad Brook — 125

EASTMAN, Sarah, of East Windsor, m. Roswell **PHELPS,** of Wilbraham, Mass., Aug. 15, 1852, by Rev. Samuel J. Andrews, of Cong. Ch. — 134

EASTON, Eliphas, of Stafford, m. Mary **BRAGG,** of East Windsor, this day, [Mar. 30, 1829], by Gurdon Robbins — 91

Jane Ann, of East Hartford, m. Warren **GRANT,** of East Windsor, [Nov.] 22, [1825], by Rev. Thomas Robbins — 88

Page

ELLSWORTH, ELSWORTH, (cont.)
    by Rev. Shubael Bartlett   59
    Elizabeth S., m. Hiram **WATSON**, b. of East Windsor, Nov. 10,
        1829, by Rev. Shubael Bartlett   92
    Erastus, of New York, m. Elizabeth S. **WOLCOTT**, of East Windsor,
        [Nov.] 23, [1820], by Rev. Thomas Robbins, of 1st Soc.   84
    Flavius J., m. Martha J. **ABBEY**, b. of East Windsor, May 1, 1853,
        by Rev. A. M. Allen   137
    Frederick, s. Abner Mosely & Alcee, b. Nov. 8, 1798   10
    Hannah, m. Chester A. **BOWERS**, Sept. 27, 1839, by Shubael Bartlett   106
    Hannah C., m. Philetus M. **BURGESS**, Jan. 1, 1846, by Shubael
        Bartlett   117
    Jane E., m. James W. **GRUSH**, Aug. 11, 1859, by Rev. Frederick
        Munson, of 1st Ch.   152
    Jason, m. Mary **PHELPS**, b. of East Windsor, May 1, 1823, by Rev.
        Shubael Bartlett of 2nd Church   85
    Jason, m. Sarah **MORTON**, b. of East Windsor, June 4, 1845, by Rev.
        James C. Houghton, of Hartland   116
    Job, Jr., m. Laura **OSBORN**, b. of East Windsor, [Oct.] 17, [1820],
        by Rev. Shubael Bartlett   59
    Job, m. Huldah **ALLEN**, b. of East Windsor, Feb. 20, 1826, by Rev.
        Shubael Bartlett   88
    Lucretia M., of East Windsor, m. Rev. Moses **STODDARD**, of the
        New England Conference, June 28, 1840, by Rev. A. Niles   108
    Lucy S., m. Samuel B. **FORBES**, Sept. 2, 1857, by W[illia]m
        Thompson   147
    Lydia, m. Lucius F. **THAYER**, [Oct.] 15, [1821], by Rev. Shubael
        Bartlett of 2nd Church   59
    Priscilla, m. Willis **MORTON**, b. of East Windsor, Apr. 6, 1830,
        by Rev. Sam[ue]l W. Whelpley   93
    Sarah E., m. Oliver C. **BUCKLAND**, b. of East Windsor, this day,
        [Apr. 9, 1840], by Rev. Moses Stoddard, of M. E. Ch.   107
    Thomas Potwine, m. Elizabeth **MORTON**, b. of East Windsor, Apr.
        7, 1829, by Rev. Shubael Bartlett   91
ELMER, Dulcinea, m. Henry **ANDERSON**, b. of East Windsor, this day,
    [Nov. 26, 1840], by Rev. Samuel Spring, of Cong. Ch., East
    Hartford   109
    Frances A., of East Windsor, m. Harvey **GOODWIN**, of West
        Hartford, Feb. 2, 1845, at the house of Horace Burnham, by Rev.
        Gurdon Robbins, of 1st Bap. Ch. Hartford   115
    Harvey, m. Clarissa **BURNHAM**, of East Hartford, Apr. 19, 1830,
        by Rev. Sam[ue]l W. Whelpley   93
    Huldah, m. Edwin **BIRGE**, b. of East Windsor, [Dec.] 23, [1823],
        by Rev. Thomas Robbins of 1st Church   87
    Martha, m. Thomas **FOSTER**, b. of East Windsor, Dec. 24, 1761   38
    Olive E., m. Francis **STOUGHTON**, b. of East Windsor, Jan. 1,
        1840, by [   ] (Entry crossed out)   115
    Orrin, of West Hartford, m. Mary **NEWBERRY**, of East Windsor, June

Page

ELMER, (cont.)
    4, 1829, by Rev. Sam[ue]l W. Whelpley   92
ELSER, ELLSER, Frederick, m. Louisa **TSCHUMI,** Dec. 22, 1857, at
    Warehouse Point, by Rev. Henry McClory, of St. John's Ch.
    (Entry crossed out)   150
    Frederick, m. Louisa **TSCHUMI** Dec. 22, 1857, at Warehouse Pt.,
    by Rev. Henry McClory, of St. John's Ch. (Elser)   149
ELY, Albert S., m. Lucinda **ABBE,** b. of East Windsor, Oct. 3, 1838,
    by Shubael Bartlett   104
    Ellas, of Springfield, m. Mary A. **BRYER,** of Albany, Aug. 15,
    1853, by Rev. Enoch Huntington of Grace Ch.   137
ENO, Laura J., of Bloomfield, m. Rufus M. **PATCHEN,** of East Windsor,
    Oct. 8, [1848], by Edward A. Lyon   124
    Philomela, d. Joab & Susanna, b. June 24, 1783   10
ENOS, Sibbel, of Hartland, Vt., m. Noadiah **BISSELL,** of East Windsor,
    July 13, 1794, by Rev. Daniel Spooner, at Hartland   32
ENSWORTH, Walter M., of Somers, m Caroline **PIERCE,** of East
    Windsor, Aug. 18, 1843, by Josiah Ellsworth, J. P.   113
ERVIN, Mary, m. Robert E. **BADER,** Mar. 31, 1850, by Shubael Bartlett   127
EVANS, [see also **EWAN**], Frederick m. Patience A. **RISLEY,** b. of
    Manchester, May 11, 1845, by Rev. B. M. Walker   116
EWAN, [see also **EVANS**], James, of Enfield, m. Ellen M. **ABBE,** of East
    Windsor, Dec. 1, 1850, by Rev. Henry H. Bates, of St. John's Ch.
    (Perhaps "EVAN")   131
FARNHAM, FARNUM, Marcus C., m. Julia Ann **ALLEN,** b. of Broad-
    Brook, Nov. 7, 1837, by Rev. John H. Willis   102
    Mariah, of East Windsor, m. Henry B. **COOLEY,** of Springfield,
    Mass., Sept. 6, 1835, by Rev. Pardon T. Keney   99
    Matilda, of East Windsor, m. Chauncey **BROWN,** of Springfield,
    Mass., Nov. 9, 1829, by Rev. Shubael Bartlett   92
FELTON, Jane, m. Michael **COSTELO,** Oct. 13, 1857, at Warehouse Point,
    by Rev. Henry McClory of St. John's Ch., at Warehouse Point   147
FENTON, Caleb, m. Electa **KING,** [Dec.] 14, [1820], by Rev. Shubael
    Bartlett   59
    Eleazer, m. Wealthy **BOWE,** b. of East Windsor, this day, [Jan.
    22, 1835], by Chauncey G. Lee   98
    Harriet N., of Vernon, m. William B. **THOMPSON,** of East Windsor,
    [Nov. 24, 1839], by Rev. Marvin Root   107
    Sarah, 2nd, of East Windsor, m. John **CHAPMAN,** of Westerly, R. I.,
    Nov. 26, 1833, by Rev. Shubael Bartlett   96
FIFIELD, Moses, s. Moses & Alice*, b. Dec. 23, 1823 *(Perhaps "Olive")   12
FILLEY, Mary M., of East Windsor, m. George M. **SESSIONS,** of Hartford,
    May 14, 1840, by Levi Smith   107
    Sarah, of East Windsor, m. Hezekiah **GAYLORD,** of Windsor, [Dec.]
    29, [1825], by Rev. Thomas Robbins of 1st Church   88
FINKLEDEY, Charles, m. Sophia **SMITH,** Aug. 17, 1856, at Warehouse
    Point, by Rev. Henry M. Clory, of St. John's Ch.   145
FINLEY, Jane, Mrs., m. Jacob **STRIFE,** Oct. 29, 1855, by Rev. W[illia]m

Page

FITCH, (cont.)

Warren, of Tolland, m. Rachel **CLARK,** of East Windsor, Feb. 12,
    1835, by Rev. Shubael Bartlett   98

FLEMING, Elliot, m. Elizabeth Louisa **NEWELL,** Mar. 1, 1852
    (see marriages recorded under May 1864)   134

FLETCHER, Maria, of East Windsor, m. Porter **CHASE,** of Vernon, June
    24, 1841, by Shubael Bartlett   110

FLINT, Charlotte, of East Windsor, m. Francis **BIRGE,** of Hartford, [Apr.]
    17, [1834], by Rev. Chauncey G. Lee   97

Elijah, s. Archelaus & Chloe, b. Feb. 7, 1773   12

James, s. Archelaus & Chloe, b. Dec. 7, 1770   12

FOOT, Lewis, of Hartford, m. Mrs. Catharine F. **ADAMS,** of East Windsor,
    this day, [Oct. 18, 1843], by Samuel Spring   113

FORBES, Albert, of East Hartford, m. Elsa **OSBORN,** of East Windsor,
    Aug. 18, 1830, by Rev. Shubael Bartlett   93

H. Almira, of Middletown, m. Franklin A. **GRANT,** of East Windsor,
    Dec. 27, 1852, by Rev. James Mather   136

Samuel B., m. Lucy S. **ELLSWORTH,** Sept. 2, 1857, by W[illia]m
    Thompson   147

FOSS, Daniel M., m. Caroline N. **BUSH,** Oct. 7, 1856, at Warehouse Pt.,
    by Rev. H. W. Conant of M. E. Ch.   145

FOSTER, Abner, s. Thomas & Martha, b. Feb. 16, 1769   12

Anna, d. Thomas & Martha, b. Feb. 14, 1765   12

Betty, d. Thomas & Martha, b. Oct. 22, 1771   12

Emily, of East Windsor, m. James **RISLEY,** of Ellington, Mar. 27,
    1845, by Rev. B. M. Walker   115

Harriet, m. Augustus **WHITON,** b. of East Windsor, May 1, 1834,
    by Rev. David L. Hunn   98

James, s. Hackaliah & Lois, b. Aug. 3, 1771   12

Martha, d. Thomas & Martha, b. Aug. 20, 1776   12

Mary, d. Thomas & Martha, b. Feb. 13, 1763   12

Mary, of East Windsor, m. Lucius **GRANT,** of East Windsor, Nov.
    22, 1838, by Rev. Freeman Nutting   104

Maryett, m. Harvey H. **BUCKLAND,** b. of East Windsor, Dec. 26,
    1841, by Rev. A. C. Wheat   110

Oliver, s. Thomas & Martha, b. Jan. 16, 1767   12

Pamela, of East Windsor, m. James **FRANCIS,** of Philadelphia,
    May 12, 1840, by Rev. Ebenezer Blake, of Wapping   107

Roswell, s. Hackaliah & Lois, b. May 28, 1768   12

Sally, d. Thomas & Martha, b. Jan. 22, 1779   12

Sally, m. Edgar **STOUGHTON,** b. of East Windsor, Nov. 29, 1832,
    by Rev. D. L. Hunn   96

Thomas, m. Martha **ELMER,** b. of East Windsor, Dec. 24, 1761   38

Thomas, s. Thomas & Martha, b. June 30, 1774   12

William, s. Thomas & Martha, b. Oct. 27, 1781   12

FOWLER, Christopher, m. Lucretia **SMITH,** Dec. 25, 1827, by G. W.
    Doane, at Warehouse Point   90

Ephraim, of New York, m. Minerva **ABBEY,** of East Windsor, Mar.

Page

FOWLER, (cont.)

9, 1833, by Rev. David L. Hunn   98

John I., of Suffield, m. Caroline **MORRAN,** of East Windsor, Jan.

23, 1848, by Shubael Bartlett   121

Minerva, wid., m. Ebenezer **AMIDON,** June 22, 1845, by Shubael

Fowler   117

FOX, Levi G., m. Elizabeth H. **BODFISH,** May 1, 1839, by Shubael Bartlett   106

Oscar, m. Eliza **WEEKS,** Aug. 23, 1846, by Rev. Henry H. Bates,

of St. John's Ch.   120

Polly, d. Jabez & Polly, b. Jan. 20, 1772   12

FRANCIS, James, of Philadelphia, m. Pamela **FOSTER,** of East Windsor,

May 12, 1840, by Rev. Ebenezer Blake, of Wapping   107

FREDERICK, John, m. Catharine **PFENING,** Dec. 24, 1855, by Rev.

Enoch Huntington of Grace Ch.   144

Philpina, m. Philip L. **BUBACH,** May 24, 1857, by Rev. W[illia]m

M. Birchard   147

FRENCH, Agnes, of East Windsor, m. Leonard **CLARK,** of Somerset, Vt.,

Jan. 14, 1822, by Rev. Shubael Bartlett of 2nd Soc.   84

Cynthia D., of East Windsor, m. Ashbel **HILLS,** of East Hartford,

Oct. 2, 1839, by Shubael Bartlett   106

Jane E., m. John H. **REED,** Dec. 8, 1859, by Rev. Warren Emerson   152

Laura H., m. James H. **SHIPMAN,** Oct. 26, 1837, by Shubael Bartlett   103

Submit, of Winchester, m. Joseph A. **HAWKINS,** of East Windsor,

[Nov.] 27, [1825], by Rev. Tho[ma]s Robbins of 1st Church   88

Thirza, m. John B. **ORCUTT,** July 13, 1841, by Shubael Bartlett   110

FRITZ, Helena Mary, m. Walter C. **MAY,** Nov. 21, 1858, at Warehouse

Point, by Rev. Henry McClory, of St. John's Ch.   152

FROST, Aaron, m. Parnal **WOOD,** b. of East Windsor, Apr. 12, 1773   38

Aaron, s. Aaron & Parnal, b. Sept. 22, 1775   12

Aaron, s. Aaron & Parnal, d. Sept. 19, 1776   67

Aaron, of East Windsor, m. Margerett **HAMMOND,** of Tolland, [his

2nd w.], Aug. 13, 1777   38

Aaron, s. Aaron & Marg[a]rett, b. Nov. 3, 1778   12

Alpha, s. Aaron & Margarett, b. July 30, 1782   12

Amos, s. Samuel & Patience, b. June 23, 1777   12

Cynthia, m. Normand **PASCO,** Apr. 24, 1834, by Rev. Shubael Bartlett   97

David P., of East Windsor, m. Sophronia **WIMAN,** of Stockbridge,

Mass., Apr. 10, 1842, by Shubael Bartlett   111

Experience, m. Anthony **SLAFTER,** b. of East Windsor, Jan. 4, 1769   53

Mary Ann, m. Calvin **COLTON,** Aug. 16, 1840, by Shubael Bartlett   108

Parnal, d. Aaron & Parnal, b. July 14, 1773   12

Parnal, w. Aaron, d. Sept. 17, 1776   67

Samuel, of East Windsor, m. Patience **HAMMOND,** of Tolland, Nov.

22, 1775   38

Sela, s. Aaron & Margaret, b. Oct. 10, 1784   12

FRYE, Barbara, of East Windsor, m. Joseph **KLERSY,** of Ellington,

Dec. 12, 1852, by Rev. Charles N. Seymour   135

FULLER, Almina, of East Windsor, m. Jonathan **WILLIAMS,** of Wales,

Page

FULLER, (cont.)

Mass., Oct. 25, 1846, by Rev. Sewall Lamberton   118

Almira, of Glastenbury, m. Austin **CRAW,** of East Windsor, [Oct.] 19,
[1820], by Rev. Shubael Bartlett   59

Amanda, of East Windsor, m. Nathan **TIFF,** of Foster, R. I., Dec.
15, 1829, by Rev. Shubael Bartlett   92

Annis, d. Horace D. & Sarah, b. Apr. 9, 1844   12

Annis, d. Horace D. & Sarah, d. June 2, 1845   67

Charlottee, of East Windsor, m. Elias **WEBSTER,** of Columbia,
[Oct.] 21, [1821], by Rev. Nathan B. Burgess   59

Florinda, m. Chaunc[e]y **CRAW,** Mar. 25, [1821], by Rev. Shubael
Bartlett of 2nd Church   59

Horace D., of Ellington, m. Mrs. Maria K. **PEMBER,** of East
Windsor, Feb. 28, 1839, by Rev. Ebenezer Blake, of Warehouse
Point   105

Horace D., m. Sally **STOUGHTON,** b. of East Windsor, June 26,
1843, by Rev. B. M. Walker   113

Lucy, m. Aurelius B. **BARBER,** b. of East Windsor, Dec. 26, 1852,
by Rev. Samuel J. Andrews, of 1st Cong. Ch.   136

Marvin, of Middletown, m. Mary **HAYES,** Oct. 5, 1831, by Rev.
Gurdon Robins, of Bap. Ch.   94

GALE, Nahum, Rev. of Ware, Mass., m. Martha **TYLER,** of East Windsor,
[Aug.] 10, [1843], by Bennet Tyler   113

GALPIN, Samuel H., of Wethersfield, m. Mary Ann **PERRIN,** of East
Windsor, Nov. 28, 1844, by William Thompson   115

GARBER, Elizabeth, of Ketch **MILLS,** m. Jacob **RIERSTEINER,** Nov. 7,
1848, by Rev. Francis J. Clerc, of Grace Ch., Broad Brook   124

GARGILE, Mary Ann, m. John **CLARK,** Aug. 6, 1849, by Rev. Henry H.
Bates, of St. John's Ch., Warehouse Point   125

GARY, Michael, m. Ellen **CARROL,** Feb. 17, 1858, at Broad Brook, by
Rev. B. Tully   148

GAY, Asahel, of Mass., m. Aurelia **PASCO,** of East Windsor, Apr. 1,
1835, by Rev. Shubael Bartlett   99

GAYLORD, Alexander, s. Charles & Margarett, b. Mar. 28, 1782   13

Anne, d. Abial & Mehetable, b. Feb. 17, 1786   13

Bets[e]y, d. Abiel & Mehetable, b. Mar. 23, 1778   13

Charles, s. Charles & Margarett, b. Dec. 12, 1779   13

Guy, s. Abial & Mehitable, b. Jan. 12, 1780   13

Henry, s. Abial & Mehetable, b. Oct. 17, 1790   13

Hezekiah, of Windsor, m. Sarah **FILLEY,** of East Windsor, [Dec.]
29, [1825], by Rev. Thomas Robbins of 1st Church   88

Horace, s. Abial & Mehetable, b. Aug. 15, 1781   13

Horatio, s. Abial & Mehetable, b. Mar. 15, 1788   13

John, s. Charles & Margarett, b. Mar. 13, 1785   13

John Lothrop, s. Abiel & Mehitable, b. Aug. 28, 1776   13

Norman, s. Abial & Mehetable, b. May 2, 1796   13

Polly, [twin with Sophia], d. Abial & Mehetable, b. July 22, 1793   13

Sophia, [twin with Polly], d. Abial & Mehetable, b. July 22, 1793   13

Page

GAYLORD, (cont.)
Stoughton, s. Abial & Mehitable, b. Aug. 17, 1784   13
Zeviah, d. Abiel & Mehitable, b. Mar. 5, 1775   13
GEAR, [see also GEIER], Edmund S., of Hebron, m. Henry Henrietta H.
HALL*, of East Windsor, July 2, 1845, by O. F. Parker. Int.
Pub. *(Written in margin "Henrietta H. HALL")   116
GEIER, [see also GEAR], Barbara, m. Albert APSTEIN, Sept. 3, 1859,
at Warehouse Point, by Rev. Henry McClory, of St. John's Ch.   152
GEISHAKER, John, m. Mrs. Eunice ALLEN, b. of East Windsor, Dec. 11,
1848, by Rev. Edward A. Lyon   124
GENTISH, Rosalia, m. Frederick KRAMER, May 7, 1855, by Rev. Enoch
Huntington of Grace Ch., Broad Brook   142
GERRISH, Mary Ann, of Broad Brook, m. Josiah EASEY, of New York,
Dec. 3, 1848, by Rev. Francis J. Clerc, of Grace Ch. Broad Brook   125
GIBBS, Ebenezer, m. Sally GRANT, b. of East Windsor, Dec. 11, 1827,
by Rev. Shubael Bartlett   89
Elizabeth, m. Beman CRANE, Apr. 15, [1821], by Rev. Shubael
Bartlett of 2nd Church   59
GILLETT, GILLETTE, Adelia, m. William PAYNE, b. of East Windsor,
this day, [Nov. 9, 1836], by Rev. Marvin Root   101
Mary Alice, of East Windsor, m. Ira HILLS, of East Hartford, this
day, Sept. 26, 1838, by Rev. Samuel Spring, of Cong. Ch. East
Hartford   104
Ozias L., m. Maria Elisabeth ELLIS, Oct. 2, 1856, at Warehouse
Point, by Rev. H. W. Conant, of M. E. Ch.   145
GLEASON, Azuba, of Enfield, m. Hezekiah ALLEN, Jr., of East Windsor,
Dec. 28, 1802   31
Charles F. Rev. of Worcester, Mass., m. Elizabeth CHARLTON*,
of East Windsor, May 14, 1845, by Bennet Tyler *(Written in
margin "Elizabeth H.")   115
Cynthia, Mrs. of East Windsor, m. [ ] PARSONS, of Plymouth,
Conn., [ ], 1830, by Rev. Gurdon Robins of Bap. Ch.   94
Eli, m. Clarissa JOHNSON, Sept. 13, 1837, by Shubael Bartlett   102
George, m. Adeline BENJAMIN, b. of East Windsor, Jan. 16, 1833,
by William Barnes, J. P.   96
Hannah, of Enfield, m. Samuel ALLEN, of East Windsor, July 15,
1841, by William Barnes, J. P.   110
Joseph, m. Laura JOHNSON, Aug. 11, 1842, by Shubael Bartlett   112
Joseph B., of Manchester, m. Caroline BUCKLAND, of East Windsor,
Apr. 1, 1833, by Rev. B. F. Northrop   96
GLYNN, Elizabeth, of East Windsor, m. Timothy ATWOOD, of Rockville,
Nov. 30, [1848], by Edward A. Lyon   124
GODDARD, John, of Roxbury, Mass., m. Catharine TYLER, of East
Windsor, this day, [Aug. 4, 1840], by Bennet Tyler   108
GOLDENBERGER, Lisetta, m. Michael ZUST, b. of Enfield, Apr. 6,
[1848], by Rev. Francis J. Clerc, of Grace Ch., Broad Brook   121
GOOD, James, m. Marcia ELLIS, Aug. 31, 1856, at Warehouse Point, by
Rev. H. W. Conant, of M. E. Ch.   145

Page

GRANT, (cont.)

by Rev. Shubael Bartlett	59
Elvira, m. Henry Chauncey **STOUGHTON**, this day, [Nov. 7, 1839],	
by Rev. Marvin Root	106
Franklin A., of East Windsor, m. H. Almira **FORBES**, of Middletown,	
Dec. 27, 1852, by Rev. James Mather	136
Frederick W., m. Ann E. **STOUGHTON**, Oct. 27, 1842, by Shubael	
Bartlett	112
Grace, m. Asahel **GREEN**, b. of East Windsor, Oct. 1, 1778	39
Hannah, of East Windsor, m. Henry **LOOMIS**, of Westfield, Mass.,	
Oct. 10, 1838, by Rev. Freeman Nutting	104
Harvey, m. Sarah Ellsworth **OSBORN**, b. of East Windsor, Jan. 22,	
1829, by Rev. Shubael Bartlett	91
Hiram, of Hartford, m. Mary **HORSMER**, of East Windsor, [Dec.] 6,	
[1821], by Rev. Thomas Robbins	84
Horace, Capt., m. Lucina **GRANT**, Jan. 6, 1835, by Rev. Sam[ue]l	
Drake	98
Jerusha, d. Azariah & Abigail, b. June 5, 1758	13
Joseph O., m. Josephine A. **MATSON**, Mar. 28, 1855, by Rev. Abel	
Gardner, at Warehouse Point	142
Laura A., of East Windsor, m. Edwin **HURLBUT**, of Enfield, Jan.	
30, 1845, by Levi Smith	115
Leonard, m. Ruth **ROCKWELL**, Sept. 15, 1836, by V. R. Osborn,	
V. D. M.	101
Lucina, m. Pelitiah **BLISS**, [June] 6, [1821], by Rev. Thomas Robbins	84
Lucina, m. Capt. Horace **GRANT**, Jan. 6, 1835, by Rev. Sam[ue]l	
Drake	98
Lucius, of East Windsor, m. Mary **FOSTER**, of East Windsor, Nov.	
22, 1838, by Rev. Freeman Nutting	104
Lucy, d. Azariah & Abigail, b. Apr. 22, 1761	13
Luther H., m. Eliza **MOODY**, b. of Ellington, Jan. 4, 1852, by Rev.	
John W. Case	132
Malinda, of East Windsor, m. Jason **CROSS**, of Perry, N. Y., Jan.	
20, 1822, by Rev. Oliver B. Cook, of East Hartford	84
Marilda, m. Horace **HORSMER**, b. of East Windsor, [July] 21,	
[1820], by Rev. Thomas Robbins of 1st Eccl. Soc.	59
Mary Ann, of Hebron, m. John W. **COON**, of East Windsor, Jan. 20,	
1830, by Rev. Samuel W. Whelpley	93
Mary Jane, of East Windsor, m. Henry **WRIGHT**, of East Hartford,	
Nov. 26, 1839, by Rev. Ebenezer Blake, of Wapping	106
Mary M., m. Andrew J. **RUSS**, Sept. 25, 1856, by W[illia]m Barnes,	
J. P.	145
Naaman, of East Windsor, m. Sarah **CLOUGH**, of Manchester, Nov.	
20, 1838, by Rev. Freeman Nutting, at Manchester	104
Nancy, m. Randolph **GRANT**, Jan. 6, 1835, by Rev. Sam[ue]l Drake	98
Nancy A., of East Windsor, m. Joseph **SHELDON**, of Manchester,	
Mar. 30, 1834, by Rev. David L. Hunn	98
Randolph, m. Nancy **GRANT**, Jan. 6, 1835, by Rev. Sam[uel]l Drake	98

48

Page

GRANT, (cont.)
Roxey, of East Windsor, m. William **NOBLE**, Jr., of Hartford, Mar.
    29, 1834, by Rev. E. M. Beebe   97
Sally, m. Ebenezer **GIBBS**, b. of East Windsor, Dec. 11, 1827, by
    Rev. Shubael Bartlett   89
Samuel, s. Azariah & Abigail, b. Mar. 6, 1752   13
Samuel, of East Windsor, m. Elizabeth **WEBSTER**, of Hartford, [Feb.]
    1, [1821], by Rev. Thomas Robbins of 1st Eccl. Soc.   84
Solyman W., m. Lucinda **ROLLO**, this day, [Sept. 28, 1836], by
    Chauncey G. Lee   101
Warren, of East Windsor, m. Jane Ann **EASTON**, of East Hartford,
    [Nov.] 22, [1825], by Rev. Thomas Robbins   88
Warren, of East Windsor, m. Jane G. **ALLEN**, of Springfield, Mass.,
    Jan. 29, 1838, by Rev. Windsor Ward   103
Wealthy, of East Windsor, m. William S. **SIMMONS**, of Bristol,
    R. I., this day, [June 21, 1844], by Rev. Charles Noble,
    Manchester   114
William, m. Eliza **HIGLEY**, b. of East Windsor, Jan. 9, 1839, by
    Rev. Freeman Nutting   105
Willys, m. Emily **BELCHER**, b. of East Windsor, July 6, [1820],
    by Rev. Thomas Robbins of 1st Eccl. Soc.   59
GRAVES, Edward H., m. Clarissa **INGOLS**, Feb. 5, 1849, by Rev. Henry
    H. Bates, of St. John's Ch., Warehouse Point   125
Lydia Barber, of Belchertown, m. Asahel **CLA[R]KE**, of Granby,
    both of Mass., Feb. 5, 1823, by Rev. William Josephus Buckley of
    Warehouse Point   85
GREEN, Asahel, m. Grace **GRANT**, b. of East Windsor, Oct. 1, 1778   39
Asahel, s. Asahel & Grace, b. Apr. 18, 1786   13
Augusta Melissa, d. William & Jane Melissa, b. Aug. 1, 1843   13
Charles, of U. S. Navy, m. Sophia H. **TUDOR**, of East Windsor,
    Dec. 16, 1840, by Levi Smith   109
Daniel, s. Jabesh & Mary, b. Dec. 22, 1802   13
Doshe, d. Asahel & Grace, b. Feb. 9, 1788   13
Eli, s. Asahel & Grace, b. Nov. 7, 1789   13
Elizabeth Jane, d. William & Jane Melissa, b. Sept. 14, 1835   13
Elizabeth Jane, d. William & Jane Melissa, d. Jan. 21, 1839   68
Eunice, d. Asahel & Grace, b. July 18, 1779   13
Eunice, of East Windsor, m. Nathaniel **NEWELL**, of Ellington, Sept.
    10, 1828, by Rev. Sam[ue]l W. Whelpley of 1st Church   91
Huldah, d. Roswell & Zebiah, b. May 23, 1792   13
Jabesh, s. Roswell & Zebiah, b. Mar. 20, 1794   13
Jabesh, of East Windsor, m. Mary **McCARTY**, of Canterbury, Nov.
    1, 1797   39
Martin, s. Asahel & Grace, b. Nov. 21, 1780   13
Mason, s. Roswell & Zebiah, b. Mar. 30, 1787   13
Olive, d. Jabesh & Mary, b. Mar. 5, 1799   13
Olive, d. Jabish & Mary, d. Oct. 16, 1801   68
Olive, d. Jabesh & Mary, b. Apr. 19, 1805   13

Page

GREEN, (cont.)

Rebecca Ann, d. Samuel, of East Windsor, m. Merrick W. **CHAPIN**, of Hartford, May 12, 1840, by Rev. George Burgess, of Christ Ch. Hartford ... 113

Richard C., m. Rosilla S. **ADAMS**, Dec. 14, 1857, by Rev. Lozien Pierce ... 148

Roswell, s. Roswell & Zebiah, b. Nov. 26, 1789 ... 13

Roxa, d. Asahel & Grace, b. July 21, 1782 ... 13

Sarah E., d. of Samuel, m. David M. **TUDOR**, b. of East Windsor, Dec. 12, 1839, by Rev. George Burgess, of Christ Ch. Hartford ... 107

Sarah Sabra, d. William & Jane Melissa, b. Nov. 23, 1837 ... 13

Thankful, d. Asahel & Grace, b. June 15, 1784 ... 13

Theodocia, m. John **STOUGHTON**, b. of East Windsor, Jan. 5, 1831, by Rev. Shubael Bartlett ... 93

William, m. Jane Melissa **BISSELL**, Apr. 29, 1834, by Rev. Shubael Bartlett ... 97

William Wolcott, s. William & Jane Melissa, b. Sept. 29, 1839 ... 13

GREENLEAF, Orick H., m. Mary Ann **POTWINE**, Jan. 31, 1847, by Shubael Bartlett ... 119

GREENWOOD, John W., m. Phebe **LONG**, May 7, 1857, by Rev. F. Munson ... 146

GRESHABO, John, m. Elisabeth **TSCHUMI**, Dec. 3, 1854, by Rev. W[illia]m K. Douglas, of St. John's Ch. ... 153

GRIFFITH, Nathaniel, m. Caroline **KILROY**, b. of Enfield, Jan. 16, 1852, by Rev. Henry H. Bates, of St. John's Ch., at Warehouse Pt. ... 132

GRIGGS, Charles,, of Tolland, m. Frances Catharine **DRAKE**, Nov. 10, 1830, by Gurdon Robbins ... 93

N. M., m. M. W. **BAILEY**, July 4, 1838, by Rev. C. A. Carter, Wapping ... 103

GRISWOLD, Jerome, of Windsor, m. Lorinda **BANCROFT**, of East Windsor, Mar. 16, 1831, by Rev. Shubael Bartlett ... 94

Roger, m. Julia A. **WELLS**, Jan. 1, 1856, by Rev. J. B. Stoddard ... 144

Sarah, of Wilbraham, Mass., m. John **BARBER**, of Palmer, Mass., Sept. 15, 1839, by Rev. Benjamin C. Phelps, of Warehouse Point ... 106

GRUBER, Christian, m. Susan **STEINMEITS**, Jan. 22, 1850, by Rev. Henry H. Bates, of St. John's Ch., Warehouse Pt. (b. of East Windsor) ... 127

Louisa, m. John **WICKLER**, b. of East Windsor, Dec. 22, 1849, by Rev. Henry H. Bates, of St. John's Ch., Warehouse Pt. ... 127

GRUSH, James W., m. Jane E. **ELLSWORTH**, Aug. 11, 1859, by Rev. Frederick Munson, of 1st Ch. ... 152

HAAG, Elizabeth, m. Michael **WHITMAER**, Jan. 16, 1849, by Rev. Henry H. Bates, of St. John's Ch., Warehouse Point ... 125

HABERMAN, Herman, m. Augusta **RIDER**, b. of East Windsor, June 19, 1853, by Rev. Charles S. Putnam of St. John's Ch. ... 137

HALE, Henry H., m. Emeline C. **HAYES**, Nov. 10, 1842, by Shubael Bartlett ... 112

EW

Page

HARRIS, (cont.)
1851, by Rev. Charles N. Seymour *(Written in margin "Rufus
A. **WHITAKER**") 131
Sidney, m. Sarah Merriam **SAWYER,** Apr. 4, 1846, by Rev. Henry
H. Bates, of St. John's Ch. 120
William, Capt. of Middletown, m. Loury* **WOOD,** of East Windsor,
Mar. 12, 1837, by Rev. Windsor Ward *(Lowry) 101
HART, Eben E., of Springfield, Mass., m. Mary A. **PEASE,** of East
Windsor, Jan. 6, 1842, by Rev. W[illia]m H. Richards 110
HARTUNG, Juliaette, of Springfield, Mass., m. Orrin N. **WOOD,** of
Somers, Conn., Feb. 7, 1839, by Rev. Ebenezer Blake, of
Warehouse Point 105
HASKELL, Edward, s. Eli B. & Sophia, b. May 8, 1813 15
Frederick, s. Eli B. & Sophia, b. Dec. 4, 1810 15
Harriss, of Windsor, m. Francis **WOLCOTT,** of East Windsor,
[Nov.] 27, [1821], by Rev. Thomas Robbins 84
Henry Tudor, s. Eli B. & Susan, b. Oct. 29, 1820 15
Rabzaman, s. Eli B. & Sophia, b. May 8, 1815 15
Sophia Bissell, d. Eli B. & Susan, b. Apr. 14, 1823 15
HATCH, Ichabod, m. Hannah **MUNSELL,** b. of East Windsor, Dec. 4, 1777 41
HATHAWAY, George M., m. Julia M. **TURPIN,** Apr. 14, 1859, by D. Ives,
M. G. 151
Mary, m. John **ABBE,** Feb. 9, 1847, by Rev. Henry H. Bates, of
St. John's Ch. 120
HAWKINS, Joseph A., of East Windsor, m. Submit **FRENCH,** of
Winchester, [Nov.] 27, [1825], by Rev. Tho[ma]s Robbins of 1st
Church 88
HAWLEY, Ebenezer Stowell, m. Rowena **PEASE,** Jan. 4, 1849, by Rev.
Henry H. Bates, of St. John's Ch., Warehouse Point 125
HAYDEN, Ann E., m. Jabez S. **ALLEN,** May 1, 1844, by Shubael Bartlett 114
Elizabeth, d. of the late Daniel, of East Windsor, m. Roswell
S. **ANDRUS,** of Hartford, Dec. 12, 1838, by Rev. O. E. Daggett
of 2nd Ch. Hartford 104
Richard N., of Norwich, m. Caroline M. **ELLSWORTH,** of East
Windsor, Nov. 10, 1829, by Rev. Shubael Bartlett 92
HAYES, HAYS, Arminda, Mrs. of East Windsor, m. Seth **HEATH,** of
Kingsville, O., June 9, 1853, by Rev. Shubael Bartlett 137
Arminda S., m. Daniel **COLEMAN,** of Vernon, Dec. 1, 1844, by
Shubael Bartlett 117
Emeline C., m. Henry H. **HALE,** Nov. 10, 1842, by Shubael Bartlett 112
Harriet Sophia, of East Windsor, m. William H. **PARMELEE,** of
Enfield, Sept. 17, 1848, by Shubael Bartlett 123
James N., m. Philura **LOOMIS,** b. of East Windsor, Apr. 11, 1837,
by Chauncey G. Lee 102
Laura, of East Hartford, m. Adolphus J. **STONE,** of East Windsor,
[Oct.] 8, [1822], by Rev. T. Robbins 85
Mary, m. Marvin **FULLER,** of Middletown, Oct. 5, 1831, by Rev.
Gurdon Robins of Bap. Ch. 94

Page

HAYNES, James, of Manchester, m. Betsey M. ALLEN, of Ellington, Oct.
   18, 1835, by Rev. Pardon T. Kenney, of M. E. Ch.   99
HAYTHORN, Joseph, m. Ellen PATTERSON, b. of Warehouse Point, Apr.
   8, 1849, in Grace Church, Broad Brook, by Rev. Francis J. Clerc   126
HAYWARD, Josiah, of Ellington, m. Thamar H. LEWIS, of East Windsor,
   Oct. 16, 1832, by Rev. Shubael Bartlett   95
HAZARD, Thomas, Capt., m. Mrs. Margaret ROCKWELL, Oct. 11, [1829],
   by Gurdon Robins   92
HAZEN, James A., Rev. of South Wilbraham, Mass., m. Helen
   ROCKWELL, of East Windsor, [Feb.] 27, [1839], by Rev.
   Jonathan Cogswell   105
HEATH, HETH, HITH, Buckley P., m. Maria BANCROFT, b. of East
   Windsor, Dec. 8, 1829, by Rev. Sam[ue]l W. Whelpley   93
Caroline B., m. William BANCROFT, s. [Isaac & Lovice], Feb. 7,
   1832   5
Caroline Louise, m. W[illia]m Harrison STUDLEY, Dec. 13, 1854,
   by Rev. W[illia]m K. Douglass, of St. John's Ch.   153
Elisha S., of Baltimore, Md., m. H. Sophia CHAPIN, of East Windsor,
   Aug. 8, 1850, by Rev. S. J. Andrews, of Cong. Ch.   129
Elizabeth Ann, m. Hollis S. CHUBBUCK, of Orwell, Penn., Oct.
   10, 1831, by Rev. Shubael Bartlett   94
Jabez, s. Stephen & Sarah, b. May 9, 1773   15
Julia Theresa, of East Windsor, m. John Ruggles BOOTH, of Enfield,
   Jan. 5, 1853, in St. John's Church, Warehouse Point, by Rev. C. S.
   Putnam   136
Mary W., of Enfield, Conn., m. Walter BUCKLAND, of Springfield,
   Mass., Jan. 1, 1840, by Rev. Benjamin C. Phelps, of Warehouse
   Point   107
Nansey, d. Stephen & Sarah, b. May 19, 1784   15
Nathaniel P., of North Troy, N. Y., m. Azuba G. ALLEN, of East
   Windsor, Apr. 29, 1840, by Rev. Benjamin C. Phelps, Warehouse
   Point   109
Penelop, d. Stephen & Sarah, b. May 19, 1771   15
Rube, d. Stephen & Sarah, b. Mar. 6, 1782   15
Sarah, d. Stephen & Sarah, b. Apr. 19, 1775   15
Seth, of Kingsville, O., m. Mrs. Arminda HAYES, of East Windsor,
   June 9, 1853, by Rev. Shubael Bartlett   137
Stephen, s. Stephen & Sarah, b. Aug. 22, 1777   15
William H., m. Elizabeth S. BARTLETT, b. of East Windsor, Nov.
   11, 1824, by Rev. Tho[ma]s C. Brownell   86
HEBARD, [see under HIBBARD]
HEIN, Conrad, m. Julia BAECKER, of Enfield, Nov. 9, 1848, by Rev.
   Francis J. Clerc, of Grace Church, Broad Brook   125
HENDER, Thomas, m. Julia Hannah POTWINE, June 27, 1844, by Shubael
   Bartlett   114
HENDRICK, Chauncey R., m. Maria SMITH, b. of East Hampton, Mass.,
   Jan. 21, 1849, by H. C. Atwater   124
Cornelia R., of East Windsor, m. David W. CORBIN, of Buffalo,

Page

HENDRICK, (cont.)
 N. Y., Dec. 13, 1846, by Rev. Robert Allyn, at Warehouse
   Point   119
 Lydia E., m. Sylvester D. ROCKWELL, Jan. 9, 1859, by Rev. John
   F. Sheffield   151
HERICK, Judson, m. Charlotte E. ALDERMAN, Oct. 21, 1846, by Rev.
   Henry H. Bates, of St. John's Ch.   120
HERRIDEN, William, m. Mary ALEXANDER, [Aug.] 12, [1821], by Rev.
   Thomas Robbins   84
HIBBARD, HEBARD, Mary Ann, m. Albert JONES, b. of Hadley, Mass.,
   Oct. 22, 1833, by Solomon Terry, Jr., J. P., at Warehouse Point 97
 Monroe, m. Elizabeth E. BISSELL, Jan. 21, 1845, by Shubael Bartlett 117
 Prudence, of Windham, m. Jacob BOTTOM, late of Norwich now of
   East Windsor, Dec. 2, 1773   ("Entered from certificate on Mar. 7,
   1775")   32
 Ruth, m. Palmer R. MOORE, of Tolland, Apr. 29, 1844, by Shubael
   Bartlett   114
HIGGINS, Lois, of Chatham, m. Caleb PARSONS, of East Windsor, Sept.
   22, 1779   49
 Margaret, m. James REED, b. of Enfield, June 15, 1851, by Rev.
   Henry H. Bates, of St. John's Ch.   131
HIGLEY, Eliza, m. William GRANT, b. of East Windsor, Jan. 9, 1839,
   by Rev. Freeman Nutting   105
 Hannah, m. Elijah ROBERTSON, b. of East Windsor, [July] 4,
   [1824], by Rev. Thomas Robbins of 1st Church   87
HILLS, HILL, Alexander, m. Joanna HUNTER, natives of Southwick, now
   of East Windsor, Sept. 26, 1839, by B. E. Northrop   106
 Amelia, m. Wareham PORTER, Jan. 31, 1831, by Rev. Gurdon Robins
   of Bap. Ch.   94
 Ashbel, of East Hartford, m. Cynthia D. FRENCH, of East Windsor,
   Oct. 2, 1839, by Shubael Bartlett   106
 Henry, m. Harriet TUCKER, b. of East Windsor, Dec. 29, 1830, by
   Rev. Asa Mead of East Hartford   93
 Ira, of East Hartford, m. Mary Alice GILLETTE, of East Windsor,
   this day, Sept. 26, 1838, by Rev. Samuel Spring, of Cong. Ch.
   East Hartford   104
 Jane Ann, m. Joel ST. CLAIR, b. of East Windsor, Jan. 11, 1842,
   by Deodate Brockway   110
 Laura, m. John M. McLACHLAN, of Hartford, [Jan. 31, 1831], by
   Rev. Gurdon Robins, of Bap. Ch.   94
 Liberty, m. Aurelia OSBORN, July 2, 1832, by Rev. Shubael Bartlett 95
 Thomas, m. Eunice RATHBUN, Nov. 28, 1822, by Isaac Dwinel   85
HITCHCOTT, Harriet, m. Samuel ROCKWELL, Mar. 25, 1821, by
   Jonathan Pasco, J. P.   59
HITH, [see under HEATH]
HODGES, Ephraim D., of Mansfield, m. Amelia S. ALLYN, of East
   Windsor, Oct. 24, 1830, by Rev. Hezekiah S. Ramsdel   93
HOGER, Margaret, m. Christian MANN, May 4, 1856, at Broad Brook, by

HOGER, (cont.)

Rev. Enoch Huntington, of Grace Ch.   144

HOITT, Joseph, of Tolland, m. Alice **DRAKE,** of East Windsor, Mar.
17, 1833, by Rev. Edmund M. Beebe   96

HOLKINS, Caroline E., m. Jehial H. **SIMONDS,** Sept. 21, 1859, at
Warehouse Point, by Rev. Henry McClory, of St. John's Ch.   152

Clarissa, m. Elisha M. **JENCKS,** June 7, 1827, by G. W. Doane, at
Warehouse Point   90

Harriet Jane, m. Frederick Eugene **PALMER,** b. of East Windsor,
Oct. 23, 1851, by Rev. Henry H. Bates, of St. John's Ch., at
Warehouse Point   132

Lydia, m. John B. **CHAPMAN,** b. of East Windsor, June 11, 1827,
by Rev. Shubael Bartlett   89

Maria, m. William **BARNES,** b. of East Windsor, Apr. 26, 1827, by
Rev. Shubael Bartlett   89

HOLLAND, Mary Ann, m. Ransom **SMITH,** b. of Hartford, Jan. 19, 1825,
by Rev. Shubael Bartlett   87

HOLLISTER, Franklin, m. Frances **PEASE,** Jan. 5, 1858, by Rev. H. W.
Conant, of M. E. Ch.   148

Rhoda C., m. William **DART,** b. of East Windsor, this day, June
6, 1837, by Rev. Marvin Root   102

HOLMAN, Ebenezer, m. Ruth **LOOMIS,** Nov. [ ], 1763   41

Ebenezer, m. Rachel **WRIGHT,** May 1, 1771   41

Ebenezer, s. [Ebenezer & Rachel], b. Dec. 8, 1778   15

Ebenezer, s. Ebenezer & Rachel, d. Mar. 27, 1780   69

John, s. [Ebenezer & Rachel], b. July 20, 1783   15

Rachel, d. Ebenezer & Rachel, b. Feb. 6, 1772   15

Ruth, w. Ebenezer, d. June 17, 1770   41

Ruth, w. Ebenezer, d. June 17, 1770   69

Ruth, d. [Ebenezer & Rachel], b. Dec. 25, 1773   15

Samuel, s. [Ebenezer & Rachel], b. Aug. 29, 1776   15

HOLSTENHOLME, Rachel, m. Samuel **SWALLOW,** Jan. 1, 1859, at
Broad Brook, by Rev. John F. Mines, of Grace Ch.   151

HOLT, Oliver A., m. Nancy A. **ABBE,** b. of East Windsor, Oct. 11, 1853,
by Rev. Enoch Huntington, of Grace Ch.   138

HOOKER, Horace, of Clyde, N. Y., m. Helen **WOLCOTT,** of East
Windsor, [Sept.] 3, [1822], by Rev. T. Robbins   85

HOPPLE, Daniel, m. Elisabeth **PIELL,** Dec. 16, 1857, at Broad Brook,
by Rev. John F. Mines, of Grace Ch.   149

HORIG, Sebastion, m. Franceska **BECKER,** May 23, 1859, at Broad Brook,
by Rev. John F. Mines, of Grace Ch.   151

HORSMER, Horace, m. Marilda **GRANT,** b. of East Windsor, [July] 21,
[1820], by Rev. Thomas Robbins of 1st Eccl. Soc.   59

Mary, of East Windsor, m. Hiram **GRANT,** of Hartford, [Dec.] 6,
[1821], by Rev. Thomas Robbins   84

Thaddeus, m. Frances **BELCHER,** [Dec.] 5, [1821], by Rev. Thomas
Robbins   84

HORTON, Alanson, m. Amilia **ALLEN,** Jan. 10, 1822, by Rev. Shubael

Page

JENCKS, (cont.)
    Pa., Sept. 27, 1850, by Henry H. Bates   129
    Elisha M., m. Clarissa HOLKINS, June 7, 1827, by G. W. Doane,
        at Warehouse Point   90
    Elisha Mowry, s. Charles & Martha, b. Oct. 21, 1797   16
    Elsey Mariah, d. Charles & Martha, b. Oct. 2, 1812   16
    Harriot, d. Charles & Martha, b. May 24, 1801   16
    Harriet Louisa, of Springfield, Mass., m. Solomon C. WARNER, May
        19, 1831, by Rev. Shubael Bartlett   94
    Laura, of East Windsor, m. Asa M. CHAMPLIN, of Lebanon, Aug. 31,
        1825, by Rev. Shubael Bartlett   87
    Martha Ann, d. Charles & Martha, b. May 19, 1810   16
    Selina L., of Enfield, m. James M. SMITH, of South Hadley, Mass.,
        Nov. 3, 1829, by Rev. Shubael Bartlett   92
JENDERVINE(?), Albert, of Charlestown, N. H., m. Chloe REED, of East
    Windsor, Nov. 10, 1834, by Rev. Shubael Bartlett   98
JENNINGS, Russell, Rev. of Weston, m. Mrs. Marcia HOUGH, of East
    Windsor, this day, [May 15, 1827], by Rev. W[illia]m Bentley   89
JEPSON, Anna, wid. of Hartford, m. George LOOMIS, of East Windsor,
    Nov. 20, 1788   44
JEWET, Jra, s. David & Elisabeth, b. Mar. 1, 1780   16
JILSON, John, of East Hartford, m. Dulcinia HURD, of East Windsor,
    [July] 10, [1820], by Rev. Thomas Robbins of 1st Eccl. Soc.   59
JOHNS, Lyllia Ann, m. John CRAWFORD, July 5, 1849, by Rev. Henry H.
    Bates, of St. John's Ch., Warehouse Point   125
JOHNSON, Caroline J., of East Windsor, m. Jesse TUCKER, of Brooklyn,
    Jan. 10, 1831, by Rev. Shubael Bartlett   94
    Celestia, of East Windsor, m. Pliny M. ALDRICH, of Woonsocket,
        R. I., Nov. 9, 1852, by Rev. James Mather   135
    Clarissa, m. Eli GLEASON, Sept. 13, 1837, by Shubael Bartlett   102
    Harriet E., of East Windsor, m. William C. LADD, of Tolland,
        May 4, 1845, by Rev. B. M. Walker, in Wapping   116
    Harriet E., m. Ransford A. PARKER, Oct. 31, 1847, by Rev. Henry H.
        Bates, of St. John's Ch., Warehouse Point   122
    Henry, m. Electa GRANT, b. of East Windsor, Oct. 15, 1820, by Rev.
        Shubael Bartlett   59
    Henry, m. Phebe BARBER, Nov. 5, 1840, by Shubael Bartlett   108
    Jane S., m. Almanzo B. VINING, May 19, 1855, by Rev. Sam[ue]l
        J. Andrews   143
    John, m. Abigail SKINNER, Nov. 12, 1823, by Rev. Shubael Bartlett   86
    Laura, m. Joseph GLEASON, Aug. 11, 1842, by Shubael Bartlett   112
    Mary, m. Walter T. BREWSTER, Jan. 1, 1838, by Shubael Bartlett   103
    Mary, m. William MARSH, b. of Vernon, Feb. 2, 1851, by Rev.
        Shubael Bartlett   130
JONES, Albert, m. Mary Ann HIBBARD, b. of Hadley, Mass., Oct. 22,
    1833, by Solomon Terry, Jr., J. P., at Warehouse Point   97
    Elnathan, of Enfield, Mass., m. Almira JENCKS, June 7, 1825, by
        G. W. Doane   87

Page

JONES, (cont.)

Harriet, m. Jesse **CHARLTON**, Mar. 24, 1830   34

Harriet, m. Jesse **CHARLTON**, b. of East Windsor, Mar. 24, 1830,
by Rev. Sam[uel]l W. Whelpley   93

Mary W. *, of Ellington, m. Spencer **BURNHAM**, of East Windsor,
Oct. 2, 1842, by Levi Smith *(Written in margin "Mrs. Mary W.
JONES")   112

W[illia]m, of Springfield, Mass., m. Elisabeth **TERRY**, of Enfield,
Conn., this day, [Jan. 7, 1836], by Solomon Terry, Jr., J. P.   100

William, m. Alice **LOUDON**, Aug. 4, 1859, at Broad Brook, by Rev.
John F. Mines, of Grace Ch.   151

JUDD, Philip S., m. Betsey **HOWD**, Sept. 29, 1833, by Rev. Lavius Hyde,
of Ellington   96

JURKINS, Catharine, m. Bernard **COOK**, b. of Broad Brook, Apr. 8,
1849, by Rev. Francis J. Clerc   126

JWATCHEN, Samuel, m. Elisheba **FISH**, b. of Warehouse Point, last
evening, [May 27, 1825], by Francis L. Robbins, Enfield   87

KAIERLOEVER, Catherine, m. Frederick **MAYER**, b. of Broad Brook,
Apr. 29, 1849, at Grace Church, by Rev. Francis J. Clerc   126

KAYLMAIRE, Joseph, m. Catharine **BREECHT**, Jan. 30, 1848, by Rev.
Henry H. Bates, of St. John's Ch., Warehouse Point   122

KEENEY, KEENY, KENEY, Aden, of Manchester, m. Sophronia **CADY**,
of East Windsor, Oct. 17, 1832, by Rev. Hezekiah S. Ramsdell   96

Alfred, of Manchester, m. Belinda **SKINNER**, of East Windsor, [Nov.
29, 1832], by Rev. D. L. Hunn   96

Ezekiel, Jr., m. Nancy **TRYON**, Mar. 2, 1829, by V. R. Osborn,
V. D. M.   91

Henry, m. Mary **GRACE**, Mar. 19, 1843, by Josiah Ellsworth, J. P.   113

Jerusha, m. Doliel **SQUIRE**, Nov. 24, 1827, by V. R. Osborn, V. D. M.   89

Mary J., of East Windsor, m. Alphonso **RISLEY**, of Ellington, Aug.
12, 1849, by Rev. Samuel J. Andrews   125

Timothy, of Manchester, m. Sophronia **BUCKLAND**, of East Windsor,
Apr. 4, 1836, by V. R. Osborn, V. D. M.   100

KEEPPORT, John, m. Teresa **KETEL**, of Enfield, Sept. 21, 1851, by
Rev. John W. Case   131

KEHLER, Michael, m. Mary **BAYER**, Aug. 8, 1848, by Rev. Francis J.
Clerc, of Grace Ch., Broad Brook   124

KELLENBERGER, Anna, m. Joseph **BONE**, b. of Thompsonville, Apr. 8,
1848, by Rev. Francis J. Clerc, of Grace Ch., Broad Brook   121

KELLOGG, William S., of Hartford, m. Margaret **BARBER**, of East
Windsor, Oct. 8, 1833, by Rev. Shubael Bartlett   97

KENNEDY, Dorothy Delina, m. Parsons **TERRY**, b. of East Windsor,
Nov. 24, 1853, by Rev. C. S. Putnam, of St. John's Ch.,
Ware'_use Point. Int. Pub.   138

James, m. Dorothy D. **WOODWORTH**, May 13, 1846, by Rev. Henry
H. Bates, of St. John's Ch.   120

Sarah, of Hartford, m. John **SKINNER**, of Windsor, now of East
Windsor, Nov. 21, 1762   53

KERN, Mary, m. Henry SMITH, Feb. 18, 1856, at Broad Brook, by Rev.
   Enoch Huntington of Grace Ch.   144
KETEL, Terresa, of Enfield, m. John KEEPPORT, Sept. 21, 1851, by Rev.
   John W. Case   131
KIBBE, KIBBY, Emeret, Mrs., m. Oscar KIBBE, b. of Somers, Nov. 25,
   1846, by Rev. Sewall Lamberton   119
   H. Eugene, m. Lydia Ann Jennette CAREW, Oct. 24, 1859, by Rev.
   Frederick Munson, of 1st Ch.   152
   Oscar, m. Mrs. Emeret KIBBE, b. of Somers, Nov. 25, 1846, by Rev.
   Sewall Lamberton   119
   Percea, d. Phillip & Thankfull, b. June 19, 1787   17
KILBOURN, Esther, m. George COTTON, Oct. 2, 1822, by Rev. Joy H.
   Fairchild of East Hartford   85
   Roxey, of East Windsor, m. Roger BURNHAM, of East Hartford,
   [Mar.] 30, [1825], by Rev. Thomas Robbins   88
KILROY, Caroline, m. Nathaniel GRIFFITH, b. of Enfield, Jan. 16,
   1852, by Rev. Henry H. Bates, of St. John's Ch., at Warehouse
   Point   132
KING, Benoni O., m. Lucina SADD, b. of East Windsor, Nov. 12, 1827,
   by Rev. Shubael Bartlett   89
   Celia, m. Lewis MILLS, b. of East Windsor, [May] 21, [1829], by
   Rev. Thomas Robbins   91
   Edwin, of Springfield, Mass., m. Charlotte C. REED, Nov. 11,
   1839, by Shubael Bartlett   106
   Electa, m. Caleb FENTON, [Dec.] 14, [1820], by Rev. Shubael Bartlett 59
   Gamaliel, of Suffield, m. Mrs. Lovicy PRIOR, of East Windsor,
   Mar. 31, 1846, by Rev. F. W. Bill, of M. E. Ch., Warehouse Point 118
   Henry M., m. Elizabeth W. STOUGHTON, b. of East Windsor, Feb.
   21, 1844, by Levi Smith   113
   Hezekiah, of Vernon, m. Wealthy WARBURTON, of East Windsor,
   [Dec.] 4, [1821], by Rev. Thomas Robbins   84
   Lavantine, of Enfield, m. Miranda SPENCER, of Somers, May 16,
   1852, by Rev. W[illia]m A. Stickney   133
   Leicester, of Suffield, m. Betsey BANCROFT, July 19, 1835, by
   Rev. Shubael Bartlett, of 2nd Church   100
   Mary, m. Aaron CHAPIN, b. of East Windsor, Sept. 11, 1777   34
KINGSBURY, Abigail H., m. John B. ABBEE, Nov. 27, 1828, by V. R.
   Osborn, V. D. M.   90
   Elisha, of Coventry, m. Betsey CHASE, of East Windsor, this day,
   [June 25, 1820], by Rev. T. C. Brownell   59
   Emily B., of East Windsor, m. Stephen AMES, of Lunenburg, Vt.,
   Oct. 3, 1827, by Rev. Shubael Bartlett   89
   Harriet E., m. Albert R. PEASE, Apr. 3, 1856, by Rev. Sam[ue]l
   H. Allen   144
   Nancy J., m. George B. BARNES, Apr. 10, 1855, in St. John's
   Ch., by Rev. W[illia]m K. Douglass   142
KINLOCK, Isabella, of Warehouse Point, m. William McKEOUN, of
   Hartford, Oct. 12, 1848, by Rev. S. H. Allen, of Cong. Ch.,

Page

KINLOCK, (cont.)

Windsor Locks 123

KINSLEY, Henry S., m. Lucretia ABBE, Jan. 1, 1841, by Waldo Lyon,
Broad Brook 109

Sarah H., m. Ralph REED, Dec. 3, 1837, by Shubael Bartlett 103

KLERSY, Joseph, of Ellington, m. Barbara FRYE, of East Windsor, Dec.
12, 1852, by Rev. Charles N. Seymour 135

KNAPS, Augusta Caroline Wilhelmina, of East Windsor, m. James
Emmanuel SEEBERGER, of New Haven, Sept. 5, 1853, by Rev.
Chares S. Putnam of St. John's Ch. 138

KNEELAND, Patience, m. Jonathan BROWN, b. of East Windsor, June 22,
1775 32

KNOWLES, Sarah, of East Windsor, m. Nathan F. STODDARD, of
Wethersfield, [May] 19, [1825], by Rev. Thomas Robbins of 1st
Church 88

KNOX, Azuba, of Manchester, m. Nathaniel WOLCOTT, Jr., of East
Windsor, Aug. 16, 1835, by Rev. Shubael Bartlett 100

KRAMER, Frederick, m. Rosalia GENTISH, May 7, 1855, by Rev. Enoch
Huntington of Grace Ch., Broad Brook 142

LADD, [see also SADD], Charles Warner, s. Ephraim & Lois, b. Sept.
5, 1781 18

Claricee, d. Elisha & Tabitha, b. Oct. 31, 1778 18

Dan, s. Jesse & Rachel, b. Mar. 5, 1772 18

Elias, s. Jesse & Rachel, b. Sept. 1, 1776 18

Elisha, m. Tabitha STRONG, b. of East Windsor, May 23, 1776 44

Elisha, s. Elisha & Tabitha, b. Oct. 24, 1780 18

Ephraim, of East Windsor, m. Lois CHAPMAN, of Bolton, July 14,
1774 44

Eunice, d. Elisha & Tabitha, b. Feb. 22, 1777 18

Horatio, s. Ephraim & Lois, b. Jan. 21, 1780 18

Jesse, s. Jesse & Rachel, b. May 13, 1768 18

Joseph L., m. Mary R. SKINNER, b. of East Windsor, May 1, 1828,
by Rev. Shubael Bartlett 90

Lucy, d. Moses & Kezia, b. Apr. 21, 1771 18

Nancey, d. Ephraim & Lois, b. Aug. 5, 1776 18

Orin, d. Moses & Kezia, b. Apr. 13, 1773 (Perhaps a son) 18

Roxcey, d. Ephraim & Lois, b. Dec. 23, 1777 18

Samuel W., of Springfield, Mass., m. Lovinia FISH, of East Windsor,
June 2, 1847, by Rev. Franklin Fisk, Warehouse Point 119

William, s. Jesse & Rachel, b. Feb. 15, 1770 18

William C., of Tolland, m. Harriet E. JOHNSON, of East Windsor,
May 4, 1845, by Rev. B. M. Walker, in Wapping 116

LAMBERTON, Matilda W., m. Naman M. PARSONS, Oct. 9, 1836, by
Rev. Shubael Bartlett 101

LANCASTER, Augustua S., mechanic, ae 24, b. Woodbury, res. Ellington,
m. Clarrissa A. THRALL, ae 18, b. Ellington, res. East Windsor,
Nov. 24, 1853, by Rev. James H. Soule 141

LASBURY, George, m. Sarah MORGAN, Apr. 5, 1855, by Rev. Enoch

Page

LASBURY, (cont.)

Huntington, of Grace Ch. Broad Brook 142

Mary Ann, of Broad Brook, m. John **BAILEY**, of Rockville, Apr. 13,

1854, by Enoch Huntington 139

LATHROP, Elizabeth, m. Maro M. **REED**, M. D., Sept. 16, 1830, by Rev.

Shubael Bartlett 93

Elisabeth, m. Charles D. **SNELL**, May 28, 1855, by Rev. W[illia]m

K. Douglass 143

Lydia, of Hartford, m. Charles C. **TYLER**, of Middletown, Nov.

24, 1830, by Rev. Shubael Bartlett 93

Sarah H., of East Windsor, m. Walter **BOOTH**, of Meriden, May 17,

1842, by Shubael Bartlett 112

LATTIMORE, Fanny, m. David **BISSELL**, b. of East Windsor, Oct. 15,

1827, by Dan[iel]l Hayden, J. P. 90

LAUBSCHER, Marian, a deaf mute of Switzerland, m. Gustavus C.

BROWN, Germany, Oct., 5, 1846, by Shubael Bartlett 118

LAW, Samuel, s. Samuel & Huldah, b. May 30, 1777 18

LEARNED, James M., m. Roxana H. **BURT**, b. of Warren, Mass., [Nov. 24,

1839, by Rev. Benjamin C. Phelps, of Warehouse Point 106

LEAVITT, Caleb, Jr., of Bath, Me., m. Delina **ROBERTSON**, Oct. 15,

1834, by Rev. Shubael Bartlett 98

L'DOIT, James Henry, s. James & Mary, b. Apr. 22, 1817 18

LEE, Alzade, of Willington, m. Eber **ROBINSON**, of East Windsor, Nov.

19, 1826, by Rev. Shubael Bartlett 88

Harriet Elizabeth, d. Smith & Submit B., b. Sept. 3, 1838 18

Lucia, 2nd, m. Ralph R. **ROLLO**, Jr., b. of East Windsor, Apr.

13, 1837, by Chauncey G. Lee 102

LEIBER, Johane, m. Charles **BOSCH**, Nov. [ ], 1850, by W[illia]m S.

Simmons 129

LENON(?), Horace, m. Angelina **ROCKWELL**, b. of East Windsor, Jan. 1,

1821, by Rev. Shubael Bartlett of 2nd Church 59

LESTER, Chauncey, m. Abigail **WOOD**, Sept. 25, 1823, by Rev. Elisha

Cushman of Bap. Ch. Hartford 86

LEWIS, Chatherine M., m. Lemuel E. **REED**, May 13, 1846, by Rev. Henry

H. Bates, of St. John's Ch. 120

Thamar H., of East Windsor, m. Josiah **HAYWARD**, of Ellington, Oct.

16, 1832, by Rev. Shubael Bartlett 95

LIEB, Matthias, m. Antionette **STEINMAN**, b. of East Windsor, Nov. 26,

1852, by Rev. C. S. Putnam, of St. John's Ch. 135

LILLIBRIDGE, Isaac B., of Chickopee, Mass., m. Martha **SWIFT**, of

Potsdam, N. Y., May 13, 1850, by Rev. Henry H. Bates, of St.

John's Ch., Warehouse Pt. 128

LITTLEFIELD, Edward H., m. Jane S. **WALDO**, b. of Newport, R. I.,

Sept. 6, 1850, by Rev. Sanford Benton 129

LIVERMORE, Russell A., of Alston, N. H., m. Mary G. **SKINNER**, of

East Windsor, this day, [Oct. 6, 1840], by Asahel Nettleton 108

LOMERILL, William Stewart, m. Lucy P. **SPERRY**, June 30, 1844, by

Shubael Bartlett 114

Page

LOOMIS, LOMIS, (cont.)

Rev. Shubael Bartlett	98
Silas, s. Elijah & Rachel, b. Mar. 24, 1770	18
Simeon, s. Luke & Experience, b. Sept. 11, 1767	18
Simeon, m. Sarah T. SKINNER, b. of East Windsor, July 15, 1829, by Rev. Samuel W. Whelpley	92
Sophia, d. Amasa & Priscilla, b. Nov. 10, 1787	18
Susan, m. Nehemiah OSBORN, May 9, 1841, by Shubael Bartlett	109
William, s. Amasa & Priscilla, b. Oct. 6, 1801	18
William, m. Agnes PEASE, b. of East Windsor, Oct. 8, 1822, by Francis L. Robbins	85
LORD, Angeline, of East Windsor, m. Randall WEST, of South Coventry, Oct. 28, 1847, by Shubael Bartlett	120
Artimesia, m. Parsons OSBORN, b. of East Windsor, Nov. 20, 1822, by Rev. Shubael Bartlett of 2nd Church	85
Asa, s. Joseph & Chloe, b. Sept. 17, 1791	18
Atkins, m. Lucretia MERAND(?), Feb. 24, 1825, by Rev. Jem. F. Bridges of Enfield	87
Charles, of East Windsor, m. Fanny B. PARSONS, of Ellington, Feb. 12, 1843, by Rev. Squire B. Hascall	113
Chester, s. Jeremiah, Jr. & Tryphena, b. Feb. 20, 1784	18
Chester A., Jr., m. Miranda A. OSBORN, b. of East Windsor, Nov. 28, 1850, by W[illia]m S. Simmons	129
Chloe, d. Joseph & Chloe, b. Oct. 5, 1785	18
Constant S., m. Mrs. Wealthy M. WALDO, Nov. 27, 1855, at Windsorville, by Rev. W[illia]m Phillips	144
Constant Shaw, of East Windsor, m. Elizabeth NYE, of Charlestown, Mass., Jan. 15, 1828, by Rev. Shubael Bartlett	90
Corodon O., m. Martha S. PARSONS, Mar. 25, 1846, by Rev. Henry H. Bates, of St. John's Ch.	120
Eleazar, of New York, m. Ruth THOMPSON, of East Windsor, Dec. 31, 1835, by W[illia]m Thompson	100
Emeline, of East Windsor, m. Edward C. CLARK, of Middletown, Nov. 4, 1849, by Rev. W[illia]m S. Simmons	126
Georg[e], s. Geor[g]e & Rana, b. Apr. 8, 1793	18
Gilbert, m. Mary A. WOLCOTT, b. of East Windsor, Oct. 21, 1849, by Rev. W[illia]m S. Simmons	126
Hiram, m. Mary OSBORN, b. of East Windsor, Oct. 24, 1827, by Rev. Shubael Bartlett	89
Horrice, s. Jeremiah, Jr. & Tryphena, b. Mar. 23, 1793	18
Horace, m. Clarissa STOUGHTON, b. of East Windsor, Jan. 21, 1827, by Rev. Shubael Bartlett	88
Horace, m. Lova PASCO, Aug. 13, 1844, by Shubael Bartlett	114
Huldah, d. Joseph & Chloe, b. Oct. 27, 1793	18
Jabez, s. Jeremiah, Jr. & Tryphena, b. Nov. 2, 1778	18
Jackson, m. Elizabeth J. SKINNER, Apr. 30, 1843, by Shubael Bartlett	113
James, m. Elizabeth HARRIS, Nov. 27, 1848, by Rev. Henry H. Bates, of St. John's Ch., Warehouse Point	125

Page

LORD, (cont.)
Jeremiah, Jr., of East Windsor, m. Tryphena PEASE, of Enfield,
  Feb. 5, 1777 — 44
Jeremiah, s. Jeremiah, Jr. & Tryphena, b. Feb. 17, 1782 — 18
Joseph, s. Joseph & Chloe, b. June 29, 1783 — 18
Lavinia H., m. Stephen CLARK, b. of East Windsor, Feb. 10, 1850,
  by W[illia]m S. Simmons — 127
Lemuel R., m. Ellen M. BARBER, Oct. 15, 1857, by Rev. Frederick
  Munson, of 1st Cong. Ch. — 147
Levi, s. Jeremiah, Jr. & Tryphena, b. Jan. 14, 1795 — 18
Levi, m. Mrs. Anna PASCO, b. of East Windsor, Apr. 2, 1854, by
  Abel Gardner — 139
Levi, m. Mary O. PHILBRICK, b. of East Windsor, July 4, 1855, at
  Enfield, by Rev. Sam[ue]l Fox — 143
Lucinda, m. Nathaniel MOSELEY, Jan. 19, 1849, by Rev. Henry H.
  Bates, of St. John's Ch., Warehouse Point — 125
Lucretia, d. Jeremiah, Jr. & Tryphena, b. Jan. 23, 1791 — 18
Luman S., m. Dorcas O. FISH, Nov. 28, 1832, by Rev. Shubael
  Bartlett — 96
Marilla B., m. David P. WALDEN, May 6, 1857, at Warehouse Point,
  by Rev. H. W. Conant of M. E. Ch. — 147
Oren, s. Jeremiah, Jr. & Tryphena, b. May 8, 1788 — 18
Orrin R., m. Sally MARBLE, b. of East Windsor, July 8, 1832,
  by Rev. Shubael Bartlett — 95
Rana, d. George & Rana, b. Apr. 2, 1791 — 18
Rhoda, d. Jeremiah, Jr. & Tryphena, b. Feb. 19, 1786 — 18
Rosannah, m. Lester DEWEY, Mar. 19, 1848, by Rev. Henry H. Bates,
  of St. John's Ch., Warehouse Point — 122
Samuel, m. Lovina MOODY, b. of East Windsor, Oct. 15, 1835, by
  Rev. Pardon T. Kenney, of M. E. Ch. — 99
Sarah, d. Jeremiah, Jr. & Tryphena, b. July 31, 1780 — 18
Sophia, d. Jeremiah, Jr. & Tryphena, b. Apr. 20, 1797 — 18
Stoddard, s. Joseph & Chloe, b. June 27, 1781 — 18
Sylvester G., of Hebron, m. Caroline S. SADD, of East Windsor,
  Nov. 28, 1855, by Rev. William Wright, of 2nd Cong. Ch. South
  Windsor — 144
Tryfena, m. Lorain WOOD, Mar. 1, 1827, by Horace Barber, J. P. — 90
Warren, s. Joseph & Cloe, b. Apr. 12, 1788 [Entry crossed out] — 4
Warren, s. Joseph & Chloe, b. Apr. 12, 1788 — 18
Zilphe, d. Joseph & Chloe, b. Dec. 9, 1789 [Entry crossed out] — 4
Zilpha, d. Joseph & Chloe, b. Dec. 9, 1789 — 18
LOUDON, Alice, m. William JONES, Aug. 4, 1859, at Broad Brook, b.
  Rev. John F. Mines, of Grace Ch. — 151
LOVELAND, Luther P., of Hartford, m. Celia A. WARD, of East Windsor,
  Feb. 11, 1844, by Rev. B. M. Walker — 113
LOWRY, Ann, m. Nathaniel E. COOMS, Nov. 25, 1847, by Rev. Henry H.
  Bates, of St. John's Ch., Warehouse Point — 122
LUCE, George, of Somers, m. Julia M. PEASE, of Enfield, June 30, 1844, — 116

Page

McMASTERS, Alexander, m. Mary Ann **ALCORNE**, b. of Thompsonville,
Mar. 30, 1848, by Rev. Francis J. Clerc, of Grace Ch., Broad
Brook   121

McMULLAN, MacMULLEN, Jane, m. John **BRIGGS**, b. of Springfield,
Mass., Sept. 10, 1849, in Grace Church, Broad Brook, by Rev.
Francis J. Clerc   126

William, m. Harriet **MURRAY**, Jan. 9, 1849, by Rev. Henry H. Bates
of St. John's Ch., Warehouse Point   125

McNALL, Lucy, of Ellington, m. Nehemiah **DANIELS**, of Vernon, Oct. 31,
1839, by Rev. Ebenezer Blake, of Wapping   106

McVINNE, James, of Hartford, m. Lydia **WHEATON**, of East Windsor,
July 9, 1833, by Rev. Salmon Hull   96

McVITTY, James, m. Mrs. Julia A. **PRIOR**, b. of East Windsor, Oct. 12,
1852, by Rev. J. Mather   134

MACVOY, Catharine, m. William **HAMPSHIRE**, b. of Enfield, July 31,
1851, by Rev. Sanford Benton   131

MAGEE, May Ann Wright, m. William Henry **WHITEHEAD**, b. of Broad
Brook, Nov. 1, 1847, at Grace Church, by Rev. Francis J. Clerc,
of Grace Ch. Broad Brook   121

MAGUIRE, McGUIRE, Andrew, m. Mary **CASEY**, b. of Enfield, Oct. 21,
1849, by Rev. Henry H. Bates, of St. John's Ch., Warehouse Pt.   127

Anna A., Mrs. of New Bedford, Mass., m. Russell T. **WARNER**, of
Springfield, Mass., Oct, 3, 1842, by Rev. J. Mather   134

Mary, m. William **TIERNEY**, Aug. 30, 1858, at Windsor Locks, by
Rev. James Smyth   150

MAINE, Nathan S., m. Cornelia E. **CARVER**, b. of Bolton, June 4, 1851,
by Rev. John W. Case   130

MALCOM, Margaret, Mrs., of Simsbury, m. George **MILLER**, of East
Windsor, Apr. 6, 1851, by Rev. Sanford Benton   130

MALONY, Elizabeth, m. George **NEWBERRY**, Jr., b. of East Windsor, Jan.
21, 1841, by Levi Smith   109

MANLY, Erastus, of West Windsor, m. Amy **GRANT**, of East Windsor,
Nov. 2, 1837, by Rev. Windsor Ward   102

John, m. Sarah **BARBER**, b. of East Windsor, June 19, 1828, by
Rev. Shubael Bartlett   90

MANN, Christian, m. Margaret **HOGER**, May 4, 1856, at Broad Brook,
by Rev. Enoch Huntington of Grace Ch.   144

Frederick, m. Barbara **SHAILER**, May 29, 1855, by Rev. Charles
W. Potter, at Cromwell   143

Gottlieb, m. Frederika **RAISH**, May 13, 1855, by Rev. Enoch
Huntington, of Grace Ch. Broad Brook   143

MARBLE, Almira, [d. William & Mary], b. Mar. 12, 1808   19

Clarissa L., of East Windsor, m. Amos **ABBEY**, of Wilbraham,
Jan. 6, 1833, by Rev. D. L. Hunn   96

Danford, [s. William & Mary], b. Apr. 27, 1810   19

Emily, [d. William & Mary], b. Apr. 22, 1806   19

Emily, of East Windsor, m. John **RICHARDSON**, of Windsor, this
day, [Mar. 31, 1823], by Rev. Tho[ma]s Robbins of 1st Soc.   86

Page

MARBLE, (cont.)
Frederick, [s. William & Mary], b. Nov. 6, 1812   19
Jason Gerry, [s. William & Mary], b. Dec. 1, 1823   19
Julia W., [d. William & Mary], b. Oct. 4, 1818   19
Laura, [d. William & Mary], b. May 6, 1821   19
Maria, [d. William & Mary], b. Feb. 22, 1802   19
Martha Jane, [d. William & Mary], b. Mar. 23, 1826   19
Mary S., [d. William & Mary], b. Feb. 31, 1815 [sic]   19
Merrow, m. Hannah BURNHAM, b. of East Hartford, this day, [May
    30, 1822], by Rev. T. Robbins of 1st Church   85
Sally, m. Orrin R. LORD, b. of East Windsor, July 8, 1832, by
    Rev. Shubael Bartlett   95
William T., [s. William & Mary], b. Apr. 26, 1804   19
MARJORUM, George S., of Trenton, N. J., m. Sarah BOOTH, of East
    Windsor, Apr. 9, 1835, by Rev. Shubael Bartlett   99
MARRAY, Susanna, of East Windsor, m. William MARRAY, of Somers,
    Sept. 28, 1851, by Rev. Henry H. Bates, of St. John's Ch.   131
William, of Somers, m. Susanna MARRAY, of East Windsor, Sept.
    28, 1851, by Rev. Henry H. Bates, of St. John's Ch.   131
MARSDEN, George, m. Mary DUNN, b. of East Windsor, Nov. 25, 1852,
    by Rev. C. S. Putnam, of St. John's Ch.   135
William, m. Grace WOODHEAD, Dec. 26, 1857, at Broad Brook, by
    Rev. John F. Mines, of Grace Ch.   148
MARSH, William, m. Mary JOHNSON, b. of Vernon, Feb. 2, 1851, by
    Rev. Shubael Bartlett   130
MARTIN, George W., m. Maria R. VANHORN, b. of Springfield, Mass.,
    Sept. 10, 1847, at Grace Church, by Rev. Francis J. Clerc of
    Grace Ch., Broad Brook. Int. Pub. in Springfield, Mass.   121
Nabbe, d. Silvanus & Ame, b. Nov. 2, 1775   19
William, s. Silvanus & Ame, b. Feb. 13, 1777   19
MASON, Isaac, of East Windsor, m. Sarah BENTON, of Toland, June 28,
    1770   46
Lydia, d. Jsaac & Sarah, b. Nov. 11, 1771   19
MATHER, W[illia]m King, of Suffield, m. Aurelia Bissell STANLEY, of
    East Windsor, this day, [Jan. 1, 1824], by Rev. Moses Fifield, Jr.   86
MATSON, Almon, of East Windsor, m. Asenath TAYLOR, of Clinton, this
    day, [Dec. 12, 1841], by Rev. John Whittlesey   110
Helena A., m. Andrew H. DAWLEY, Apr. 5, 1860, at Windsorville,
    by A. Booth   153
Josephine A., m. Joseph O. GRANT, Mar. 28, 1855, by Rev. Abel
    Gardner at Warehouse Point   142
MAY, Betsey S., of East Windsor, m. Allen OSBORN, of Middletown,
    [Oct. 31, 1825], by Rev. Thomas Robbins   88
Charles B., m. Abigail L. WALDEN, b. of East Hartford, Aug. 11,
    1844, by Rev. B. M. Walker   115
Harriet, of Ellington, m. Stephen CADY, Sept. 21, 1851, by Rev.
    John W. Case   131
Julia, of East Windsor, m. Joseph CURTIS, of Hampton, Nov.

Page

MAY, (cont.)
    9, 1831, by Rev. Augustus Bolles   94
    Walter C., m. Helena Mary **FRITZ,** Nov. 21, 1858, at Warehouse
        Point, by Rev. Henry McClory, of St. John's Ch.   152
MAYER, MAIR, Frederick, m. Catherine **KAIERLOEVER,** b. of Broad
    Brook, Apr. 29, 1849, at Grace Church, by Rev. Francis J. Clerc   126
    John S., m. Catharine **PIKE,** Mar. 25, 1848, at Rev. Henry H.
        Bates, of St. John's Ch., Warehouse Point   122
MEACHAM, Elijah, of Tolland, m. Lucina **ALLEN,** Apr. 19, 1840, by
    Shubael Bartlett   107
    Lucina, Mrs., m. Austin **CARVER,** June 17, 1855, by Rev. L. D.
        Bentley   143
MELONA, Sally, of East Windsor, m. George **HARPER,** of Enfield, Sept.
    17, 1837, by Rev. Windsor Ward   102
MENSCHING, Dorothea, m. Frederick **SCHMIDT,** b. of Warehouse Point,
    July 30, 1848, in Grace Church, Broad Brook, by Rev. Francis J.
    Clerc, of Grace Ch.   124
MENTIS, Adelaide, m. Philip **MOESER,** Aug. 27, 1859, at Warehouse
    Point, by Rev. Henry McClory, of St. John's Ch.   152
MERAND(?), Lucretia, m. Atkins **LORD,** Feb. 24, 1825, by Rev. Jem,
    F. Bridges, of Enfield   87
MERRICK, Cresentia, m. Andon **PFEIFFER,** May 3, 1857, by Rev.
    W[illia]m M. Birchard   147
    Gideon, of East Windsor, m. Mary E. **HUTCHINSON,** of Andover,
        Dec. 21, 1853, by Rev. Shubael Bartlett of 1st ch.   138
MERRILL, David K., of New England Conference, m. Delina J. **ALLEN,**
    of East Windsor, this day, [Sept] 12, [1842], by Rev. Moses
    Stoddard   112
MERRIMAN, Ruth, m. George V. **BUSKIRK,** Oct. 16, 1854, by Rev.
    W[illia]m K. Douglass of St. John's Ch.   152
MIGLER, Dexter R., m. Maria H. **PHELPS,** Feb. 3, 1848, by Rev. Henry
    H. Bates, of St. John's Ch., Warehouse Point   122
MILLARD, Calven, s. Jason & Rachel, b. June 28, 1769   19
    Jason, s. Jason & Rachel, b. Mar. 12, 1766   19
MILLER, Chauncey B., of West Windsor, m. Elizabeth **BELCHER,** of East
    Windsor, Apr. 1, 1822, by Rev. Elisha B. Cook, of East Hartford   84
    Elizabeth, m. Robert **BRAMAN,** b. of East Windsor, Jan. 2, 1853,
        by Rev. James Mather   136
    George, of East Windsor, m. Mrs. Margaret **MALCOM,** of Simsbury,
        Apr. 6, 1851, by Rev. Sanford Benton   130
    Selah, of Farmington, m. Elizabeth **OSBORN,** of East Windsor,
        Jan. 6, 1828, by Rev. Shubael Bartlett   90
    William H., of Hartford, m. Mary M. **STRONG,** of East Windsor,
        Nov. 28, 1844, by Levi Smith   115
MILLION, Margaret, m. Joseph **FISHER,** Aug. 21, 1858, at Broad Brook,
    by Rev. John F. Mines, of Grace Ch.   149
MILLS, Lewis, m. Celia **KING,** b. of East Windsor, [May] 21, [1829],
    by Rev. Thomas Robbins   91

Page

MILLS, (cont.)

Philemon, m. Elizabeth **STRONG**, b. of East Windsor, Feb. 26,
1829, by Rev. Shubael Bartlett   91

MINER, Ann, m. Eli W. **DANIELS**, Dec. 30, 1838, by Rev. John W.
Handy, Wilbraham   105

MITCHEL, Simon, of East Windsor, m. Therecia **SINKEL**, Mar. 24, 1858,
at Hartford, by Rev. Enest Berger of the German Cong. Rockville   148

MOESER, Philip, m. Adelaide **MENTIS**, Aug. 27, 1859, at Warehouse
Point, by Rev. Henry McClory, of St. John's Ch.   152

MONGER, Sarah Ann, m. James **CRAMER**, b. of East Windsor, July 8,
1834, by Rev. Chauncey G. Lee   97

MONTAGUE, Charles, of Lenox, Mass., m. Harriet G. **BLODGET**, of
Amherst, Mass., Nov. 19, 1840, by Shubael Bartlett   108

MOODY, Azubah, m. Samuel **ALLEN**, b. of East Windsor, this day, [Jan.
12, 1824], by Asher Allen, J. P.   86

Eliza, m. Luther H. **GRANT**, b. of Ellington, Jan. 4, 1852, by
Rev. John W. Case   132

Henry, m. Candace **WOLCOTT**, b. of East Windsor, Apr. 20, 1825,
by Rev. Shubael Bartlett   87

Lovina, m. Samuel **LORD**, b. of East Windsor, Oct. 15, 1835, by
Rev. Pardon T. Kenney, of M. E. Ch.   99

Marilla, of Ellington, m. Henry M. **SHEPARD**, of Northampton,
Mass., July 5, 1852, by Rev. Edmund A. Standish   133

MOORE, John, m. Eliza **PORTER**, [May] 7, [1821], by Rev. Thomas
Robbins   84

Palmer R., of Tolland, m. Ruth **HIBBARD**, Apr. 29, 1844, by Shubael
Bartlett   114

Sam[ue]l, m. Lydia **STOUGHTON**, b. of East Windsor, Nov. 18, 1828,
by Rev. Samuel W. Whelpley of 1st Church   91

MORELL, Alvah, of Hartford, m. Mary Bartlett **BLODGETT**, of East
Windsor, Feb. 8, 1832, by Rev. Shubael Bartlett   95

Amelia R., m. Edwin F. **THOMPSON**, Oct. 7, 1857, by Rev. F.
Munson, of Cong. Ch.   147

MORGAN, Charlotte A., of Springfield, Mass., m. Charles C. **DOLE**, of
Hartford, Mar. 13, 1842, by Rev. W[illia]m H. Richards   111

Clark H., m. Charlotte E. **McFALL**, Feb. 21, 1859, by Rev.
Frederick Munson   151

Darius, m. Elisabeth **WEBSTER**, Oct. 7, 1856, at Windsorville,
by Rev. G. D. Boynton   145

Sarah, m. George **LASBURY**, Apr. 5, 1855, by Rev. Enoch
Huntington, of Grace Ch., Broad Brook   142

MORGANVECK, Charles, m. Amanda **BOING**, Nov. 11, 1856, at
Warehouse Point, by Rev. Henry M. Clory of St. John's Ch.   146

MORMANN, Qunigunde, m. Philip **ZIMMERMAN**, Mar. 20, 1860, at
Broad Brook, by T. A. Hazen   153

MORRAN, [see also **MURRAN**], Caroline, of East Windsor, m. John I.
FOWLER, of Suffield, Jan. 23, 1848, by Shubael Bartlett   121

MORRIS, Melissa M., of Vernon, m. Horatio N. **WEED**, of Bridgeport,

Page

MORRIS,(cont.)
Nov. 10, 1844, by Rev. Benjamin F. Walker   115
MORRISON, John, m. Jane **WATT**, b. of Enfield, Sept. 4, 1853, by Rev.
Enoch Huntington, of Grace Ch.   138
William T., of Enfield, m. Tamar **THOMPSON***, of East Windsor,
Feb. 17, 1831, by Rev. Shubael Bartlett   *(Tamar **BANCROFT**
in margin)   94
MORROW, William, of Suffield, m. Nancy Anne **DUFFON**, of East
Windsor, Feb. 6, 1853, by Rev. Charles N. Seymour   136
MORTIER, Joseph, m. Ann **NAYLOR,** b. of Enfield, Dec. 25, 1851, by
Rev. Henry H. Bates, of St. John's Ch., at Warehouse Pt.   132
MORTON, Elisha G., m. Mabel **THOMPSON**, b. of East Windsor, Dec. 12,
1826, by Rev. Shubael Bartlett   88
Elisha G., m. Clarrissa Ann **TARBOX**, Feb. 8, 1849, by Shubael
Bartlett   124
Eliza Ann, m. Willard Hall **BANCROFT**, [s. Isaac & Lovice], [   ]   5
Elizabeth, m. Thomas Potwine **ELLSWORTH**, b. of East Windsor,
Apr. 7, 1829, by Rev. Shubael Bartlett   91
Elisabeth M., m. Francis H. **GRANGER**, Aug. 17, 1849, by Shubael
Bartlett   126
Emiline, m. Charles L. **BARTLETT**, Dec. 20, 1832, by Rev. Shubael
Bartlett   96
Joanna, m. Bissell **BANCROFT**, s. [Isaac & Lovice], Nov. 24, 1824   5
Joanna, m. Bissell **BANCROFT**, b. of East Windsor, Nov. 24, 1824,
by Rev. Shubael Bartlett of 2nd Church   87
Julia, m. James C. **HOUGHTON**, of Hallifax, Vt., Nov. 4, 1840,
by Shubael Bartlett   108
Lavinia, of Leaveret, Mass., m. Stephen **ADAMS***, of Broome, N. Y.,
Nov. 3, 1842, by Rev. Joseph Scott of St. John's Ch.   *(Written in
margin "**BROOME**")   113
Mary, m. Daniel **TAGERT**, b. of East Windsor, Jan. 3, 1847, by Rev.
Sewall Lamberton   119
Maryette, of East Windsor, m. Hiram **HOUGHTON**, of Enfield, July
4, 1847, by Rev. Franklin Fisk, Warehouse Point   120
Sarah, m. Jason **ELLSWORTH**, b. of East Windsor, June 4, 1845,
by Rev. James C. Houghton, of Hartland   116
Susan, m. Caleb **BENJAMIN**, b. of East Windsor, May 23, 1839, by
Shubael Bartlett   106
Willis, m. Priscilla **ELLSWORTH**, b. of East Windsor, Apr. 6,
1830, by Rev. Sam[ue]l W. Whelpley   93
MOSELEY, Nathaniel, m. Lucinda **LORD**, Jan. 19, 1849, by Rev. Henry H.
Bates, of St. John's Ch., Warehouse Point   125
MOULTEN, Phildelia, m. Hosmer P. **STEDMAN**, Nov. 7, 1836, by J.
Cogswell   101
MOWRY, Martha, of Smithfield, R. I., m. Charles **JENCKS**, of East
Windsor, Jan. 22, 1797   42
MUMFORD, Mary, m. Oliver **WOLCOTT**, b. of East Windsor, Apr. 27,
1826, by Rev. Shubael Bartlett   88

Page

NASH, Aaron, s. Joel & Sarah, b. Oct. 12, 1770   20
    Abner, s. Joel & Sarah, b. Aug. 29, 1776   20
    Joel, m. Sarah **POALK**, of East Windsor, Mar. 30, 1769   47
    Samuel, s. Joel & Sarah, b. May 1, 1774   20
    Stedman, of Quincy, Ill., m. Abigail R. **BLODGETT**, of East
      Windsor, Apr. 14, 1840, by Shubael Bartlett   106
NAYLOR, Ann, m. Joseph **MORTIER**, b. of Enfield, Dec. 25, 1851, by
    Rev. Henry H. Bates, of St. John's Ch., at Warehouse Point   132
NEEDHAM, Mary A., of Warehouse Pt., m. William C. **BALLARD**, of
    Maine, Mar. 3, 1850, by Rev. Henry H. Bates, of St. John's Ch.
    Warehouse Pt.   128
NESSBAUMER, Albertine, m. Joseph **ANDEREAU**, Nov. 20, 1856, at
    Warehouse Pt., by Rev. Henry McClory of St. John's Ch.   146
NEWBURY, NEWBERRY, Dyer, m. Lucy **TERRY**, b. of East Windsor,
    Nov. 29, 1827, by Rev. Russell Jennings   89
    George, Jr., m. Elizabeth **MALONY**, b. of East Windsor, Jan. 21,
      1841, by Levi Smith   109
    James M., m. Harriet Maria **ALEXANDER**, Dec. 22, 1841, by Levi
      Smith   112
    Jerusha, of East Windsor, m. Zimri **SKINNER**, of Harwinton, this
      day, [Sept. 7, 1835], by Rev. C. G. Lee   99
    Joseph E., m. Erocia E. **ALLEN**, of East Windsor, Aug. 17, 1848,
      by S. R. Brown. Witnesses: E. G. Brown, Fanny Bartlett   123
    Lucy, of East Winsor, m. Sylvester **CHAPIN**, of Springfield, Mass.,
      Dec. 2, 1827, by Rev. Shubael Bartlett   89
    Mary, of East Windsor, m. Orrin **ELMER**, of West Hartford, June
      4, 1829, by Rev. Sam[ue]l W. Whelpley   92
NEWELL, NEWEL, Elizabeth Louisa, m. Elliot **FLEMING**, Mar. 1, 1852
    (See marriages recorded under May 1864)   134
    John A., of New Britain, m. Mary A. **SADD**, of East Windsor, Apr.
      8, 1851, by Rev. Sam[ue]l J. Andrews, of Cong. Ch.   131
    Nathaniel, of Ellington, m. Eunice **GREEN**, of East Windsor, Sept.
      10, 1828, by Rev. Sam[ue]l W. Whelpley of 1st Church   91
NEVERS, Sarah B., of East Windsor, m. Nathan D. **WORK**, of Somers,
    Aug. 28, 1831, by Rev. Shubael Bartlett   94
NICHOLS, NICKOLS, Elisabeth Ann, m. Sanford **AMADON**, Apr. 4,
    1847, by Shubael Bartlett   119
    Lucretia L., m. Henry H. **PAYNE**, b. of East Windsor, Nov. 25,
      1852, by Rev. Edmund A. Standish   135
NILES, Sleuman, m. Lucinda **COMSTOCK**, Sept. 10, 1846, by Rev. Henry
    H. Bates, of St. John's Ch.   120
    Vernum, m. Mary Angelina **WHEELER**, Oct. 2, 1848, by Rev. Henry
      H. Bates, of St. John's Ch., Warehouse Point   125
NOBLE, NOBLES, Alman, m. Mary Ann **BARTLETT**, Sept. 7, 1831, by
    Rev. Shubael Bartlett   94
    Alman, m. Eunice K. **BARTLETT**, b. of East Windsor, Mar. 1, 1849,
      by Shubael Bartlett   125
    Elizabeth Bartlett, m. Sam[ue]l W[illia]m **BARTLETT**, Sept. 29,

Page

OSBORN, OSBORNE, ORSBORN, (cont.)

Stephen, s. Daniel & Hannah, b. June 4, 1770   21

Susanna, d. Thomas & Lovise, b. Oct. 24, 1781   21

Susanna, d. Thomas & Lovise, d. Dec. 15, 1794   75

Sylvia, m. Algernon Sidney **BARTLETT**, of Granby, Mass., Nov. 23, 1843, by Shubael Bartlett   113

Thomas, s. Benjamin & Sarah, b. Mar. 25, 1757   21

Wyllys, s. Ezra & Abigail, b. Dec. 21, 1801   21

PACKARD, Abel A., m. Harriet L. **PHILLIPS**, b. of East Windsor, Oct. 24, 1849, by Rev. Samuel J. Andrews, of Cong. Ch.   127

Angeline H., m. Norris B. **PIERCE**, Jan. 1, 1850, by Rev. Shubael Bartlett   127

Charles, of Springfield, Mass., m. Emeline **BLODGETT**, of East Windsor, Apr. 19, 1827, by Rev. Shubael Bartlett   89

Mary Jane, d. Henry & Jane, b. Mar. 29, 1833   30

PAGE, Priscilla, see Priscilla **BIRGE**   44

PAHLE, Appollonia, m. Frederick T. **WILLIS**, Aug. 6, 1857, at Broad Brook, by Rev. John F. Mines, of Grace Ch.   149

PALMER, Epaphroditus, m. Sophronia W. **WOODWARD**, Dec. 9, 1824, by Rev. Shubael Bartlett of 2nd Church   87

Esther, m. Caleb **STOCKBRIDGE**, Mar. 14, 1838, by Shubael Bartlett   103

Frederick Eugene, m. Harriet Jane **HOLKINS**, b. of East Windsor, Oct. 23, 1851, by Rev. Henry H. Bates, of St. John's Ch., at Warehouse Point   132

Harrison, of Cherry Valley, N. Y., m. Nancy M. **WOODARD**, of East Windsor, Sept. 23, 1850, by Rev. Sanford Benton   129

Levi, m. Mrs. Sophronia W. **PALMER**, b. of East Windsor, Mar. 23, 1842, by Rev. W[illia]m H. Richards   111

Maria L., m. William W. **HUNTINGTON**, Jan. 8, 1855, by Rev. W[illia]m M. Birchard   142

Mary, m. George D. **WOODWARD**, b. of East Windsor, Feb. 3, 1825, by Rev. Shubael Bartlett   87

Mary D., of East Windsor, m. George **ASPINWALL**, of Providence, R. I., June 27, 1849, by Rev. Samuel J. Andrews   125

Rev. Moses, of Yarmouth, Mass., m. Elizabeth Jane **HOSMER**, of East Windsor, July 16, 1840, by Rev. Ezra S. Cook   108

Sophronia W., Mrs., m. Levi **PALMER**, b. of East Windsor, Mar. 23, 1842, by Rev. W[illia]m H. Richards   111

PARKER, Almond, m. Sarah **STONE**, b. of Mass., Sept. 8, 1837, by Solomon Terry, Jr., J. P.   102

Elisha H., of Stoughton, Mass., m. Charlotte **SKINNER**, of East Windsor, this day, [July 1, 1832], by Horace Hooker, Hartford   95

Elmira L., of Warehouse Point, m. William Henry **ZIMMERMAN**, [May 28, 1848], by Rev. Frances J. Clerc   123

Harriet S., m. Charles **THOMAS**, b. of East Windsor, Apr. 14, 1847, by Rev. Francis J. Clerc, of Grace Ch., Broad Brook, at Grace Church   121

Joseph, of East Windsor, m. Clarissa L. **SANBORN**, of Strafford, Vt.,

Page

PARSONS, (cont.)
    of Cong. Ch. Enfield, at Warehouse Point   104
    Solomon G., m. Rhoda A. BISSELL, Mar. 28, 1858, by Rev. W. M.
        Birchard   149
    Sophronia M., m. Elihu COOK, b. of East Windsor, May 31, 1837,
        by B. Tyler   103
    ----, of Plymouth, Conn., m. Mrs. Cynthia GLEASON, of East
        Windsor, [   ], 1830, by Rev. Gurdon Robins of Bap. Ch.   94
PASCO, Anna, Mrs., m. Levi LORD, b. of East Windsor, Apr. 2, 1854,
    by Abel Gardner   139
    Aurelia, of East Windsor, m. Asahel GAY, of Mass., Apr. 1, 1835,
        by Rev. Shubael Bartlett   99
    Charlotte R., m. William W. ALLEN, Dec. 30, 1858, by Rev. John F.
        Sheffield   150
    Eliza, m. Charles A. ABBEY*, Mar. 30, 1843, by Shubael Bartlett
        *(Written in margin "ABBE")   113
    Fluvia, of East Windsor, m. Wyllys PHELPS, of Enfield, Jan. 18,
        1832, by Rev. Shubael Bartlett   94
    James, m,. Elizabeth VINING, b. of East Windsor, Sept. 25, 1832,
        by Rev. Edmund M. Beebe   95
    Jonathan, s. James & Abigail, b. Sept. 29, 1760   22
    Jonathan, m. Elisabeth ALLIN, b. of East Windsor, Apr. 29, 1784   49
    Jonathan, s. Jonathan & Elisabeth, b. Mar. 12, 1785   22
    Lova, m. Horace LORD, Aug. 13, 1844, by Shubael Bartlett   114
    Melissa C., m. Levi BLANCHARD, Mar. 18, 1851, by Rev. Sanford
        Benton   130
    Normand, m. Cynthia FROST, Apr. 24, 1834, by Rev. Shubael Bartlett   97
    Sarah, m. Horace GRANGER, b. of East Windsor, Dec. 19, 1824,
        by Rev. Shubael Bartlett   87
    Sarah A., of East Windsor, m. Albert C. WHITE, of Long Meadow,
        Mass., Jan. 6, 1842, by Shubael Bartlett   111
    Zilphia L., m. Shadrach D. FISH, May 27, 1841, by Shubael Bartlett   109
PATCHEN, Caroline C., m. Luke D. ALLEN, b. of East Windsor, Apr. 10,
    1853, by Rev. James Mather   136
    Rufus M., of East Windsor, m. Laura J. ENO, of Bloomfield, Oct.
        8, [1848], by Edward A. Lyon   124
    Samuel, m. Dorothy BENJAMIN, b. of East Windsor, July 11, 1838,
        by Rev. Ebenezer Blake, of Warehouse Point   105
PATTERSON, Ellen, m. Joseph HAYTHORN, b. of Warehouse Point, Apr.
    8, 1849, in Grace Church, Broad Brook, by Rev. Francis J. Clerc   126
    Harriet M., m. Lucius PHELON, Sept. 16, 1832, by Rev. D. L. Hunn   96
    James, m. Agnes CRAGE, Apr. 4, 1851, by Rev. Shubael Bartlett   130
PAYNE, Aurel, d. Eleazer & Aurel, b. Sept. 15, 1798   22
    Charles Cook, s. Eleazer & Aurel, b. May 6, 1793   22
    Eleazer, s. Eleazer & Aurel, b. Nov. 10, 1795   22
    Franklin, s. Eleazer & Aurel, b. Jan. 15, 1791   22
    Hendrick, s. Eleazer & Aurel, b. Feb. 14, 1789   22
    Henry H., m. Lucretia L. NICKOLS, b. of East Windsor, Nov. 25,

Page

PEASE, (cont.)

Joel, s. Joel & Lois, b. Nov. 6, 1764   22

Julia M., of Enfield, m. George **LUCE**, of Somers, June 30, 1844,
   by Rev. Henry H. Bates, of St. John's Ch.   116

Kellogg, m. Jane **PEASE**, of Enfield, Sept. 9, 1840, by Shubael Bartlett   108

Laphineas, b. Mar. 27, 1813   30

Lemuel, s. Peter & Desire, b. Jan. 20, 1792   22

Lemuel F., of East Windsor, m. Mary Ann **COON**, of Palmer, Mass.,
   July 9, 1848, by Rev. C. W. Stearns   123

Lois, d. Joel & Lois, b. Jan. 7, 1763   22

Lorenzo, of Enfield, m. Mary **PEASE**, of East Windsor, Nov. 28,
   1850, by Rev. Sanford Benton   130

Loring, s. Peter & Desire, b. Apr. 30, 1802   22

Lovice, of Enfield, m. Alexander **VINING**, of East Windsor, Nov.
   22, 1786   54

Lucina, d. Peter & Desire, b. May 8, 1794   22

Lucy, d. Joel & Lois, b. Oct. 30, 1780   22

Lucy, d. James & Lucy, b. Nov. 22, 1788   22

Lyman F., of Enfield, m. Polly M. **OSBORN**, of East Windsor, Oct.
   5, 1851, by Shubael Bartlett   131

Mary, m. Henry **BARBER**, b. of East Windsor, May 10, 1827, by
   Rev. Shubael Bartlett   89

Mary, of East Windsor, m. Lorenzo **PEASE**, of Enfield, Nov. 28,
   1850, by Rev. Sanford Benton   130

Mary A., of East Windsor, m. Eben E. **HART**, of Springfield, Mass.,
   Jan. 6, 1842, by Rev. W[illia]m H. Richards   110

Nancy, d. James & Lucy, b. Oct. 2, 1792   22

Olive, of Enfield, m. Alexander **VINING**, of East Windsor, Sept.
   19, 1774   56

Orrin, s. Peter & Desire, b. Jan. 28, 1788   22

Peter, s. Peter & Desire, b. Jan. 7, 1790   22

Rowena, m. Ebenezer Stowell **HAWLEY**, Jan. 4, 1849, by Rev. Henry
   H. Bates, of St. John's Ch., Warehouse Point   125

Rufus, s. James & Lucy, b. June 1, 1790   22

Tryphena, of Enfield, m. Jeremiah **LORD**, Jr., of East Windsor, Feb.
   5, 1777   44

Wyllys, s. Peter & Desire, b. Apr. 16, 1798   22

Zina K., m. L. Louisa **CHAPMAN**, Sept. 29, 1858, at Warehouse
   Pt., by Rev. Henry McClory of St. John's Ch.   150

PECK, Robert G., of Vernon, m. Julia A. **LOOMIS**, of East Windsor,
   Aug. 13, 1834, by Rev. David L. Hunn   98

PEEBLES, Ann, of East Windsor, m. John E. **BRAMBLE**, of Norwich,
   [Sept.] 9, [1838], by Rev. Marvin Root   104

PELTON, Austin, m. Charlotte **PELTON**, [Jan.] 1, [1822], by Rev.
   Thomas Robbins of 1st Eccl. Soc.   85

Charlotte, m. Austin **PELTON**, [Jan.] 1, [1822], by Rev. Thomas
   Robbins of 1st Eccl. Soc.   85

Enoch, s. Nathan & Ruth, b. Aug. 7, 1770   22

Page

PELTON, (cont.)

Harriet F., m. Daniel G. SPERRY, b. of East Windsor, Mar. 30,
1834, by Rev. Chauncey G. Lee   97

James, s. Nathan & Ruth, b. Oct. 20, 1778   22

James, m. Mrs. Betsey BISSELL, [Feb.] 23, [1834], by Rev. Chauncey
G. Lee   97

John, s. Nathan & Ruth, b. July 29, 1772   22

John, m. Mary BULKLEY, Jan. 24, 1847, by Shubael Bartlett   119

Lucy, d. Nathan & Ruth, b. Nov. 7, 1774   22

Ruth, d. Nathan & Ruth, b. Sept. 19, 1768   22

Sarah, d. Nathan & Ruth, b. Oct. 12, 1780   22

Susan, m. Elihu DRAKE, b. of East Windsor, Apr. 9, 1829, by
Rev. S. W. Whelpley   92

PEMBER, Austin, of Ellington, m. Rhoda Maria BLODGETT, of East
Windsor, Aug. 3, 1825, by Rev. Shubael Bartlett   87

Maria K. Mrs., of East Windsor, m. Horace D. FULLER, of Ellington,
Feb. 28, 1839, by Rev. Ebenezer Blake, of Warehouse Point   105

PERKINS, Harriet, m. James COOK, b. of East Windsor, Nov. 26, 1837,
by Rev. J. Cogswell   103

PERRIN, Marette, of East Windsor, m. Edwin G. BRIGHAM, of Vernon,
this day, [Nov. 28, 1839], by Bennet Tyler   106

Mary Ann, of East Windsor, m. Samuel H. GALPIN, of Wethersfield,
Nov. 28, 1844, by William Thompson   115

Sarah Roselle, of East Windsor, m. David BANCROFT, of Grafton,
Vt., this day, [Jan. 15, 1839], by Bennet Tyler   105

PERRY, William, m. Elizabeth P. ELLSWORTH, Nov. 13, 1842, by
Shubael Bartlett   112

PERSSE, Margaret E., m. Rev. Henry McCLORY, May 25, 1857, at
Warehouse Point, by John Williams, Asst. Bishop of Conn.   147

PETTIBONE, Giles, m. Mary G. PARSONS, Apr. 11, 1838, by Shubael
Bartlett   103

PFEIFFER, PEEIFER, Andon, m. Cresentia MERRICK, May 3, 1857, by
Rev. W[illia]m M. Birchard   147

John, m. Catharine WAGNER, Nov. 21, 1858, at Broad Brook, by
Rev John F. Mines, of Grace Ch.   150

Katharin, m. Fertinam BAKER, Apr. 8, 1855, by Rev. Enoch
Huntington of Grace Ch., Broad Brook   142

PFENING, Catharine, m. John FREDERICK, Dec. 24, 1855, by Rev.
Enoch Huntington of Grace Ch.   144

PFENNICH, Anna Mary, m. Matthias ZAHN, Jan. 8, 1859, by Rev.
W[illia]m M. Birchard   151

PHELON, Lucius, m. Harriet H. PATTERSON, Sept. 16, 1832, by Rev. D.
L. Hunn   96

PHELPS, Almira J., of East Windsor, m. Chauncey WINCHELL, Jr., of
Vernon, Oct. 18, 1853, by Rev. Abel Gardner   138

Benjamin, s. Daniel & Hulday, b. June 27, 1795   22

Charlotte, of East Windsor, m. Benjamin ALLEN, of Warren, N. Y.,
May 11, 1828, by Rev. Shubael Bartlett   90

Page

PHELPS, (cont.)

Daniel, s. Daniel & Huldah, b. Jan. 11, 1792   22

Elizabeth, m. Ashbel **BARBER**, Sept. 4, 1823, by Rev. Shubael Bartlett
of 2nd Church   85

Horace, of Enfield, m. Laura **ALLEN**, of East Windsor, May 10,
1827, by Rev. Shubael Bartlett   89

Huldah, d. Daniel & Huldah, b. Aug. 2, 1793   22

Jabez, m. Mary **ALLEN**, Dec. 27, 1821, by Rev. Shubael Bartlett,
of 2nd Church   84

Jabez, m. Mrs. Laura **CHAMPLIN**, b. of East Windsor, Sept. 12,
1841, by Rev. W[illia]m H. Richards, Warehouse Point   110

Jabez, m. Mrs. Sarah **COOK**, b. of East Windsor, May 25, 1842,
by Rev. W[illia]m H. Richards, Warehouse Point   112

Jane E., m. Isaac **BRADBURY**, Jr., Feb. 9, 1858, at Warehouse Point,
by Rev. H. W. Conant, of M. E. Ch.   148

Levi C., m. Martha **FISH**, May 13, 1821, by Rev. Shubael Bartlett
of the 2nd Church   59

Lucy Elizabeth, m. George **WATSON**, Feb. 25, 1847, by Shubael
Bartlett   119

Maria H., m. Dexter R. **MIGLER**, Feb. 3, 1848, by Rev. Henry H.
Bates, of St. John's Ch., Warehouse Point   122

Mary, m. Jason **ELLSWORTH**, b. of East Windsor, May 1, 1823, by
Rev. Shubael Bartlett of 2nd Church   85

Melinda, m. Albert A. **SPERRY**, Nov. 21, 1859, by Rev. Frederick
Munson   152

Noah, m. Lucy **BARBER**, Dec. 5, 1820, by Rev. Shubael Bartlett   59

Rachel, of Enfield, m. Abner **BLODGETT**, of East Windsor, Mar.
23, 1768   32

Roswell, of Wilbraham, Mass., m. Sarah **EASTMAN**, of East Windsor,
Aug. 15, 1852, by Rev. Samuel J. Andrews, of Cong. Ch.   134

Salome P., of Windsor, m. Moseley A. **OSBORN**, of East Windsor,
May 27, 1841, by Levi Smith   112

Wyllys, of Enfield, m. Fluvia **PASCO**, of East Windsor, Jan. 18,
1832, by Rev. Shubael Bartlett   94

PHILBRICK, Mary O., m. Levi **LORD**, b. of East Windsor, July 4, 1855,
at Enfield, by Rev. Sam[ue]l Fox   143

PHILLIPS, Harriet L., m. Abel A. **PACKARD**, b. of East Windsor, Oct.
24, 1849, by Rev. Samuel J. Andrews, of Cong. Ch.   127

PICKHARDT, Hellena, m. Peter **SNYDER**, b. of Warehouse Pt., Apr. 14,
1850, by Rev. Henry H. Bates, of St. John's Ch., Warehouse Pt.   128

PIELL, Elisabeth, m. Daniel **HOPPLE**, Dec. 16, 1857, at Broad Brook,
by Rev. John F. Mines, of Grace Ch.   149

PIERCE, Anne, d. Daniel & Bethiah, b. Sept. 18, 1770   22

Benjamin, Jr., m. Chloe Mary **AVERY**, b. of East Windsor, this
day, [Apr. 9, 1839], by Rev. Marvin Root   105

Caroline, of East Windsor, m. Walter M. **ENSWORTH**, of Somers,
Aug. 18, 1843, by Josiah Ellworth, J. P.   113

Daniel, s. Dan[ie]ll & Bethiah, b. May 13, 1775   22

Page

PIERCE, (cont.)

Eliza, m. Silas MUNSELL, b. of East Windsor, Aug. 17, 1829, by
W[illia]m Cooley, J. P.   92

Elisabeth, d. Daniel & Bethiah, b. May 12, 1765   22

Ephraim G., m. Cordelia McKINNEY, [Apr.] 10, [1842], by Rev.
Marvin Root   111

Hiram, of Plymouth, m. Charlotte BANCROFT, of East Windsor,
Nov. 6, 1828, by Rev. Samuel W. Whelpley, of 1st Church   91

Joseph, s. Daniel & Bethiah, b. Oct. 11, 1767   22

Joseph, s. Joseph & Sarah, b. Apr. 1, 1774   22

Luther, s. Daniel & Bethiah, b. Sept. 6, 1772   22

Mary, m. James BARKER, b. of Somers, Sept. 28, 1851, by Rev.
Henry H. Bates, of St. John's Ch.   131

Norris B., m. Angeline H. PACKARD, Jan. 1, 1850, by Rev. Shubael
Bartlett   127

Sarah, d. Joseph & Sarah, b. Feb. 19, 1777   22

Theodotia, d. Joseph & Sarah, b. May 30, 1781   22

PIKE, Catharine, m. John S. MAIR, Mar. 25, 1848, by Rev. Henry H.
Bates, of St. John's Ch., Warehouse Point   122

Mary E., m. George H. BUGBEY, May 24, 1857, at Warehouse Point,
by Rev. Henry McClory of St. John's Ch.   147

PINNEY, Achsah, d. Lemuel & Zeruiah, b. Mar. 29, 1780   22

Allison, s. Jonathan & Martha, b. Sept. 7, 1794   30

Benjamin, s. Eleazer & Eunice, b. July 4, 1780   22

Elisabeth, d. Jonathan, d. Dec. 5, 1768   76

Gurdon, of Granby, Mass., m. Eunice WARD, of Torringford, Nov.
30, 1848, by H. C. Atwater   124

Huldah, of East Windsor, m. David ELLSWORTH, of Windsor, Apr.
4, 1832, by Rev. J. W. Case   95

Julia, m. Francis BANCROFT, b. of East Windsor, Apr. 11, 1844,
by Levi Smith   114

Lemuel, s. Lemuel & Zeruiah, b. Nov. 3, 1776   22

Levi, s. Jonathan & Martha, b. Jan. 3, 1786   30

Lydia, d. Eleazer & Eunice, b. Oct. 9, 1776   22

Nansey, d. Lemuel & Zeruiah, b. Mar. 23, 1782   22

Nancy, d. Jo[na]th[a]n & Martha, b. Nov. 18, 1790   30

Persis, d. Eleazer & Eunice, b. Sept. 6, 1778   22

Roxana, d. Lemuel & Zeruiah, b. Aug. 3, 1778   22

Samuel B., of Ellington, m. Nancy P. ALLEN, of East Windsor, this
day, [Mar. 17, 1842], by Rev. Edwin C. Brown   111

Sophia R., m. Ebenezer S. CLAPP, b. of East Windsor, Apr. 17,
1832, by Rev. John W. Case   95

Thankfull, d. Lemuel & Zeruiah, b. Jan. 29, 1784   22

PITCHER, David, of Lebanon, m. Mary B. HURLBUT, of Hartford, Apr.
14, 1835, by Rev. Shubael Bartlett   99

PITKIN, Everlyn, m. Esther J. STILES, July 11, 1843, by Shubael Bartlett   113

POLK, POALK, Cyrus, s. Noah & Rachel, b. Dec. 26, 1769   22

Noah, s. Noah & Rachel, b. July 16, 1767   22

Page

POLK, POALK, (cont.)
Sarah, of East Windsor, m. Joel NASH, Mar. 30, 1769   47
PORTER, Abiezer, s. Hezekiah & Sarah, d. Oct. 30, 1776, in the 19th
y. of his age   76
Abiezer, m. Sophia WOOD, [Oct.] 9, [1820], by Rev. Thomas Robbins
of 1st Eccl. Soc.   59
David, s. Reuben & Ruth, b. Sept. 6, 1780   22
Elijah, m. Olive DIGGINS, Sept. 2, [1821], by Rev. Thomas Robbins   84
Eliza, m. John MOORE, [May] 7, [1821], by Rev. Thomas Robbins   84
Elizabeth, of East Windsor, m. Zebulon CROCKER, of Ellington,
Oct. 11, 1830, by Rev. Shubael Bartlett   93
Eunice, d. Reuben & Ruth, b. Nov. 26, 1778   22
George, s. Joseph & Naomi, b. Feb. 1, 1767   22
Jephthah, s. Joseph & Naomi, b. Jan. 21, 1776   22
Joel M., of Glastenbury, m. Cordelia L. BOLYER, of Enfield,
Apr. 24, 1850, by Rev. Shubael Bartlett   128
Joseph, s. Joseph & Naomi, b. Apr. 9, 1771   22
Lusina, d. Joseph & Naomi, b. Feb. 6, 1765   22
Malvina S., m. Thomas Hall POTWINE, Oct. 15, 1839, by Shubael
Bartlett   106
Martha P., m. George M. SHIPMAN, Mar. 27, 1844, by Shubael
Bartlett   114
Mary B., m. Horace CHIPMAN, Oct. 7, 1832, by Rev. Chauncey G.
Lee, of 1st Church   95
Naomi, d. Joseph & Naomi, b. Mar. 5, 1769   22
Reuben, s. Joseph & Naomi, b. Oct. 17, 1773   22
Rumah, d. Hezekiah & Sarah, b. Feb. 26, 1775   22
Ruth, d. Reuben & Ruth, b. Dec. 14, 1776   22
Wareham, m. Amelia HILLS, Jan. 31, 1831, by Rev. Gurdon Robins,
of Bap. Ch.   94
POST, Charlotte Elizabeth, of East Windsor, m. Charles DAVIS,
of Bristoll, July 31, 1853, by Rev. Charles S. Putnam of St. John's
Ch.   137
Josephine, m. Almanzo B. VINING, Jan. 31, 1856, at Warehouse Pt.
by W[illia]m Barnes, J. P.   144
POTTER, Orvillia, m. John R. OSBORN, b. of Warehouse Point, Feb. 23,
1854, by Rev. Abel Gardner   139
POTWINE, Ann, of East Windsor, m. Orrin CLARK, of Utica, N. Y., Sept.
2, 1833, by Rev. Shubael Bartlett   96
Caleb, Jr., m. Clarissa TRUMBULL, b. of East Windsor, Apr. 15,
1835, by Rev. Shubael Bartlett   99
Caroline E., m. Lewis H. TAYLOR, Sept. 4, 1844, by Shubael Bartlett   117
David, s. John, Jr. & Eunice, d. Sept. 29, 1775, in the 11th
y. of his age   76
Edward L., m. Mary K. BARTLETT, Sept. 19, 1839, by Shubael
Bartlett   106
Eunice, m. Robert WATSON, b. of East Windsor, Dec. 24, 1772   56
George C., m. Ruth W. HULL, b. of East Windsor, Apr. 25, 1833,

Page

POTWINE, (cont.)

by Rev. Shubael Bartlett 96

Hannah C., m. Samuel H. WELLS, Jan. 3, 1860, by Rev. Frederick
Munson, of 1st Ch. 153

Israel, m. Mary F. POTWINE, b. of East Windsor, Nov. 6, 1828,
by Rev. Shubael Bartlett 90

John, s. John, Jr. & Eunice, d. Aug. 22, 1775, in the 21st y. of his age 76

John, Jr., d. Aug. 10, 1785, in the 57th y. of his age 76

John T., m. Sophronia BELKNAP, May 17, 1837, by Rev. Shubael
Bartlett 102

Julia Hannah, m. Thomas HENDER, June 27, 1844, by Shubael
Bartlett 114

Lucinda W., m. William N. WELLS, b. of East Windsor, Sept. 3,
1850, by Rev. S. J. Andrews, of Cong. Ch. 129

Mary, m. Dea. Noah ALLEN, Apr. 2, 1822, by Rev. Shubael Bartlett
of 2nd Church 84

Mary Ann, m. Orick H. GREENLEAF, Jan. 31, 1847, by Shubael
Bartlett 119

Mary F., m. Israel POTWINE, b. of East Windsor, Nov. 6, 1828,
by Rev. Shubael Bartlett 90

Nathaniel, m. Sophia M. CLARK, [Oct.] 16, [1821], by Rev. Shubael
Bartlett of 2nd Church 59

Thomas, m. Sarah STOUGHTON, b. of East Windsor, May 22, 1828,
by Rev. Shubael Bartlett 90

Thomas, m. Margaret BARTLETT, Feb. 15, 1849, by Shubael Bartlett 124

Thomas Hall, m. Jane S. TRUMBULL, Apr. 29, 1834, by Rev.
Shubael Bartlett 97

Thomas Hall, m. Malvina S. PORTER, Oct. 15, 1839, by Shubael
Bartlett 106

William, m. Mary A. WATERS, b. of East Windsor, Jan. 18, 1852,
by Rev. Sanford Benton 132

POWERS, Albert B., of Westfield, Mass., m. Frances B. DANFORTH, of
Cabotville, Mass., Aug. 11, 1844, by Rev. Henry H. Bates, of St.
John's Ch. 116

PRATT, David M., of New York City, m. Clarissa WILLSON, of South
Hadley, Mass., Oct. 14, 1849, by Shubael Bartlett 126

PRENTISS, Hugh K., of Salem, Mass., m. Laura H. WATSON, of East
Windsor, Feb. 21, 1844, by Bennet Tyler 113

PRESTON, Harriet, d. Earl C. & Harriet, b. Apr. 27, 1824 27

PRIOR, Abigail, d. Joel & Jerusha, b. Nov. 27, 1773 22

Asa, s. Joel & Jerusha, b. Sept. 13, 1788 22

Agustus, s. Joel & Jerusha, b. Apr. 16, 1769 22

Augustus, s. Joel & Jerusha, b. Aug. 21, 1780 (Line drawn
through entry) 22

Augustus, s. Joel & Jerusha, b. Aug. 21, 1780 22

Clarissa, d. Joel & Jerusha, b. May 21, 1777 22

Ellen, [see under Helen]

Frederick, s. Joel & Jerusha, b. Apr. 18, 1771 22

Page

REED, READ, (cont.)

18, 1778   34

Celina, m. Henry M. **BISSELL,** Apr. 4, 1858, by Rev. F. Munson,
of 1st Ch.   149

Charlotte C., m. Edwin **KING,** of Springfield, Mass., Nov. 11,
1839, by Shubael Bartlett   106

Charlotte Sophia, of East Windsor, m. Samuel **STILES,** of Utica,
N. Y., [June] 12, [1825], by Rev. Thomas Robbins of 1st Church 88

Chloe, of East Windsor, m. Albert **JENDERVINE**(?), of Charlestown,
N. H., Nov. 10, 1834, by Rev. Shubael Bartlett   98

Francis M., m. Elisabeth W. **HOUSE,** Feb. 22, 1846, by Shubael
Bartlett   118

Jacob, late of Norwich, d. May 25, 1774   78

James, m. Margaret **HIGGINS,** b. of Enfield, June 15, 1851, by Rev.
Henry H. Bates, of St. John's Ch.   131

Jane Ann Maria, of East Windsor, m. Edward **BISSELL,** of Rochester,
N. Y., [Sept.] 15, [1823], by Rev. Thomas Robbins of 1st Church 86

John H., m. Jane E. **FRENCH,** Dec. 8, 1859, by Rev. Warren Emerson 152

Joseph, lately removed from Norwich ot East Windsor, d. Apr.
24, 1774, in the 67th y. of his age   78

Judith, d. Jedediah & Judith, b. Oct. 23, 1773   23

Lemuel E., m. Catherine M. **LEWIS,** May 13, 1846, by Rev. Henry H.
Bates, of St. John's Ch.   120

Maro M., M. D., m. Elizabeth **LATHROP,** Sept. 16, 1830, by Rev.
Shubael Bartlett   93

Mary, w. Ebenezer, d. Nov. 11, 1774   78

Ralph, m. Sarah H. **KINSLEY,** Dec. 3, 1837, by Shubael Bartlett 103

Rosanna, of East Windsor, m. Stanley **WHITE,** of Andover, town
of Coventry, Oct. 17, 1838, by Allen McLean   104

Rusha, d. Ebenezer & Mary, b. Aug. 10, 1773   23

Rusha, d. Ebenezer & Mary, d. Mar. 2, 1777   78

REINTANZ, Frank, m. Mary Elizabeth **ABBE,** b. of East Windsor, Oct.
10, 1852, by Rev. C. S. Putnam, of St. John's Ch., Warehouse Pt. 134

RELKE, Christiana, m. Daniel **SCHAFFER,** Dec. 17, 1848, at the house of
Rev. H. H. Bates, Warehouse Point, by Rev. Francis J. Clerc, of
Grace Ch., Broad Brook   125

REYNOLDS, George, of Long Meadow, Mass., m. Mary **COOK,** of East
Windsor, May 16, 1838, by Asahel Nettleton   103

RHONER, William, m. Lamira Amelia **BARKER*,** b. of East Windsor,
Dec. 15, 1851, by Rev. Henry H. Bates, of St. John's Ch., at
Warehouse Point *(Written in margin " Lamira A. **BARNES"**) 132

RICE, Josiah S., of Hartford, m. Eleanor P. **BISSELL,** of East Windsor,
Apr. 24, 1832, by Rev. Shubael Bartlett   95

RICH, William, of Manchester, m. Minerva **BLINN,** of East Windsor, this
day, [Jan. 31, 1825], by Rev. Thomas Robbins, of 1st Church 88

RICHARDS, Mary S., [m.] Mahlon H. **BANCROFT,** [s. William &
Caroline B.], June 27, 1762   5

RICHARDSON, Emeline, of Ludlow, Mass., m. Ezra **WRIGHT,** of Ludlow,

Page

RICHARDSON, (cont.)

    Mass., June 18, 1843, by Josiah Ellsworth, J. P.   113

    Hugh J., of Springfield, Mass., m. Abigail **ROBINSON,** of West
    Springfield, Mass., Jan. 1, 1843, by Rev. Joseph Scott, of St.
    John's Ch.   113

    John, of Windsor, m. Emily **MARBLE,** of East Windsor, this day,
    [Mar. 31, 1823], by Rev. Tho[ma]s Robbins, of 1st Soc.   86

    Lorenzo D., of Hartford, m. Louisa **BURNHAM,** of East Windsor,
    this day, [Oct. 13, 1840], by Rev. Samuel Spring, of Cong. Ch.
    East Hartford   108

RIDER, Augusta, m. Herman **HABERMAN,** b. of East Windsor, June 19,
    1853, by Rev. Charles S. Putnam, of St. John's Ch.   137

    Zenas, m. Julia **LOOMIS,** Sept. 12, 1832, by Rev. Chauncey G.
    Lee, of 1st Church   95

RIERSTEINER, Jacob, m. Elizabeth **GARBER,** of Ketch Mills, Nov. 7,
    1848, by Rev. Francis J. Clerc, of Grace Ch., Broad Brook   124

RIGGS, Andrew, of Wilmington, Del., m. Lucinda **CHASE,** of Warehouse
    Point, Apr. 2, 1843, by Rev. Joseph Scott, of St. John's Ch.   113

RILEY, Mary Kane, m. William **TROY,** b. of Enfield, Dec. 30, 1849, by
    Rev. Henry H. Bates, of St. John's Ch., Warehouse Pt.   127

    William, m. Ellen **CARPENTER,** July 11, 1852, by Rev. Enoch
    Huntington, of Grace Ch.   134

RISLEY, Alphonso, of Ellington, m. Mary J. **KEENEY,** of East Windsor,
    Aug. 12, 1849, by Rev. Samuel J. Andrews   125

    Amelia N., of East Windsor, m. Bickford **ABBOT,** of Vernon,
    [May] 21, [1835], by Chester Humphrey, Vernon   99

    Elizur, m. Amanda P. **ALLEN,** Jan. 4, 1847, by Shubael Bartlett   119

    Hester R., of East Windsor, m. William C. **BURNHAM,** of East
    Haddam, Aug. 6, 1834, by Rev. Salmon Hull   98

    James, of Ellington, m. Emily **FOSTER,** of East Windsor, Mar. 27,
    1845, by Rev. B. M. Walker   115

    Joshua, m. Betseyann **CRANE,** b. of East Windsor, Aug. 30, 1829,
    by Rev. George Sutherland   92

    Maria S., of East Windsor, m. William W. **DAVIS,** of New York,
    Apr. 2, 1840, by Rev. Ebenezer Blake, of Wapping   107

    Martin, of Manchester, m. Mary E. **GOODALE,** of East Windsor, this
    day, [Nov. 16, 1836], by Rev. Marvin Root   101

    Patience A., m. Frederick **EVANS,** b. of Manchester, May 11, 1845,
    by Rev. B. M. Walker   116

    Peter H., m. Clarissa **WOLCOTT,** Jan. 17, 1857, by Rev. Frederick
    Munson of 1st Ch.   146

    Selden N., m. Louisa **BELKNAP,** b. of East Windsor, June 19, 1838,
    by Shubael Bartlett   104

    Sylvester, m. Martha A. **ALLEN,** Dec. 31, 1841, by Shubael Bartlett
    (Perhaps 1840?)   109

ROACH, David, m. Mary **MacHILCUDDY,** Nov. 20, 1858, at Windsor
    Locks, by Rev. James Smyth   148

ROBERTS, Elizaabeth D., d. William, b. Dec. 2, 1831 (colored)   23

Page

ROBERTS, (cont.)

Mary, m. Morgan STRONG, b. of East Windsor, May 1, 1842, by Rev.
Andrew M. Smith   111

ROBERTSON, Delina, m. Caleb LEAVITT, Jr., of Bath, Me., Oct. 15,
1834, by Rev. Shubael Bartlett   98

Elijah, m. Hannah HIGLEY, b. of East Windsor, [July] 4, [1824],
by Rev. Thomas Robbins of 1st Church   87

Elmina, m. Gardner CHILD, of Green Bay, Wis., July 29, 1840, by
Shubael Bartlett   108

John C., of South Windsor, m. Marietta ALLEN, of East Windsor, Apr.
12, 1853, by Rev. Samuel J. Andrews, of Cong. Ch.   137

Miranda, m. Charles SEWALL, of Bath, Me., Sept. 9, 1835, by
Rev. Shubael Bartlett   100

ROBINS, Clarissa Ann, Mrs., m. James LUDLOW, of Charleston, S. C.,
Aug. 17, 1831, by Rev. Gurdon Robins of Bapt. Ch.   94

ROBINSON, Abigail, of West Springfield, Mass., m. Hugh J.
RICHARDSON, of Springfield, Mass., Jan. 1, 1843, by Rev.
Joseph Scott, of St. John's Ch.   113

Caroline, of East Windsor, m. W[illia]m ALLEN, of Enfield, Nov. 17,
1839, by Rev. Benjamin C. Phelps, of Warehouse Point   106

Eber, of East Windsor, m. Alzade LEE, of Willington, Nov. 19,
1826, by Rev. Shubael Bartlett   88

Fanny W., m. George W. CADWELL, b. of East Windsor, May 9,
1853, by Charles Bartlett, J. P.   137

Lucinda, m. Walter WELDEN, Apr. 6, 1858, at Scantic, by Rev.
John F. Mines, of Grace Ch.   148

ROCKWELL, Aaron, s. Samuel & Sarah, b. Oct. 2, 1777   23

Angelina, m. Horace LENOM(?), b. of East Windsor, Jan. 1, 1821,
by Rev. Shubael Bartlett of 2nd Church   59

Betsey, of Warehouse Point, m. Aaron CHAMPION, of Lebanon,
Sept. 10, 1823, by Rev. W[illia]m J. Bulkeley of Warehouse Point   85

Charles, s. Charles & Abigail, b. July 2, 1765   23

Charles, m. Rhoda BROWN, [Mar. 25, 1821], by Jonathan Pasco, J. P.   59

Chloe, d. Jsaac & Desire, b. June 16, 1780   23

Chloe A., m. Harvey H. BUCKLAND, May 14, 1844, by Rev. B. M.
Walker   114

Clarissa, of East Windsor, m. William COOMS, of Enfield, Conn.,
Mar. 8, 1826, by Horace Barber, J. P.   88

Desire, w. Isaac, d. Aug. 19, 1782   78

Edward Frances, m. Ann Maria WILLEY, b. of East Windsor, this day,
[Sept. 16, 1841], by Rev. Abijah C. Wheat, of M. E. Ch.   110

Elihu, s. Charles & Abigail, b. Oct. 16, 1770   23

Elijah, s. Samuel & Sarah, b. Oct. 16, 1788   23

Harriet T., m. Seth F. WOODFORD, May 18, 1842, by Levi Smith   112

Helen, of East Windsor, m. Rev. James A. HAZEN, of South
Wilbraham, Mass., [Feb.] 27, [1839], by Rev. Jonathan Cogswell   105

Jsaac, s. Jsaac & Desire, b. Nov. 16, 1769   23

Jerusha, d. Samuel & Sarah, b. June 8, 1780   23

Page

ROLLO, (cont.)

Ralph R. Jr., m. Lucia **LEE**, 2nd, b. of East Windsor, Apr. 13,
1837, by Chauncey G. Lee   102

ROOT, Ann, of Westfield, m. Oliver **BARBER**, of Windsor, now of East
Windsor, Jan. 30, 1766   32

[ROWE], [see under **ROE**]

RUDD, James, of Becket, Mass., m. Elizabeth **VINING**, of East Windsor,
June 8, 1788   51

RUSS, Andrew J., m. Mary M. **GRANT**, Sept. 25, 1856, by W[illia]m
Barnes, J. P.   145

RUSSELL, George, m. Joan **WATTS**, of Thompsonville, July 25, 1852, by
Rev. Enoch Huntington, of Grace Ch.   134

Rufus, of Sunderland, Mass., m. Dolly S. **BISSELL**, of East Windsor,
Dec. 8, 1833, by Ebenezer Pinney, J. P.   97

Wyllys, s. Ebenezer, Jr. & Hannah, b. Jan. 9, 1770   23

RUTHERFORD, Andrew, m. Ellen **WELCH**, b. of East Windsor, Dec. 15,
1842, by Levi Smith   112

SADD, [see also **LADD**], Amanda, m. Joseph **SADD**, b. of East Windsor,
Apr. 30, 1834, by Rev. David L. Hunn   98

Caroline S., of East Windsor, m. Sylvester G. **LORD**, of Hebron,
Nov. 28, 1855, by Rev. William Wright, of 2nd Cong. Ch. South
Windsor   144

Emily C., of East Windsor, m. Daniel N. **CONE**, of Linklaen, N. Y.,
Aug. 25, 1831, by Rev. Shubael Bartlett   94

Emily C., m. William W. **SADD**, b. of South Windsor, May 2, 1850,
by Rev. Shubael Bartlett   128

Frederick H., m. Hannah **COLLINS**, b. of East Windsor, May 6,
1840, by W[illia]m Thompson, at Wapping   107

John, m. Emeline **CLARK**, b. of East Windsor, Nov. 28, 1826, by
Rev. Shubael Bartlett   88

Joseph, m. Amanda **SADD**, b. of East Windsor, Apr. 30, 1834, by
Rev. David L. Hunn   98

Lucina, m. Benoni O. **KING**, b. of East Windsor, Nov. 12, 1827,
by Rev. Shubael Bartlett   89

Maria, of East Windsor, m. Dan Terry **CHAPIN**, of Enfield, Oct.
31, 1832, by Rev. Shubael Bartlett   95

Mary A., of East Windsor, m. John A. **NEWEL**, of New Britain,
Apr. 8, 1851, by Rev. Sam[ue]l J. Andrews, of Cong. Ch.   131

William W., m. Emily C **SADD**, b. of South Windsor, May 2, 1850,
by Rev. Shubael Bartlett   128

ST. CLAIRE, ST. CLAIR, Aurelia, m. George W. **BARBER**, Sept. 22,
1844, by Shubael Bartlett   117

Joel, m. Jane Ann **HILLS**, b. of East Windsor, Jan. 11, 1842,
by Deodate Brockway   110

Marble G., of East Windsor, m. Mary Ann **WALES**, of Portland,
May 3, 1843, by Josiah Ellsworth, J. P.   113

Sarah, of East Windsor, m. Harlow **TOPLIFF**, of Coventry, May
16, 1841, by Rev. John Whittlesey   109

Page

SANBORN, Clarissa L., of Strafford, Vt., m. Joseph **PARKER**, of East
    Windsor, Apr. 13, 1838, by William Barnes, J. P.   104
    Susan, of East Windsor, m. William R. **OLDS**, of Ludlow, Mass.,
    Mar. 31, 1842, by William Barnes, J. P.   111
SANDERSON, George, of Rockville, m. Elizabeth **ATWOOD**, of East
    Windsor, Oct. 14, 1849, by Rev. Samuel J. Andrews, of Cong.
    Ch.   126
SANGER, Parmelia, d. Jonathan & Lucy, b. Nov. 18, 1784   25
SARGENT, Sophia, Mrs., m. Reuel **THRALL**, Nov. 14, 1856, at Warehouse
    Point, by Rev. Henry McClory of St. John's Ch.   146
SAUNDERS, Peggy, m. Nath[anie]ll **BARBER**, Nov. 4, [1821], by Rev.
    Shubael Bartlett of 2nd Church   59
SAUVAN, John J., m. Mary A. **RAMSDELL**, Nov. 15, 1857, at Warehouse
    Pt., by Rev. Henry McClory of St. John's Ch. **(RAMSELL)**   147
SAWYER, Sarah Merriam, m. Sidney **HARRIS**, Apr. 4, 1846, by Rev.
    Henry H. Bates, of St. John's Ch.   120
SAXTON, Sarah, d. Jonathan & Susanna, b. Aug. 1, 1777   25
SCHAFFER, Daniel, m. Christiana **RELKE**, Dec. 17, 1848, at the house
    of Rev. H. H. Bates, Warehouse Point, by Rev. Francis J. Clerc,
    of Grace Ch., Broad Brook   125
    Elizabeth, m. Lewis **SCHAFFER**, Dec. 17, 1848, at the house of Rev.
    H. H. Bates, Warehouse Point, by Rev. Francis J. Clerc, of Grace
    Ch., Broad Brook   125
    Lewis, m. Elizabeth **SCHAFFER**, Dec. 17, 1848, at the house of Rev.
    H. H. Bates, Warehouse Point, by Rev. Francis J. Clerc, of Grace
    Ch. Broad Brook   125
SCHMAHLFELDT, Christine M. E., m. Christian H. F. **BOLTE**, Mar. 28,
    1848, in Grace Church, Broad Brook, by Rev. Frances J. Clerc   123
SCHMIDT, Frederick, m. Dorothea **MENSCHING**, b. of Warehouse Point,
    July 30, 1848, in Grace Church, Broad Brook, by Rev. Francis J.
    Clerc, of Grace Ch.   124
SCHOLL, George, m. Ann **AUER**, Sept. 13, 1856, by Rev. Enoch
    Huntington, of Grace Ch. Broad Brook (1855?)   143
SCHRIER, Sophia, m. Henry **BRAUTYMAN**, June 9, 1856, at Warehouse
    Pt., by Rev. Henry M. Clory of St. John's Ch.   145
SCHUMAN*, Henry, m. Josephine **WERG**, Apr. 26, 1860, by Rev. F.
    Munson, of 1st Ch. *(In margin "TSCHUMANN")   153
SCHUSTER, Johan, m. Louisa **BENDER**, Apr. 23, 1854, by Rev. W[illia]m
    K. Douglass, of St. John's Ch.   152
SCOVEL, Hepzibath, m. Samuel **OSBORN**, Jr., b. of Windsor, Nov. 20,
    1766   48
SEDGEWICK, Catharine F., of East Windsor, m. Benjamin W. **ADAMS**, of
    Uxbridge, Mass., Apr. 16, 1833, by Rev. Russell Jennings   96
    Maria, m. George **BURNHAM**, b. of East Windsor, Mar. 18, 1832,
    by Rev. George Goodyear   95
SEEBERGER, James Emmanuel, of New Haven, m. Augusta Caroline
    Wilhelmina **KNAPS**, of East Windsor, Sept. 5, 1853, by Rev.
    Charles S. Putnam, of St. John's Ch.   138

Page

SEIBEL, Conrad, m. Eva WOOSTER, Feb. 13, 1859, at Broad Brook, by
    Rev. John F. Mines, of Grace Ch.   151
Louisa, m. Lawrence WOLF, May 4, 1856, at Broad Brook, by Rev.
    Enoch Huntington, of Grace Ch.   144
SENGLE, Palthas, m. Mary WAGNER, Apr. 29, 1860, at Broad Brook, by
    T. A. Hazen   153
SENNEWALD, Eustina, m. John TSCHUMI, Jan. 21, 1858, at Broad
    Brook, by Rev. John F. Mines, of Grace Ch.   148
SENNHAUSER, Augustus, m. Margaret WILLEY, of Enfield, Oct. 21,
    1848, by Rev. Francis J. Clerc, of Grace Ch., Broad Brook   124
SESSIONS, Anne, d. Samuel & Abigail, b. May 5, 1776   25
    George M., of Hartford, m. Mary M. FILLEY, of East Windsor,
    May 14, 1840, by Levi Smith   107
    Hannah, d. Samuel & Abigail, b. Aug. 22, 1778   25
    Nabby Ruggles, d. Samuel & Abigail, b. June 18, 1774   25
    Persa, d. Samuel & Abigail, b. Mar. 19, 1781   25
    Samuel, s. Samuel & Abigail, b. Aug. 31, 1783   25
    William Vine, of Wilbraham, Mass., m. Lydia AMES, of East Windsor,
    Nov. 26, 1829, by Rev. Shubael Bartlett   92
SEWALL, Charles, of Bath, Me., m. Miranda ROBERTSON, Sept. 9, 1835,
    by Rev. Shubael Bartlett   100
SEXTON, Chauncey, m. Henrietta BISSELL, Nov. 27, 1845, by Shubael
    Bartlett   117
    Chauncey C., m. Jemima S. BISSELL, Nov. 28, 1839, by Shubael
    Bartlett   108
    Henry, of East Windsor, m. Harriet A. BUTLER, of St. Lawrence
    Co., N. Y., Sept. 30, 1851, by Rev. Henry H. Bates, of St. John's
    Ch.   131
    Lucinda, m. Alpheus Harris BARBER, b. of East Windsor, July 2,
    1851, by Rev. Henry H. Bates, of St. John's Ch.   131
    Susan M., of Warehouse Point, m. Benjamin F. CUNNINGHAM, of
    Norwalk, O., Mar. 15, 1854, by Abel Gardner   139
SHAILER, SHALER, Barbara, m. Frederick MANN, May 29, 1855, at
    Cromwell, by Rev. Charles W. Potter, of Bapt. Ch.   143
    David, m. Flora BROWN, b. of East Windsor, Oct. 31, 1852, by Rev.
    Enoch Huntington, of Grace Ch.   135
SHAW, Mary, d. David & Mary, b. May 1, 1775   25
    Mary, d. David, m. Moses OSBORN, s. Daniel, Aug. 27, 1794   48
    Mary S.*, m. Joseph BUCKLIN, b. of Holyoke, Mass., Oct. 12, 1853,
    by Rev. Abel Gardner *(In margin "J")   138
SHELDON, George, of Mantua, O., m. Fanny G. WILKINSON, of East
    Windsor, Oct. 8, 1834, by Rev. Chauncey G. Lee   98
    Joseph, of Manchester, m. Nancy A. GRANT, of East Windsor,
    Mar. 30, 1834, by Rev. David L. Hunn   98
    Sarah, m. Samuel ROCKWELL, b. of East Windsor, Feb. 16, 1775   51
SHEPARD, SHEPHERD, Francis W., of Northampton, Mass., m. Adelia
    BISSELL, Apr. 29, 1844, by Shubael Bartlett   114
    Henry M., of Northampton, Mass., m. Marilla MOODY, of Ellington,

Page

SHEPARD, SHEPHERD, (cont.)
   July 5, 1852, by Rev. Edmund A. Standish   133
   Lucy, of East Hartford, m. Ezra **HORTON**, of East Windsor, Mar.
     18, [1821], by Rev. Thomas Robbins of 1st Eccl. Soc.   84
   Maria A., m. Nathaniel M. **CHAPIN**, Nov. 7, 1836, by Rev. Shubael
     Bartlett   101
   Mary E., m. Daniel **CHAPIN**, Jr., Jan. 19, 1859, by Rev. W[illia]m
     M. Birchard   151
   Sally, m. David **WHEELER**, [Feb.] 21, [1839], by Bennet Tyler   105
SHIPMAN, George M., m. Martha P. **PORTER**, Mar. 27, 1844, by Shubael
   Bartlett   114
   James H., m. Laura H. **FRENCH**, Oct. 26, 1837, by Shubael Bartlett   103
SHUMWAY, Susan, m. Edwin **CHAPMAN**, Mar. 15, 1848, by Rev. Henry
   H. Bates, of St. John's Ch., Warehouse Point   122
SHUTTLEWORTH, Betsey, of Dedham, Mass., m. Noadiah **BISSELL**, of
   East Windsor, Jan. 29, 1797, by Rev. Thomas Thacher, at
   Dedham   32
SIEGLER, Heinrich, m. Josepha **DINKLER**, Oct. 21, 1855, by Rev.
   W[illia]m K. Douglass, of St. John's Ch. Warehouse Pt.   143
SIKES, Harvey, of Springfield, Mass., m. Julia E. **BONINVILLE**, of
   Springfield, Mass., Sept. 5, 1844, by Rev. Henry H. Bates, of St.
   John's Ch.   116
SILL, Daniel, s. Jabez & Hannah, b. July 26, 1797   25
   Sedley, s. Jabez & Hannah, b. Sept. 13, 1795   25
SIMMONS, [see also **SIMONDS**], William S., of Bristol, R. I., m.
   Wealthy **GRANT**, of East Windsor, this day, [June 21, 1844], by
   Rev. Charles Noble, Manchester   114
SIMONDS, [see also **SIMMONS**], Jehial H., m. Caroline E. **HOLKINS**,
   Sept. 21, 1859, at Warehouse Point, by Rev. Henry McClory, of
   St. John's Ch.   152
SIMPSON, Ellen Maria, m. Ebenezer B. **STEDMAN**, of Springfield, Mass.,
   Mar. 30, 1842, by J. Cogswell   111
   James, of Enfield, m. Nancy **DUNN**, of Cabotville, Mass., Oct.
     24, 1852, by Rev. C. S. Putnam, of St. John's Ch., Warehouse Pt.   134
   Mary A., m. Thomas E. **MUNSELL**, b. of East Windsor, Mar. 5, 1834,
     by Rev. David L. Hunn   98
SINKEL, Therecia, m. Simon **MITCHEL**, Mar. 24, 1858, at Hartford, by
   Rev. Enest Berger of the German Cong., Rockville   148
SKINNER, Abigail, m. John **JOHNSON**, Nov. 12, 1823, by Rev. Shubael
   Bartlett   86
   Almina, m. [   ], b. of East Windsor, Oct. 9, 1822, by Rev.
     Shubael Bartlett of 2nd Church   85
   Ann, m. Hiram **STRONG**, Sept. 23, 1823, by Deodate Brockway, at
     his house, Ellington   86
   Belinda, of East Windsor, m. Alfred **KEENEY**, of Manchester,
     [Nov. 29, 1832], by Rev. D. L. Hunn   96
   Benjamin, m. Eliza **COLSON**, b. of East Windsor, Dec. 15, 1822,
     by Joseph Russell, J. P.   85

Page

SPARHAWK, (cont.)
    of 2nd Cong. Ch. Middletown   110
SPARROW, George E., of Tolland, m. Eliza SNOW, of Willington,
    Mar. 19, 1849, by Rev. Francis J. Clerc, of Grace Ch., Broad
    Brook   125
SPEAR, John, of Ellington, m. Mary OSBORN, of East Windsor, Aug. 23,
    1813   53
SPENCER, Miranda, of Somers, m. Lavantine KING, of Enfield, May 16,
    1852, by Rev. W[illia]m A. Stickney   133
    Parmelia, m. Seth BOOTH, Mar. 26, 1860, by Harvey Pease, J. P. 153
SPERRY, Abigail, m. Samuel YOUNG, July 4, 1852, by Rev. C. S. Putnam,
    of St. John's Ch., at Warehouse Pt. Int. Pub.   133
    Albert A., m. Melinda PHELPS, Nov. 21, 1859, by Rev. Frederick
    Munson   152
    Daniel G., m. Harriet F. PELTON, b. of East Windsor, Mar. 30,
    1834, by Rev. Chauncey G. Lee   97
    Davis, of East Windsor, m. Julia AUSTIN, of Suffield, Oct. 6,
    1833, by Solomon Terry, Jr., J. P.   96
    Elizabeth Jane, of Warehouse Pt., m. Stephen D. THAYER, of Mass.,
    Oct. 27, 1850, by Henry H. Bates   129
    Jeremiah, of New Haven, m. Jerusha P. O[S]BORN, of East Windsor,
    Jan. 6, 1825, by Rev. Shubael Bartlett of 2nd Church   87
    Lucy P., m. William Stewart LOMERILL, June 30, 1844, by Shubael
    Bartlett   114
    Mary, m. Solomon AARONS, May 15, 1858, by Josiah Ellsworth, J. P. 149
    Persis Ann, m. John H. BANCROFT, Feb. 28, 1858, at Warehouse Pt.,
    by Josiah Ellsworth, J. P.   149
    Ransom, of New Haven, m. Henrietta BUTTON, of East Windsor,
    Apr. 2, 1829, by Rev. Shubael Bartlett   91
    Stephen W., m. Sarah F. ARCHER, b. of Suffield, Mar. 4, 1852,
    by Rev. Henry H. Bates, of St. John's Ch., at Warehouse Point 133
SPRING, Horace, m. Minerva FISH, Mar. 3, 1824, by Rev. Shubael Bartlett
    of 2nd Church   86
SQUIRE, Doliel, m. Jerusha KENEY, Nov. 24, 1827, by V. R. Osborn,
    V. D. M.   89
STANGLE, STANGEL, Conrad, m. Margaret STEINMETZ, Mar. 18,
    1855, by Rev. W[illia]m K. Douglass, of St. John's Ch.   142
    William, m. Mary MUSTER, Mar. 18, 1858, at Broad Brook, by Rev.
    John F. Mines of Grace Ch.   148
STANLEY, Aurelia Bissell, of East Windsor, m. W[illia]m King MATHER,
    of Suffield, this day, [Jan. 1, 1824], by Rev. Moses Fifield, Jr. 86
    Mary, of East Windsor, m. Loring E. COE, of Granvill, Mass.,
    [May] 11, [1824], by Rev. Thomas Robbins   87
STARK, STARKS, Austin Tucker, [s. Charles I. & Prudence], b. June 1,
    1812 (Entry marked "mistake")   6
    Austin Tucker, s. [Charles I. & Prudence], b. June 1, 1812   25
    Charles, s. Charles I. & Prudence, b. May 12, 1806
    (entry marked "mistake")   6

Page

STARK, STARKS, (cont.)

Charles, s. Charles I. & Prudence, b. May 12, 1806   25

Cynthia, d. [Charles I. & Prudence], b. Nov. 5, 1807 (Entry
marked "mistake")   6

Cynthia, d. [Charles I. & Prudence], b. Nov. 5, 1807   25

Diantha T., m. Russell **ROCKWELL,** Jr., b. of East Windsor, this day,
[Nov. 10, 1841], by Rev. A. C. Wheat   110

Wareham Bissell, s. [Charles I. & Prudence], b. Feb. 10, 1810
(Entry marked "mistake")   6

Wareham Bissell, s. [Charles I. & Prudence], b. Feb. 10, 1810   25

STARR, Charles, of Hartford, m. Eveline **MUNSELL,** of East Windsor,
Oct. 19, 1834, by Rev. David L. Hunn   98

ST. CLAIR, [see under **SAINT CLAIR**]

STEBBINS, STEBINS, Albert, of Springfield, m. Laura Ann **CHARTER,**
of Ellington, Mar. 22, 1830, by Horace Barber, J. P.   93

Benjamin, of Enfield, m. Mrs. Rachel **STEBINS,** of East Windsor,
Sept. 19, 1841, by Rev. W[illia]m H. Richards, Warehouse Point   110

Caroline, of Wilbraham, m. Luther **BRIDGES,** of Warren, Mass.,
Nov. 24, 1839, by Rev. Benjamin C. Phelps, of Warehouse Point   106

Rachel, Mrs. of East Windsor, m. Benjamin **STEBINS,** of Enfield,
Sept. 19, 1841, by Rev. W[illia]m H. Richards, Warehouse Point   110

Sophronia, m. Abiel **PEASE,** Jr., b. of Enfield, this day, [May
25, 1824], by Asher Allen, J. P.   86

William P., m. Evelina **COLSON,** b. of East Windsor, Mar. 31, 1833,
by Rev. Chauncey G. Lee   96

STEDMAN, STEADMAN, STEDDMAN, Charlotte A., of East Windsor,
m. George **WARREN,** of East Hartford, Nov. 25, 1858, at
Windsorville, by Rev. Lozien Pierce   150

Ebenezer B., of Springfield, Mass., m. Ellen Maria **SIMPSON,**
Mar. 30, 1842, by J. Cogswell   111

Hosmer P., m. Phildelia **MOULTEN,** Nov. 7, 1836, by J. Cogswell   101

Morgan, see Morgan **STEDDMAN**   97

Morgan, m. Esther **CHILDS,** of Manchester, Nov. 12, 1833, by Rev.
Hezekiah S. Ramsdell (Morgan **STEADMAN** in margin)   97

STEEL, Aaron, s. James & Abigail, b. Dec. 4, 1777   25

Abigail, d. James & Abigail, d. Aug. 9, 1777   80

Solomon, s. James & Abigail, b. June 16, 1780   25

STEINMAN, Antoinette, m. Matthias **LIEB,** b. of East Windsor, Nov. 26,
1852, by Rev. C. S. Putnam, of St. John's Ch.   135

STEINMETZ, STEINNITTS, STEINMEITS, Cecelia, m. Frederick
Charles **WERNER,** b. of East Windsor, Sept. 27, 1853, by Rev.
Charles S. Putnam, of St. John's Ch. (In margin
"STEINMITTS")   138

Margaret, m. Conrad **STANGLE,** Mar. 18, 1855, by Rev. W[illia]m
K. Douglass, of St. John's Ch.   142

Susan, m. Christian **GRUBER,** b. of East Windsor, Jan. 22, 1850,
by Rev. Henry H. Bates, of St. John's Ch., Warehouse Pt.   127

STEVENS, STEPHENS, Charles, m. Charlotte R. **ALLEN,** Apr. 14, 1858,

STEVENS, STEPHENS, (cont.)
    by Rev. W[illia]m M. Birchard   149
    Cornelius R., of Martinsburg, N. Y., m. Caroline P. COHOON, of
      Granby, Conn., Nov. 24, 1847, by Rev. J. H. Farnsworth of
      Somersville   121
STILES, Asahel C., m. Eliza I. BELKNAP, b. of East Windsor, Jan. 31,
    1832, by Rev. Shubael Bartlett   94
    Chloe A., m. John ROE, Apr. 25, 1860, by Rev. F. Munson, of 1st Ch. 153
    Esther J., m. Everlyn PITKIN, July 11, 1843, by Shubael Bartlett   113
    Israel, m. Eunice M. AVERY, b. of East Windsor, this day, [Nov.
      15, 1836], by Rev. Marvin Root   101
    James H., [m.] Marilla* M. SKINNER, b. of East Windsor, [May]
      11, [1836], by Rev. Marvin Root   *(Murilla?)   100
    Jared, s. John & Jemima, b. Mar. 25, 1785   25
    John, of East Windsor, m. Jemima ALLIS, of Bolton, Aug. 3, 1784   53
    John Morton, m. Julia A. GOWDY, Dec. 14, 1843, by Shubael Bartlett
      (Written John Morton BARTLETT in margin)   113
    Marilla M., m. Lewis TROWBRIDGE, Mar. 28, 1847, by Shubael
      Bartlett   119
    Robert, late of Stafford, now of East Windsor, d. Dec. 19, 1774   80
    Samuel, of Utica, N. Y., m. Charlotte Sophia REED, of East Windsor,
      [June] 12, [1825], by Rev. Thomas Robbins of 1st Church   88
    Samuel, m. Roxa SKINNER, b. of East Windsor, [Mar.] 4, [1840],
      by Marvin Root   107
    Samuel, m. Ann BOWERS, Dec. 10, 1843, by Shubael Bartlett   113
    Sarah Matilda, m. Hiram SKINNER, b. of East Windsor, July 1,
      1835, by Rev. Shubael Bartlett   100
STOCKBRIDGE, Caleb, m. Esther PALMER, Mar. 14, 1838, by Shubael
    Bartlett   103
STODDARD, Moses, Rev. of the New England Conference, m. Lucretia M.
    ELLSWORTH, of East Windsor, June 28, 1840, by Rev. A.
    Niles   108
    Nathan F., of Wethersfield, m. Sarah KNOWLES, of East Windsor,
      [May] 19, [1825], by Rev. Thomas Robbins of 1st Church   88
STONE, Adolphus J., of East Windsor, m. Laura HAYES, of East Hartford,
    [Oct.] 8, [1822], by Rev. T. Robbins   85
    Sarah, m. Almond PARKER, b. of Mass., Sept. 8, 1837, by Solomon
      Terry, Jr., J. P.   102
STORMS, Mary A., m. John BANKS, Aug. 5, 1858, by Rev. John F.
    Sheffield   149
    Mary A., m. John BANKS, Aug. 5, 1858, by Rev. John F. Sheffield
      (Entry crossed out)   150
STOUGHTON, Amanda, of East Windsor, m. James M. TALCOTT, of
    Hartford, [Jan.] 13, [1841], by W[illia]m Thompson   109
    Amelia, m. Oliver STOUGHTON, b. of East Windsor, [May] 4,
      [1841], by Rev. Marvin Root   109
    Ann E., m. Frederick W. GRANT, Oct. 27, 1842, by Shubael Bartlett   112
    Clarissa, m. Horace LORD, b. of East Windsor, Jan. 21, 1827, by

Page

STOUGHTON, (cont.)

Rev. Shubael Bartlett   88

Cynthia, of East Windsor, m. Samuel WILLIAMS, of East Hartford,
[Feb.] 17, [1825], by Rev. Thomas Robbins   88

Edgar, m. Sally FOSTER, b. of East Windsor, Nov. 29, 1832, by
Rev. D. L. Hunn   96

Elizabeth W., m. Henry M. KING, b. of East Windsor, Feb. 21,
1844, by Levi Smith   113

Francis, m. Olive E. LOOMIS, b. of East Windsor, Jan. 1, 1840,
by Levi Smith   107

Francis, m. Olive E. ELMER, b. of East Windsor, Jan. 1, 1840, by
[   ] (Entry crossed out)   115

Frank E., m. Sarah L. CLARK, Apr. 21, 1859, by Rev. John F.
Sheffield   151

Hardin, m. Emeline ANDRUS, b. of East Windsor, June 9, [1836],
by Rev. Marvin Root   100

Henrietta, of East Windsor, m. Samuel B. SMITH, of Bristol,
Apr. 23, 1845, by O. F. Parker   116

Henry Chauncey, m. Elvira GRANT, this day, [Nov. 7, 1839], by
Rev. Marvin Root   106

Irena, of East Windsor, m. Henry WARD, [Oct.] 4, [1820], by Rev.
Thomas Robbins of 1st Eccl. Soc.   59

John, m. Theodocia GREEN, b. of East Windsor, Jan. 5, 1831, by
Rev. Shubael Bartlett   93

John P., of Wethersfield, Vt., m. Laura HULL, of East Windsor,
Oct. 13, 1847, by Shubael Bartlett   120

Lemuel, m. Hannah BLODGET, Dec. 29, 1841, by Shubael Bartlett   111

Lucy, m. Homer D. ALLEN, of Scantic, Sept. 24, 1844, by O. F.
Parker, in Wapping   115

Lucy W., m. Abner M. ELLSWORTH, Jr., Apr. 26, 1832, by Rev.
Shubael Bartlett   95

Lydia, m. Sam[ue]l MOORE, b. of East Windsor, Nov. 18, 1828, by
Rev. Samuel W. Whelpley of 1st Church   91

Maria, m. William DOBSON, b. of Vernon, this day, Nov. 3, 1837,
by Rev. Marvin Root   102

Maria Ann, m. Julius BIRGE, b. of East Windsor, [Nov.] 25,
[1824], by Rev. Thomas Robbins of 1st Church   87

Martha J., m. Charles SOUTHMAYDE, June 17, 1845, by Shubael
Bartlett   117

Mary S., of East Windsor, m. Samuel S. TERRY, of Plymouth, Nov.
28, 1827, by Rev. Shubael Bartlett   89

Oliver, m. Amelia STOUGHTON, b. of East Windsor, [May] 4,
[1841], by Rev. Marvin Root   109

Sally, m. Horace D. FULLER, b. of East Windsor, June 26, 1843, by
Rev. B. M. Walker   113

Sarah, m. Thomas POTWINE, b. of East Windsor, May 22, 1828, by
Rev. Shubael Bartlett   90

William, of East Windsor, m. Jerusha ABBEY, of East Hartford,

Page

STOUGHTON, (cont.)

    Nov. 3, 1844, by Levi Smith   115

    Willis, m. Mary B. **BIRGE**, b. of East Windsor, Nov. 23, 1824,

        by Rev. Francis L. Robbins of Enfield   86

STOWELL, Marilla, m. Harvey B. **ALLEN**, Nov. 24, 1836, by Rev.

    Shubael Bartlett   101

STRICKLAND, Mary Ann, m. Justus D. **CHAPMAN**, of Hartford, June 15,

    1842, by Shubael Bartlett   112

STRIFE STREIF, Jacob, m. Mrs. Jane **FINLEY**, Oct. 29, 1855, by Rev.

    W[illia]m K. Douglass, of St. John's Ch. Warehouse Pt.   143

    Jacob, m. Barbara **MYER**, May 1, 1859, by Rev. John F. Mines, of

        Grace Ch., at Broad Brook   151

STRONG, Charlotte W., m. Luther **BABBIT**, b. of East Windsor, Oct. 2,

    1836, by W[illia]m Thompson   101

    Elizabeth, m. Philemon **MILLS**, b. of East Windsor, Feb. 26, 1829,

        by Rev. Shubael Bartlett   91

    Emeline, m. Joseph S. **BARTLETT**, Nov. 23, 1833, by Rev. Shubael

        Bartlett   96

    Hannah, of East Windsor, m. Jourdan **ROGERS**, of Plymouth, [Nov.]

        17, [1824], by Rev. Thomas Robbins of 1st Church   87

    Hiram, m. Ann **SKINNER**, Sept. 23, 1823, by Deodate Brockway at

        his house, Ellington   86

    Ira, s. Jacob & Elizabeth, b. Aug. 27, 1788   25

    Jacob, of East Windsor, m. Elizabeth **LOOMIS**, Nov. 1, 1787   53

    Mary M., of East Windsor, m. William H. **MILLER**, of Hartford,

        Nov. 28, 1844, by Levi Smith   115

    Morgan, m. Mary **ROBERTS**, b. of East Windsor, May 1, 1842, by

        Rev. Andrew M. Smith   111

    Nathaniel C., m. Rossanna E. **ALLEN**, b. of East Windsor, May 30,

        1850, by Rev. John Cadwell   128

    Tabitha, m. Elisha **LADD**, b. of East Windsor, May 23, 1776   44

STUDLEY, W[illia]m Harrison, m. Caroline Louise **HEATH**, Dec. 13, 1854,

    by Rev. W[illia]m K. Douglass, of St. John's Ch.   153

SULLIVAN, Joseph, m. Cordelia **TERRY**, Nov. 24, 1844, by Shubael

    Bartlett   117

SUNDERLAND, Ann, m. William **BAKER**, May 27, 1849, by Rev. Henry

    H. Bates, of St. John's Ch., Warehouse Point   125

    John, m. Sarah **WOODHOUSE**, Mar. 28, 1848, by Rev. Henry H.

        Bates, of St. John's Ch., Warehouse Point   122

SWALLOW, Samuel, m. Rachel **HOLSTENHOLME**, Jan. 1, 1859, at

    Broad Brook, by Rev. John F. Mines, of Grace Ch.   151

SWAN, Sarah D., m. William N. **COOMES**, Aug. 28, 1855, by Rev. L. D.

    Bentley of M. E. Ch.   143

SWEET, Mary M., Mrs., m. Hiram M. **SMITH**, Nov. 28, 1850, by Rev.

    Shubael Bartlett   129

SWETLAND, Alvah, s. Benjamin & Rosanner, b. Oct. 31, 1795   25

    Cynth[i]a, d. Benjamin & Rosanner, b. May 12, 1793   25

    James, s. Benjamin & Rosanner, b. Mar. 31, 1791   25

Page

SWETLAND, (cont.)

Polly, d. Benjamin & Rosanner, b. Oct. 20, 1797   25

SWIFT, Martha, of Potsdam, N. Y., m. Isaac B. **LILLIBRIDGE**, of
Chickopee, Mass., May 13, 1850, by Rev. Henry H. Bates, of St.
John's Ch., Warehouse Pt.   128

TAGERT, Daniel, m. Mary **MORTON**, b. of East Windsor, Jan. 3, 1847,
by Rev. Sewall Lamberton   119

TAIT, James M., m. Mary **McIIROY**, b. of Enfield, Mar. 12, 1854, by Rev.
Charles R. Fisher, of Hartford, Int. Pub.   139

TALCOTT, Anson F., m. Mary **COOK**, June 10, 1841, by Shubael Bartlett   109

Charles H., of Glastenbury, m. Cornelia M. **BISSELL**, of East
Windsor, Jan. 8, 1851, by Rev. Samuel J. Andrews, of Cong. Ch.   130

Francis, m. Harriet A. **CHASE**, b. of East Windsor, Mar. 21, 1838,
by Shubael Bartlett   103

James M., of Hartford, m. Amanda **STOUGHTON**, of East Windsor,
[Jan.] 13, [1841], by W[illia]m Thompson   109

TARBOX, Clarrissa Ann, m. Elisha G. **MORTON**, Feb. 8, 1849, by Shubael
Bartlett   124

Octavia C., m. Samuel W. **BARTLETT**, Sept. 14, 1843, by Shubael
Bartlett   113

Thomas C., m. Harriet H. **BILLINGS**, b. of East Windsor, May 20,
1852, by Rev. Samuel J. Andrews, of Cong. Ch.   134

TAYLOR, Asenath, of Clinton, m. Almon **MATSON**, of East Windsor, this
day, [Dec. 12, 1841], by Rev. John Whittlesey   110

George H.*, m. Ruth T. **SMITH**, Nov. 1, 1857, at Broad Brook, by
Rev. John F. Mines, of Grace Ch. *(In margin "K")   149

Lewis H., m. Caroline E. **POTWINE**, Sept. 4, 1844, by Shubael
Bartlett   117

TENANT, Abram, m. Achsah **CRANE**, Nov. 27, 1823, by Rev. Shubael
Bartlett   86

TERRY, Cordelia, m. Joseph **SULLIVAN**, Nov. 24, 1844, by Shubael
Bartlett   117

Elisabeth, of Enfield, Conn., m. W[illia]m Jones, of Springfield,
Mass., this day, [Jan. 7, 1836], by Solomon Terry, Jr., J. P.   100

James U., m. Julia A. **ALLEN**, Nov. 28, 1844, by Shubael Bartlett   117

Joseph, m. Mary M. **FITCH**, Oct. 8, [1821], by Rev. Thomas Robbins   84

Lucy, m. Dyer **NEWBERRY**, b. of East Windsor, Nov. 29, 1827, by
Rev. Russell Jennings   89

Parsons, m. Dorothy Delina **KENNEDY**, b. of East Windsor, Nov.
24, 1853, by Rev. C. S. Putnam, of St. John's Ch., Warehouse
Point. Int. Pub.   138

Reuben, s. Reuben & Abia, b. June 30, 1768   26

Samuel S., of Plymouth, m. Mary S. **STOUGHTON**, of East Windsor,
Nov. 28, 1827, by Rev. Shubael Bartlett   89

THAYER, Lucius F., m. Lydia **ELLSWORTH**, [Oct.] 15, [1821], by Rev.
Shubael Bartlett of 2nd Church   59

Stephen D., of Mass., m. Elizabeth Jane **SPERRY**, of Warehouse
Pt., Oct. 27, 1850, by Henry H. Bates   129

Page

THOMAS, Charles, m. Harriet S. PARKER, b. of East Windsor, Apr. 14,
    1847, by Rev. Francis J. Clerc, of Grace Ch., Broad Brook, at
    Grace Church   121
Rebecca M., m. Jesse CHARLTON, Nov. 2, 1809   34
THOMPSON, THOMSON, Abigail O., m. Jairus BARBER, June 16, 1842,
    by Shubael Bartlett   112
Alexander, m. Amanda CRANE, May 1, 1832, by Rev. Shubael
    Bartlett   95
Almena S., m. George PARSONS, July 4, 1841, by Shubael Bartlett   110
Asahel, of Ellington, m. Mrs. Diadema BELKNAP, of East Windsor,
    Aug. 26, 1832, by Rev. Edmund M. Beebe   95
Edwin F., m. Amelia R. MORELL, Oct. 7, 1857, by Rev. F. Munson
    of Cong. Ch.   147
Elizabeth, m. John BISSELL, 2nd, [Dec.] 12, [1820], by Rev.
    Shubael Bartlett   59
Elizabeth, of East Windsor, m. George BEEBEE, of West Springfield,
    Mass., Jan. 13, 1825, by Rev. Shubael Bartlett   87
Elcee, m. Abner Moseley ELSWORTH, b. of East Windsor, Dec. 31,
    1797   37
Henrietta, m. Alfred ALLEN, Apr. 17, 1834, by Rev. Shubel Bartlett   97
Jair, s. Elec, b. Apr. 15, 1790   26
James A., m. Maria BARBER, b. of East Windsor, Jan. 8, 1829,
    by Rev. Shubael Bartlett   91
John, 2nd, m. Ann ELLSWORTH, b. of East Windsor, Jan. 6, 1823,
    by Rev. Shubael Bartlett of 2nd Church   85
John Terry, m. Sarah Maria BLODGETT, b. of East Windsor, Jan.
    6, 1831, by Rev. Shubael Bartlett   93
Mabel, m. Elisha G. MORTON, b. of East Windsor, Dec. 12, 1826,
    by Rev. Shubael Bartlett   88
Margaret, m. David Talcott SMITH, of Vernon, June 28, 1832, by
    Rev. Shubael Bartlett   95
Margaret, of East Windsor, m. Leonard BILLINGS, of Somers, Apr.
    14, 1836, by Rev. Shubael Bartlett   101
Mary Ann, m. Winthrop ALLEN, July 5, 1848, by Shubael Bartlett   122
Needham A., manufacturer, ae 21, b. Wales, res. Monson, Mass.,
    m. Mary A. CHURCH, ae 22, b. Wales, res. Broad Brook, Nov.
    17, 1853, by Rev. James H. Soule   141
Ruth, of East Windsor, m. Eleazer LORD, of New York, Dec. 31,
    1835, by W[illia]m Thompson   100
Sabra, m. Isaac G. ALLEN, Oct. 20, 1831, by Rev. Shubael Bartlett   95
Samuel W., m. Mary A. BARBER, Dec. 25, 1834, by Rev. Shubael
    Bartlett   98
Sarah E., of East Windsor, m. James G. HARPER, of Enfield, Apr.
    23, 1833, by Rev. Shubael Bartlett   96
Susan E., m. Allen P. BARBER, Feb. 12, 1846, by Shubael Bartlett   117
Tamar*, of East Windsor, m. William T. MORRISON, of Enfield,
    Feb. 17, 1831, by Rev. Shubael Bartlett *(Tamar BANCROFT in
    margin)   94

Page

THOMPSON, THOMSON, (cont.)

Warren, Jr., of East Windsor, m. Ruth ELLIS, of Barnard, Vt.,
   this day, [Nov. 24, 1839], by Marvin Root   107

William B., of East Windsor, m. Harriet N. FENTON, of Vernon,
   [Nov. 24, 1839], by Rev. Marvin Root   107

William H., m. Huldah CHAPIN, Jan. 28, 1836, by Rev. Shubael
   Bartlett   101

THRALL, THALL, Alvah, [s. Ruel & Elisabeth], b. Mar. 15, 1813   26

Charles, [s. Ruel & Elisabeth], b. May 8, 1810   26

Clarrissa A., ae 18, b. Ellington, res. East Windsor, m. Augustus
   S. LANCASTER, mechanic, ae 24, b. Woodbury, res. Ellington,
   Nov. 24, 1853, by Rev. James H. Soule   141

Curtis, s. [Ruel & Elisabeth], b. Apr. 2, 1807   26

Harriet, d. Ruel & Elisabeth, b. Feb. 16, 1798   26

Harriet, m. Alanson HORTON, Sept. 14, 1824, by Rev. Shubael
   Bartlett   86

Harriet A., of East Windsor, m. Myron F. GOWDY, of Somers, Apr.
   21, 1853, by Rev. Samuel J. Andrews, of Cong. Ch.   137

Horatio, m. Sibyl CLARK, [Oct.] 17, [1821], by Rev. Shubael Bartlett
   of 2nd Church   59

Lemuel, s. [Ruel & Elisabeth], b. Jan. 18, 1801   26

Marilla, d. [Ruel & Elisabeth], b. Sept. 24, 1805   26

Merrick, of East Windsor, m. Juliaette WILLIAMS, of Tolland,
   Oct. 31, 1839, by Rev. Ebenezer Blake, of Wapping   106

Orren M., [s. Ruel & Elisabeth], b. Nov. 16, 1818   26

Philo, [s. Ruel & Elisabeth], b. Nov. 15, 1802   26

Philo, m. Cyndona ALLEN, b. of East Windsor, Jan. 1, 1827, by
   Rev. Shubael Bartlett   88

Ruel, s. Ruel & Elisabeth, b. Sept. 28, 1799   26

Reuel, m. Mrs. Sophia SARGENT, Nov. 14, 1856, at Warehouse Point,
   by Rev. Henry McClory of St. John's Ch.   146

William, Jr., of Ellington, m. Amanda M. HYDE, of East Windsor,
   June 24, 1835, by Rev. Deodate Brockway, of Cong. Ch.
   Ellington   99

THRESHER, Rufus P., of Enfield, m. Elizabeth PEASE, of East Windsor,
   Dec. 18, 1851, by Rev. Sanford Benton   132

TIERNEY, TIRNEY, John, m. Ann CORKINS, June 30, 1852, by Rev. C.
   S. Putnam, of St. John's Ch., at Warehouse Pt. Int. Pub.   133

William, m. Mary MAGUIRE, Aug. 30, 1858, at Windsor Locks, by
   Rev. James Smyth   150

TIFF, Nathan, of Foster, R. I., m. Amanda FULLER, of East Windsor,
   Dec. 15, 1829, by Rev. Shubael Bartlett   92

TOPLIFF, Harlow, of Coventry, m. Sarah ST. CLAIRE, of East Windsor,
   May 16, 1841, by Rev. John Whittlesey   109

TORBUSH, Henry, Rev. of Windham, m. Chloe GRANT, of East Windsor,
   June 4, 1838, by Rev. Windsor Ward   103

TREADWAY, Hannah, of Colchester, m. Timothy SKINNER, of East
   Windsor, Sept. 21, 1774   53

Page

TREAT, Henry, Jr., of East Hartford, m. Abigail BELCHER, of East
    Windsor, Aug. 28, 1822, by Rev. Elisha B. Cook, of East Hartford   85
TREMAIN, William H., M. D., of New Mareboroug*, Mass., m. Lavinia A.
    BELKNAP, of East Windsor, Mar. 15, 1842, by Shubael Bartlett
    *(Marlborough?)   111
TROWBRIDGE, Lewis, m. Marilla M. STILES, Mar. 28, 1847, by Shubael
    Bartlett   119
TROY, William, m. Mary Kane RILEY, b. of Enfield, Dec. 30, 1849, by
    Rev. Henry H. Bates, of St. John's Ch., Warehouse Pt.   127
TRUMBULL, Clarissa, m. Caleb POTWINE, Jr., b. of East Windsor, Apr.
    15, 1835, by Rev. Shubael Bartlett   99
    David, s. David & Sarah, b. Mar. 20, 1773   26
    Harriet, m. Joel ALLEN, of Springfield, Mass., Sept. 6, 1837,
    by Shubael Bartlett   102
    Jane E., m. Thomas Hall POTWINE, Apr. 29, 1834, by Rev. Shubael
    Bartlett   97
TRYON, Nancy, m. Ezekiel KENEY, Jr., Mar. 2, 1829, by V. R. Osborn,
    V. D. M.   91
TSCHUMI, Elisabeth, m. John GRESHABO, Dec. 3, 1854, by Rev.
    W[illia]m K. Douglass, of St. John's Ch.   153
    John, m. Eustina SENNEWALD, Jan. 21, 1858, at Broad Brook, by
    Rev. John F. Mines, of Grace Ch.   148
    Louisa, m. Frederick ELLSER, Dec. 22, 1857, at Warehouse Pt.,
    by Rev. Henry McClory, of St. John's Ch. (ELSER)   149
    Louisa, m. Frederick ELSER, Dec. 22, 1857, at Warehouse Point,
    by Rev. Henry McClory, of St. John's Ch. (Entry crossed out)   150
TUCKER, Daniel, of Vernon, m. Hannah CORCORAN, of East Windsor,
    July 21, 1833, by Rev. David L. Hunn   98
    Harriet, m. Henry HILL, b. of East Windsor, Dec. 29, 1830, by
    Rev. Asa Mead of East Hartford   93
    Jesse, of Brooklyn, m. Caroline J. JOHNSON, of East Windsor,
    Jan. 10, 1831, by Rev. Shubael Bartlett   94
TUDOR, Abigail, m. Abner Loring REED, b. of East Windsor, Oct. 15,
    1828, by Rev. Samuel W. Whelpley of 1st Church   91
    David M., m. Sarah E. GREEN, d. of Samuel, b. of East Windsor,
    Dec. 12, 1839, by Rev. George Burgess, of Christ Ch. Hartford   107
    Edward, Dr., of East Windsor, m. Elizabeth DABNEY, of Salem,
    Mass., [June] 23, [1822], by Rev. Tho[ma]s Robbins   85
    Elihu, Dr., had negro Prince, b. Mar. 3, 1787   20
    Eliza, of East Windsor, m. John HORTON, of Providence, R. I.,
    [Dec.] 3, [1820], by Rev. Thomas Robbins of 1st Soc.   84
    Mary Ann, of East Windsor, m. Parmenio WHELPLEY, of New York,
    this day, [Jan. 17, 1831], by Rev. Samuel Spring, of North
    Church, Hartford   93
    Sophia H., of East Windsor, m. Charles GREEN, of U. S. Navy,
    Dec. 16, 1840, by Levi Smith   109
TURNER, Josiah W., Rev. of Great Barrington, Mass., m. Almana W.
    GRANT, of East Windsor, Nov. 24, 1836, by B. Tyler   103

Page

TURPIN, Frances A., m. Lorenzo J. **DENISON**, Apr. 14, 1859, by D.
  Ives, M. G.   151
  Julia M., m. George M. **HATHAWAY**, Apr. 14, 1859, by D. Ives,
    M.G.   151
TUTTLE, Sarah, of East Windsor, m. James **GOODMAN**, of West
  Hartford, [Mar.] 29, [1843], by Rev. Chester Humphrey, of 1st
  Cong. Ch., Vernon   113
TYLER, Catharine, of East Windsor, m. John **GODDARD**, of Roxbury,
  Mass., this day, [Aug. 4, 1840], by Bennet Tyler   108
  Charles C., of Middletown, m. Lydia **LATHROP**, of Hartford, Nov.
    24, 1830, by Rev. Shubael Bartlett   93
  Martha, of East Windsor, m. Rev. Nahum **GALE**, of Ware, Mass.,
    [Aug.] 10, [1843], by Bennet Tyler   113
VANHORN, Maria R., m. George W. **MARTIN**, b. of Springfield, Mass.,
  Sept. 10, 1847, at Grace Church, by Rev. Francis J. Clerc, of
  Grace Ch., Broad Brook. Int. Pub. in Springfield, Mass.   121
VINING, Alexander, of East Windsor, m. Olive **PEASE**, of Enfield, Sept.
  19, 1774   56
  Alexander, s. Alexander & Olive, b. Mar. 11, 1781   27
  Alexander, of East Windsor, m. Lovice **PEASE**, of Enfield,
    Nov. 22, 1786   54
  Almanzo B., m. Jane S. **JOHNSON**, May 19, 1855, by Rev. Sam[ue]l
    J. Andrews   143
  Almanzo B., m. Josephine **POST**, Jan. 31, 1856, at Warehouse Pt.,
    by W[illia]m Barnes, J. P.   144
  Alven, s. Alexander & Olive, b. May 29, 1783   27
  Ann, of East Windsor, m. Horace **PEASE**, of Middlefield, Mass.,
    Apr. 29, 1829, by Rev. Shubael Bartlett   91
  Elem, s. Alexander & Olive, b. Dec. 25, 1778   27
  Elizabeth, of East Windsor, m. James **RUDD**, of Becket, Mass., June
    8, 1788   51
  Elizabeth, m. James **PASCO**, b. of East Windsor, Sept. 25, 1832, by
    Rev. Edmund M. Beebe   95
  Elkanah, s. Alexander & Olive, b. Dec. 27, 1776   27
  James, m. Almira **BUCKLAND**, b. of East Windsor, Sept. 26, 1832,
    by Rev. Edmund M. Beebe   95
  Olive, w. Alexander, d. May 29, 1786   82
  Roxavene, d. Alexander & Olive, b. May 20, 1775   27
  Samuel, s. John & Rosanna, b. Oct. 12, 1770   27
VINTON, Chester Crandal, s. W[illia]m & Esther, b. June 19, 1826   27
  Elizabeth, w. William, d. Sept. 24, 1820   82
  Seth, s. William & Esther, b. July 7, 1824   27
  William, m. Elizabeth **COLLINS**, May 5, 1819   56
  William, m. Esther **CRANDAL**, Apr. 11, 1822   56
  William, m. Esther **CRANDALL**, b. of East Windsor, Apr. 11, 1822,
    by Rev. Shubael Bartlett, of 2nd Church   84
  William, s. William & Esther, b. Jan. 12, 1823   27
  William, of South Windsor, m. Delia E. **BARBER**, of East Windsor,

VINTON, (cont.)

Nov. 29, 1849, by Rev. Samuel J. Andrews, of Cong. Ch.   127

WAGNER, Anna, m. George BROWN, b. of Broad Brook , June 25, 1854,
    by Enoch Huntington   139

Catharine, m. John PFEIFER, Nov. 21, 1858, at Broad Brook, by Rev.
    John F. Mines, of Grace Ch.   150

Jacob, m. Mary BADER, July 19, 1856, by Rev. W[illia]m M. Birchard   145

Mary, m. Palthas SENGLE, Apr. 29, 1860, at Broad Brook, by T. A.
    Hazen   153

WAITE, Ann Jane, of East Windsor, m. Francis BANCRAFT, of South
    Windsor, Nov. 24, 1853, by Rev. Shubael Bartlett, of 1st Cong.
    Ch.   138

WALDEN, Abigail L., m. Charles B. MAY, b. of East Hartford, Aug. 11,
    1844, by Rev. B. M. Walker   115

David P., m. Marilla B. LORD, May 6, 1857, at Warehouse Point,
    by Rev. H. W. Conant, of M. E. Ch.   147

WALDO, Bethuel, of East Windsor, m. Ruth WHE[E]LER, of Stafford,
    Dec. 23, 1775   56

Jane S., m. Edward H. LITTLEFIELD, b. of Newport, R. I.,
    Sept. 6, 1850, by Rev. Sanford Benton   129

Wealthy M., Mrs., m. Constant S. LORD, Nov. 27, 1855, at
    Windsorville, by Rev. W[illia]m Phillips   144

WALES, Mary Ann, of Portland, m. Marble G. ST. CLAIR, of East
    Windsor, May 3, 1843, by Josiah Ellsworth, J. P.   113

WALLACE, Molla, d. Abraham, Jr. & Elisabeth, b. Feb. 7, 1776   27

William, s. Daniel & Ruth, b. Dec. 14, 1781   27

WALTON, Sarah Ann, m. Robert COOK, Dec. 6, 1846, by Rev. Henry H.
    Bates, of St. John's Ch.   120

WARBURTON, Eliza, of East Windsor, m. Silas DRAKE, Jr., of Hartford,
    Sept. 25, [1821], by Rev. Thomas Robbins   84

Wealthy, of East Windsor, m. Hezekiah KING, of Vernon, [Dec.]
    4, [1821], by Rev. Thomas Robbins   84

WARD, Celia A., of East Windsor, m. Luther P. LOVELAND, of Hartford,
    Feb. 11, 1844, by Rev. B. M. Walker   113

Charlotte, m. Henry DEWEY, b. of Windsor, Nov. 1, 1844, or
    about that date, by Rev. Henry H. Bates, of St. John's Ch.   116

Elijah, m. Jane McFALL, Apr. 11, 1848, by Shubael Bartlett   122

Eunice, of Torringford, m. Gurdon PINNEY, of Granby, Mass.,
    Nov. 30, 1848, by H. C. Atwater   124

Giles, s. Giles & Eunice, b. Oct. 12, 1798   28

Henry, s. Giles & Eunice, b. Mar. 5, 1795   28

Henry, m. Irena STOUGHTON, of East Windsor, [Oct.] 4, [1820],
    by Rev. Thomas Robbins of 1st Eccl, Soc.   59

Irene, m. Ozias BISSELL, b. of East Windsor, May 14, 1833, by
    Rev. David L. Hunn   98

Nancy, m. James Munroe WOLCOTT, Nov. 26, 1857, by Rev. Henry
    W. Conant, of M. E. Ch.   153

WARE, Gilbert, m. Caroline PEASE, b. of East Windsor, Dec. 11, 1854,

Page

WATSON, (cont.)

Hannah, m. Dr. Horatio A. **HAMILTON**, of Enfield, Dec. 10, 1840,
    by Shubael Bartlett   108

Harriet, d. John & Anne, b. Sept. 17, 1786   28

Hiram, m. Elizabeth S. **ELLSWORTH**, b. of East Windsor, Nov. 10,
    1829, by Rev. Shubael Bartlett   92

Hulda, d. Robert & Eunice, b. July 27, 1788   28

James, s. Ebenezer & Sarah, b. May 15, 1787   28

Jane, d. Robert & Eunice, b. Dec. 31, 1781   28

Jerusha, d. Timothy & Anne, b. Aug. 1, 1776   27

Jerusha, m. Reuben **CAHOON**, Apr. 16, 1842, by Shubael Bartlett   111

John, s. John & Anne, b. June 17, 1770   27

Julia, of East Windsor, m. Leverett **BIDDELL**, of Toledo, O., this day
    [Nov. 26, 1840], by Bennet Tyler   108

Laura H., of East Windsor, m. Hugh K. **PRENTISS**, of Salem, Mass.,
    Feb. 21, 1844, by Bennet Tyler   113

Lucy Elizabeth, m. Sam[ue]l **WATSON**, b. of East Windsor, Aug.
    3, 1851, by Rev. Sam[ue]l J. Andrews, of Cong. Ch.   131

Mary, m. William **WOODHOUSE**, Dec. 19, 1857, at Broad Brook, by
    Rev. John F. Mines of Grace Ch.   148

Nancy, of East Windsor, m. William **HALL**, Jr., of Rockingham, Vt.,
    May 28, 1822, by Nath[anie]ll S. Wheaton   84

Nathaniel, s. Ebenezer & Anne, d. Dec. 3, 1775   83

Natha[n]iel, s. Ebenezer, Jr. & Sarah, b. Feb. 4, 1777   28

Polly, d. John & Anne, b. Dec. 8, 1775   27

Polly, d. John & Anna, b. Dec. 8, 1775   27

Robert, m. Eunice **POTWINE**, b. of East Windsor, Dec. 24, 1772   56

Robert, s. Robert & Eunice, b. Apr. 25, 1774   27

Roderick, s. Eben[eze]r, Jr. & Sarah, b. Oct. 15, 1782   28

Ruth, d. Robert & Eunice, b. Apr. 8, 1784   28

Sally, d. John & Anne, b. Aug. 30, 1784   28

Sally, m. Seth **BOOTH**, Jr., [Oct.] 29, [1820], by Rev. Thomas
    Robbins of 1st Eccl. Soc.   59

Sam[ue]l, m. Lucy Elizabeth **WATSON**, b. of East Windsor, Aug. 3,
    1851, by Rev. Sam[ue]l J. Andrews, of Cong. Ch.   131

Sarah, 2nd, m. Ebenezer **WATSON**, Jr., b. of East Windsor, Jan.
    13, 1774   56

Sarah, d. Eben[eze]r, Jr. & Sarah, b. Dec. 29, 1784   28

Sarah, d. Ebenezer & Sarah, d. Apr. 23, 1787   83

Timothy, d. Feb. 1, 1777, in the 25th y. of his age   83

Timothy, s. Eben[eze]r, Jr. & Sarah, b. Oct. 2, 1779   28

William, s. John & Anne, b. Mar. 25, 1773   27

WATTS, WATT, Jane, m. John **MORRISON**, b. of Enfield, Sept. 4, 1853,
    by Rev. Enoch Huntington, of Grace Ch.   138

Joan, of Thompsonville, m. George **RUSSELL**, July 25, 1852, by
    Rev. Enoch Huntington, of Grace Ch.   134

WAY, Ambrose, of Windsor, m. Anna **CAESAR**, of East Windsor,
    (colored), [May] 8, [1823], by Rev. Thomas Robbins   86

Page

WEAVER, Erastus, of Plainfield, m. Carile M. HOSMER, of East Windsor,
    Apr. 14, 1845, by Rev. B. M. Walker, in Wapping   116
WEBSTER, Chloe, d. Cyrenus & Prudence, b. Mar. 8, 1772   27
    Clark, s. Samuel & Lucy, b. Jan. 4, 1772   27
    Dosha, d. Cyrenus & Prudence, b. Feb. 26, 1778   27
    Elias, of Columbia, m. Charlottee FULLER, of East Windsor,
      [Oct.] 21, [1821], by Rev. Nathan B. Burgess   59
    Elizabeth, of Hartford, m. Samuel GRANT, of East Windsor, [Feb.]
      1, [1821], by Rev. Thomas Robbins of 1st Eccl. Soc.   84
    Elisabeth, m. Darius MORGAN, Oct. 7, 1856, at Windsorville, by
      Rev. G. D. Boynton   145
    Emily, of East Windsor, m. Henry M. COLLUM, of Vernon, May 29,
      1842, by Levi Smith, at his house   112
    Grove, s. Samuel & Lucy, b. Dec. 31, 1767   (Entry marked "mistake")   3
    Grove, s. Samuel & Lucy, b. Dec. 31, 1767   27
    James, s. Cyrenus & Prudence, b. May 7, 1776   27
    Lucy, d. Samuel & Lucy, b. Sept. 2, 1763   27
    Lucy, d. Samuel & Lucy, b. Sept. 2, 1763   (Entry marked "mistake")   3
    Naomi, d. Cyrenus & Prudence, b. Apr. 24, 1782   27
    Salla, d. Cyrenus & Prudence, b. Jan. 16, 1780   27
    Walter, s. Samuel & Lucy, b. July 21, 1765   27
    Walter, s. Samuel & Lucy, b. July 21, 1765   (Entry marked "mistake")   3
    Welthy, d. Samuel & Lucy, b. Nov. 9, 1769   27
    Welthy, d. Samuel & Lucy, b. Nov. 9, 1769   (Entry marked "mistake")   3
WEED, Horatio N., of Bridgeport, m. Melissa M. MORRIS, of Vernon,
    Nov. 10, 1844, by Rev. Benjamin F. Walker   115
WEEKS, Eliza, m. Oscar FOX, Aug. 23, 1846, by Rev. Henry H. Bates, of
    St. John's Ch.   120
    William H., m. [Mary M. ALLEN], Nov. 24, 1858, at the home of
    Luke Allen, by Rev. E. J. Avery   150
WELCH, Ellen, m. Andrew RUTHERFORD, b. of East Windsor, Dec. 15,
    1842, by Levi Smith   112
WELDEN, Walter, m. Lucinda ROBINSON, Apr. 6, 1858, at Scantic, by
    Rev. John F. Mines, of Grace Ch.   148
WELLER, Lodowick, m. Eliza WHIPPLE, Feb. 12, 1847, by Rev. Henry
    H. Bates, of St. John's Ch.   120
WELLS, WELLES, Albert S., of Enfield, m. Caroline BOOTH, of East
    Windsor, Jan. 8, 1851, by Rev. Samuel J. Andrews, of Cong. Ch.   130
    Ann, m. Erastus BUCKLAND, Oct. 9, 1834, by Rev. Shubael Bartlett   98
    Ann Maria, of East Windsor, m. Zachariah SNYDER, of Germantown,
    N. Y., [Oct.] 24, [1820], by Rev. Thomas Robbins, of 1st Eccl.
    Soc.   59
    Charles H., m. Elisabeth H. WELLS, Feb. 25, 1858, by Rev.
    Frederick Munson, of 1st Ch.   148
    Cynthia, m. Henry CLARK, July 27, 1837, by Shubael Bartlett   102
    Elisabeth H., m. Charles H. WELLS, Feb. 25, 1858, by Rev. Frederick
    Munson of 1st Ch.   148
    Emily H., of East Windsor, m. Isaac WOOD, of Wilksbarre, Penn.,

WILLEY, (cont.)

Margaret, of Enfield, m. Augustus **SENNHAUSER,** Oct. 21, 1848,
by Rev. Francis J. Clerc, of Grace Ch., Broad Brook   124
WILLIAMS, Harriet, of Willington, m. Addison **MURRAN,** of Suffield,
June 10, 1830, by Rev. Shubael Bartlett   93
Harriet, of East Windsor, m. John F. **BINGHAM,** of Andover, Sept.
14, 1835, by C. G. Lee   99
Jonathan, of Wales, Mass., m. Almina **FULLER,** of East Windsor,
Oct. 25, 1846, by Rev. Sewall Lamberton   118
Juliaette, of Tolland, m. Merrick **THALL,** of East Windsor, Oct. 31,
1839, by Rev. Ebenezer Blake, of Wapping   106
Lucy, of East Hartford, m. John **CROSSETT,** Jr., of East Windsor,
Dec. 16, 1834, by Rev. Shubael Bartlett   98
Margaret B., m. Richard A. **BURLINGAME,** b. of East Windsor, Aug.
25, 1840, by Benjamin C. Phelps   109
Samuel, of East Hartford, m. Cynthia **STOUGHTON,** of East Windsor,
[Feb.] 17, [1825], by Rev. Thomas Robbins   88
William, of Willington, m. Mary **BURNHAM,** of East Windsor, Mar.
12, 1832, by Rev. Geo[rge] Goodyear   95
WILLIS, [see also **WYLLYS**], Frederick T., m. Appollonia **PAHLE,** Aug.
6, 1857, at Broad Brook, by Rev. John F. Mines, of Grace Ch.   149
WILSON, WILLSON, Clarissa, of South Hadley, Mass., m. David M.
PRATT, of New York City, Oct. 14, 1849, by Shubael Bartlett   126
James, of Springfield, Mass., m. Sarah **PARSONS,** of Warehouse Point,
yesterday, [Nov.] 5, [1838], by Rev. Francis L. Robbins, of Cong.
Ch. Enfield, at Warehouse Point   104
Mary, m. James **WRIGHT,** b. of Enfield, Aug. 19, 1849, by Rev.
Henry H. Bates, of St. John's Ch. Warehouse Pt.   127
Mary, m. Spencer **ALLEN,** b. of Suffield, Jan. 5, 1851, by Rev.
Sanford Benton   130
WIMAN, Sophronia, of Stockbridge, Mass., m. David P. **FROST,** of East
Windsor, Apr. 10, 1842, by Shubael Bartlett   111
WINCHELL, Chauncey, Jr., of Vernon, m. Almira J. **PHELPS,** of East
Windsor, Oct. 18, 1853, by Rev. Abel Gardner   138
WINTER, Eliza, of East Windsor, m. William R. **BROWN,** of Southwick,
Mass., Oct. 1, 1833, by Rev. Shubael Bartlett   97
Emily, of Enfield, m. Charles H. F. **RANNENBERG,** Nov. 14, 1848,
by Rev. Francis J. Clerc, of Grace Ch. Broad Brook   125
WOLCOTT, Anson, s. James & Mariam, b. Apr. 9, 1787   28
Betty, d. Henry & Dorcas, b. Sept. 14, 1771   27
Candace, m. Henry **MOODY,** b. of East Windsor, Apr. 20, 1825, by
Rev. Shubael Bartlett   87
Chloe, d. Erastus, Jr. & Chloe, b. Apr. 19, 1786   28
Chloe, of East Windsor, m. Caleb Jones **BANCROFT,** of Enfield,
Oct. 5, 1831, by Rev. Shubael Bartlett   94
Clarissa, of East Windsor, m. Samuel **GOULD,** of Manchester, May
1, 1831, by Rev. Shubael Bartlett   94
Clarissa, m. Peter H. **RISLEY,** Jan. 17, 1857, by Rev. Frederick

Page

WOLCOTT, (cont.)

Munson, of 1st Ch.   146

Cynthia, of East Windsor, m. Warren **SKINNER**, of Vernon, this
day, Apr. 4, 1838, by Asahel Nettleton   103

Edward, s. Capt. Erastus & Cloe, b. Oct. 12, 1788   28

Elihu, m. Julia **WOLCOTT**, b. of East Windsor, [May] 13, [1823],
by Rev. Thomas Robbins   86

Elizabeth S., of East Windsor, m. Erastus **ELLSWORTH**, of New
York, [Nov.] 23, [1820], by Rev. Thomas Robbins of 1st Soc.   84

Emily L., m. William C. **COVELL**, Nov. 26, 1857, by Rev. Henry W.
Conant, of M. E. Ch.   153

Epaphras, s. James & Mariam, b. Apr. 7, 1789   28

Erastus, Jr., Capt., m. Chloe **BISSELL**, b. of East Windsor, Dec.
27, 1783   56

Erastus, s. Erastus, Jr. & Chloe, b. Oct. 7, 1784   28

Francis, of East Windsor, m. Harriss **HASKELL**, of Windsor, [Nov.]
27, [1821], by Rev. Thomas Robbins   84

Gideon, s. Henry & Dorcas, b. May 26, 1769   27

Hannah, w. Albert & d. of Amasa & Hannah **LOOMIS**, d. Jan. 11,
1807, in her 42nd y.   72

Harlow, m. Mary **WOLCOTT**, Sept. 11, 1856, by Rev. F. Munson   145

Hellen, d. Erastus & Chloe, b. Mar. 9, 1794   28

Helen, of East Windsor, m. Horace **HOOKER**, of Clyde, N. Y.,
[Sept.] 3, [1822], by Rev. T. Robbins   85

Henry, s. Henry & Dorcas, b. May 27, 1779   27

Hiram, m. Sophronia **CRANE**, b. of East Windsor, [Sept.] 23,
[1824], by Rev. Thomas Robbins   87

Hopefull, m. Nathaniel **DRAKE**, Jr., of East Windsor, Apr. 4, 1774   35

James, s. Epaphras & Mable, b. Apr. 19, 1766   27

James, s. James & Mariam, b. May 29, 1791   28

James Munroe, m. Nancy **WARD**, Nov. 26, 1857, by Rev. Henry W.
Conant, of M. E. Ch.   153

Jenny, d. Henry & Dorcas, b. Jan. 13, 1777   27

Julia, m. Elihu **WOLCOTT**, b. of East Windsor, [May] 13, [1823],
by Rev. Thomas Robbins   86

Julia, of East Windsor, m. Warren **SKINNER**, of Vernon, Mar. 13,
1833, by Rev. Chauncey G. Lee   96

Julia R., m. Chauncey **BANCROFT**, s. Isaac & Lovice, Jan. 5, 1860   5

Julia R., m. Chauncey **BANCROFT**, Jan. 5, 1860, by Rev. Silas P.
Babcock   153

Juliana, d. Erastus, Jr. & Chloe, b. Apr. 9, 1791   28

Mable, d. Epaphras & Mable, b. Mar. 17, 1770   27

Mary, d. Epapras & Mable, b. July 26, 1773   27

Mary, m. Harlow **WOLCOTT**, Sept. 11, 1856, by Rev. F. Munson   145

Mary A., m. Gilbert **LORD**, b. of East Windsor, Oct. 21, 1849, by
Rev. W[illia]m S. Simmons   126

Nathaniel, Jr., of East Windsor, m. Azuba **KNOX**, of Manchester,
Aug. 16, 1835, by Rev. Shubael Bartlett   100

Page

WOLCOTT, (cont.)

Oliver, m. Mary **MUMFORD,** b. of East Windsor, Apr. 27, 1826, by
Rev. Shubael Bartlett   88

Peter, of Jersey, Ohio, m. Laura **INGERSOLL,** of East Windsor,
Dec. 17, 1823, by Rev. Shubael Bartlett of 2nd Church   86

Sarah, d. Epaphras & Mable, b. Jan. 10, 1764   27

Warren, m. Hannah Adelia **BILLINGS,** b. of East Windsor, Feb. 15,
1846, by Rev. F. W. Bill, of M. E. Ch. Warehouse Point   118

WOLF, Lawrence, m. Louisa **SEIBEL,** May 4, 1856, at Broad Brook, by
Rev. Enoch Huntington, of Grace Ch.   144

WOOD, Abigail, m. Chauncey **LESTER,** Sept. 25, 1823, by Rev. Elisha
Cushman of Bap. Ch. Hartford   86

Isaac, of Wilksbarre, Penn. m. Emily H. **WELLS,** of East Windsor,
June 1, 1842, by Shubael Bartlett   112

John, Col. of Greenfield, N. Y., m. Eliza **COGSWELL,** Nov. 14,
1836, by J. Cogswell   101

Jonathan, m. Rachel **CRAW,** b. of East Windsor, Apr. 13, 1767   56

Levi, s. Jonathan & Rachel, b. Jan. 17, 1768   27

Lorain, m. Tryfena **LORD,** Mar. 1, 1827, by Horace Barber, J. P.   90

Loury, of East Windsor, m. William **HARRIS,** (Capt.), of Middletown,
Mar. 12, 1837, by Rev. Windsor Ward   101

Lucy, d. Jonathan & Rachel, b. Dec. 27, 1770   27

Orrin N., of Somers, Conn., m. Juliaette **HARTUNG,** of Springfield,
Mass., Feb. 7, 1839, by Rev. Ebenezer Blake, of Warehouse Point   105

Parnal, m. Aaron **FROST,** b. of East Windsor, Apr. 12, 1773   38

Reuben, m. Amy **BELNAP,** Sept. 17, 1821, by Rev. Shubael Bartlett of
2nd Church   59

Sophia, m. Abiezer **PORTER,** [Oct.] 9, [1820], by Rev. Thomas
Robbins of 1st Eccl Soc.   59

Tryphena, Mrs., m. Parsons **OSBORN,** b. of East Windsor, Apr. 25,
1842, by Rev. W[illia]m H. Richards, Warehouse Point   112

William, of East Hartford, m. Abigail **CRAW,** of East Windsor,
Oct. 22, 1843, by Josiah Ellsworth, J. P.   113

WOODBRIDGE, Deodat, Jr., of East Hartford, m. Jerusha **LOOMIS,** of
East Windsor, [Aug.] 9, [1821], by Rev. Thomas Robbins   84

WOODFORD, Seth F., m. Harriet T. **ROCKWELL,** May 18, 1842, by Levi
Smith   112

WOODHEAD, Grace, m. William **MARSDEN,** Dec. 26, 1857, at Broad
Brook, by Rev. John F. Mines, of Grace Ch.   148

WOODHOUSE, Sarah, m. John **SUNDERLAND,** Mar. 28, 1848, by Rev.
Henry H. Bates, of St. John's Ch., Warehouse Point   122

William, m. Mary **WATSON,** Dec. 19, 1857, at Broad Brook, by Rev.
John F. Mines of Grace Ch.   148

WOODRUFF, Erastus, m. Candace **COHOON,** Sept. 29, 1824, by Rev.
Shubael Bartlett   86

WOODWARD, WOODARD, Abigail, m. Henry **McKINNEY,** b. of East
Windsor, Nov. 16, 1826, by Rev. Shubael Bartlett   88

George D., m. Mary **PALMER,** b. of East Windsor, Feb. 3, 1825,

ELLINGTON VITAL RECORDS
PART 1
1786 - 1850

Page

BINGHAM, (cont.)

Orra, d. [Ithamar & Hannah], b. June 23, 1793   2

Persis, m. Ebenezer NASH, Jr., Sept. 19, 1791   14

Sarah, Mrs., d. Apr. 6, 1805   2

Sophia, d. [Ithamar & Hannah], b. Nov. 23, 1786   2

BISSELL, BEYSELL, Anne, d. July 24, 1812   2

Elihu, m. Ann **HYDE,** Nov. 6, 1782   2

Harry*, s. Joseph W. & Mary An[n], b. Aug. 4, 1840 (*Perhaps
"Henry"?)   31

Henry, s. [Elihu & Ann], b. Aug. 20, 1785   2

Henry, d. Aug. 25, 1839   21

Henry Hyde, s. Joseph W. & Mary An[n], b. Oct. 1, 1838   31

Joseph Wadsworth, s. Elihu & Ann, b. June 15, 1784   2

Roxa, d. [Elihu & Ann], b. Dec. 11, 1789   2

Sarah, m. John **CHARTER,** Jr., Nov. 7, 1777   4

BLODGETT, BLODGET, Cynthia, m. Benjamin **HAMILTON,** Jr., Oct. 7,
1817   9

Harriot, d. Sept. 13, 1834   21

Harvey, d. Nov. 19, 1827 (Perhaps "Henry")   21

Janet, d. Elihu & Mary, b. Oct. 8, 1813   21

Jerusha, m. Benjamin **HAMILTON,** Nov. 17, 1790   9

Jerusha, Mrs., d. Jan. 11, 1822   21

Josiah, d. Dec. 19, 1823   21

Miranda, d. Elihu & Mary, b. Oct. 10, 1818   21

Nelson, s. Elihu & Mary, b. Aug. 20, 1820   21

BLOOD, Jonathan Erskine, s. Simeon & Elsey, b. Jan. 18, 1811   21

Simeon, d. Nov. 7, 1817   2

Simeon Upham, s. Simeon & Elsey, b. Apr. 27, 1809   21

BOOTH, Abi, m. Eli **GIFFORD,** Jan. 24, 1804   8

BOSWORTH, Levina T., d. Elijah T. & Tirzah, b. July 1, 1828   31

BOWEN*, Joseph Baldwin, s. Zelotes & Fanny, b. Jan. 5, 1829
(*BOWERS?)   31

Nicholas Theophilus, s. Zelotes & Fanny, b. May 2, 1832   31

Zelotes Berthret(?), s. Zelotes & Fanny, b. Nov. 28, 1825   31

BOWERS, [see under **BOWEN**]

BOYNTON, Anna Fidelia, d. Moses D. & Mary, b. July 10, 1821   21

Benjamin Chapman, s. Moses D. & Mary, b. Feb. 1, 1812   21

Lovina Cassandra, d. Moses D. & Mary, b. Nov. 1, 1814   21

Philo Dorastus, s. Moses D. & Mary, b. Mar. 27, 1816   21

Sally Miranda, d. Moses D. & Mary, b. Feb. 23, 1819   21

BRADLEY, Austin, s. [Reuben & Grace], b. Oct. 30, 1803   2

Betsey, [d. Reuben & Grace], b. Oct. 30, 1800   2

Clarissa, d. [Reuben & Grace], b. Oct. 16, 1788   2

Grace, w. Reuben, d. Nov. 5, 1814   2

Huldah, d.[Reuben & Grace], b. Nov. 6, 1785   2

Jason, s. [Reuben & Grace], b. Aug. 29, 1794   2

Josiah, d. Apr. 1, 1826   21

Leonard, s. [Reuben & Grace], b. Nov. 4, 1791   2

BRADLEY, (cont.)
Polly, d. [Reuben & Grace], b. Aug. 17, 1797 — 2
Reuben, d. Apr. 26, 1759 — 2
Reuben, m. Grace **HILLS**, Apr. 14, 1785 — 2
BRAMAN, Joseph, s. Isaac & Sarah, b. Jan. 29, 1809 — 21
BROCKWAY, Deodate, m. Miranda **HALL**, Oct. 29, 1799 — 2
Diodate, Rev., d. Jan. 27, 1849 — 21
Emeline, d. John H. & Flavia F., b. Dec. 5, 1829 — 31
Francis, s. Diodate & Miranda, b. Aug. 23, 1812 — 21
Francis, s. Diodate, d. July 19, 1816 — 2
Jane Eunice, d. [Diodate & Miranda], b. May 8, 1814 — 21
Jane Matilda, d. Diodate, d. Feb. 5, 1808 — 2
Mary Field, d. John H. & Flavia F., b. Mar. 3, 1839 — 31
Matilda, d. [Diodate & Miranda], b. [   ] — 2
Miranda, d. Diodate, d. Aug. 4, 181[ ] — 2
Miranda, Mrs., d. Mar. 21, 1824 — 21
Miranda, d. Diodate & Miranda, b. Mar. 20, 18[ ] — 2
-----ll, s. Deodath & Miranda, b. Jan. 31, 1801 — 2
---, s. Deodath & Miranda, b. Dec. 20, 1802 — 2
---, s. [Diodate & Miranda], b. Aug. 2, [   ] — 2
BROWN, Hannah Whiting, d. Timothy H. & Phebe, b. July 18, 1816 — 31
Jonathan, d. Aug. 29, 1821 — 21
Lydia Emeline, Mrs., d. June 17, 1832 — 21
Mary Colton, d. Timothy H. & Phebe H., b. Dec. 9, 1814 — 31
BUCKLAND, Alexander, d. Nov. 26, 1815 — 2
Anson, s. Leveritt & Doxey, b. June 9, 1820 — 21
Betsey, [twin with Polly], d. Walter & Elisabeth, b. Mar. 8, 1792 — 2
Epaphras, s. Walter & Elisabeth, b. Feb. 3, 1791 — 2
Fanny, d. Leveritt & Doxey, b. Apr. 10, 1814 — 21
Fanny, d. Apr. 15, 1814 — 2
Junises(?)*, s. Leverett & Doxey, b. Apr. 23, 1816   (*Junius?) — 21
Leveritt, m. Desey* **PARKER**, Oct. 2, 1813   (*Doxey?) — 2
Polly, [twin with Betsey], d. Walter & Elisabeth, b. Mar. 8, 1792 — 2
Sarah, Mrs., d. Jan. 20, 1824 — 21
Walter, m. Elisabeth **KROW**, July 11, 1790 — 2
BUCKLEY, [see under **BULKLEY**] — 2
BULKLEY, BUCKLEY, Daniel, m. Rhoda **PRESTON**, Oct. 7, 1807 — 2
Daniel, d. Nov. 2, 1830 — 21
Elisha, s. Dan[ie]ll & Anna, b. Sept. 28, 1801 — 21
Mary Anna, d. Dan[ie]ll & Anna, b. June 25, 1805 — 21
Nelson, s. Daniel & Anna, b. June 6, 1793 — 21
Nelson, d. July 2, 1818 — 21
BULL, Clarissa, d. Moses B. & Sally, b. Oct. 17, 1821 — 21
Elizabeth, d. Moses B. & Sally, b. Apr. 5, 1824 — 31
Henry Symonds, s. Moses B. & Sally, b. Oct. 31, 1825 — 31
Julia Ann, d. Moses B. & Sally, b. Nov. 12, 1829 — 31
Mary, d. Moses B. & Sally, b. Mar. 11, 1827 — 31
Rebec[c]a Lyman, d. Moses B. & Sally, b. Aug. 5, 1820 — 21

Page

BULL, (cont.)
    Sarah-Butler, d. Moses Butler & Sally, b. June 29, 1819   21
BURCH*, Cynthia Ingals, of Phillipsburg, Canada, E., [m. as 3d
    w. Silvester **NASH**, eldest s. of Ebenezer, Jr. & Paris], June 15,
    1838 (***RUNNELL?**)   42
BURDICK, Walter, d. Sept. 1, 1831   21
BURLEY, Asaph, d. Sept. 20, 1808   2
BURNSS(?), Rebecca, m. Roswell **STANLEY**, Dec. 21, 1800   18
BURROUGHS, Abner, d. Oct. 15, 1810   2
    Eunice, Mrs., d. Nov. 21, 1820   21
BURT, Eunice, Mrs., d. Feb. 12, 1823   21
BUTTON, Hannah, m. Ithamar **BINGHAM,** Jan. 15, 1784   2
    Naomi, Mrs., d. Nov. 28, 1832   21
CARPENTER, Delford, s. [Ruggles & Julana], b. Mar. 18, 180[ ]   3
    Joel, Dr., d. Jan. 25, 1789   4
    Mary, d. Dec. 27, 1799   4
    Mary, d. Salmon & Rhoda, b. Aug. 21, 1817   29
    Miriva, d. [Ruggles & Julana], b. Apr. 28, 18[ ]   3
    Polly, m. Converse **JOHNSON,** July 29, 1787   10
    Ruggles, s. Eunice **WALDOW,** b. Aug. 17, 1798   20
    Ruggles, m. Julana **PEARCE,** Oct. 15, 1799   4
    Salmon, m. Rhoda **RICHARDSON,** Dec. 26, 1816   4
    Salmon, Jr., s. Salmon & Rhoda, b. June 9, 1819   29
    Seymour, s. Salmon & Rhoda, b. Oct. 19, 1821   29
    Zunder, s. [Ruggles & Julana], b. May 28, 180[ ]   3
CHADWICK, Ann M., m. Obadiah **WARD,** Sept. 1, 1816   20
CHAPMAN, Alexander, m. Huldah **LEE,** Nov. 6, 1809   4
    Anna, d. [Samuel & Polly], b. Oct. 14, 1791   3
    Anna, Mrs., d. Mar. 21, 1810   4
    Anna, m. Seth **PARKER,** Dec. 29, 1812   15
    Austin, s. [Hosea & Mary], b. Jan. 1, 1780   3
    Betsey, [d. Samuel & Polly], b. May 10, 1787   3
    Chaunc[e]y Putnam, s. Thomas W. & Sophia, b. Jan. 22, 1818   29
    Chester, s. [Samuel & Polly], b. June 24, 1799   3
    Damaris, m. Eleazer **PINNEY,** Jr., Sept. 25, 1818   15
    Damaris Holton, d. John & Ann, b. Oct. 15, 1819   29
    Delmore, s. [Hosea & Patty], b. Dec. 28, 1804   4
    Dilson, s. [Hosea & Patty], b. Apr. 28, 1806   4
    Emeline, d. Perley & Roxa, b. Oct. 6, 1809   4
    Erastus Wolcott, s. Thomas W. & Sophia, b. Aug. 19, 1814   29
    George, s. Aaron & Susan, b. Dec. 11, 1815   29
    Henry, s. Alex[ande]r & Huldah, b. Apr. 4, 1812   4
    Henry, s. Alexander, d. Sept. 27, 1813   4
    Hosea, m. Patty **CONVERSE,** Dec. 22, 1803   4
    Jabez, m. Damarus **HOLTON,** Dec. 15, 1785   4
    John, s. [Jabez & Damarus], b. June 15, 1793   3
    John, s. [Samuel & Polly], b. June 25, 1797   3
    John, m. Ann **PITKIN,** Jan. 21, 1819   4

Page

CHAPMAN, (cont.)
Juliann, d. Aaron & Susan, b. Aug. 16, 1812   29
Laura, d. [Jabez & Damarus], b. June 18, 1791   3
Laura, d. Roxa LOVETT, b. June 3, 1814   12
Lydia, d. [Samuel & Polly], b. Aug. 8, 1794   3
Martha, Mrs., d. May 22, 1825   29
Mary, m. Timothy PITKIN, May 15, 1816   15
Mary Ann, d. John & Ann, b. Aug. 27, 1822   38
Mary Sophia, d. Thomas W. & Sophia, b. May 22, 1820   29
Melissa, d. Aaron & Susan, b. Aug. 12, 1810   29
Nancy, d. [Samuel & Polly], b. Oct. 14, 1791   3
Nelson Cortland, s. Alexander & Huldah, b. Aug. 21, 1810   4
Orlow, s. Calvin & Artimesia, b. Jan. 7, 1832   38
Parly, s. [Jabez & Damarus], b. Jan. 19, 1789   3
Perley, m. Roxania McKNIGHT, Mar. 31, 1809   4
Polly, d. [Hosea & Mary], b. May 6, 1782   3
Polly, d. [Samuel & Polly], b. June 16, 1785   3
Polly, w. Samuel, d. Mar. 8, 1809   4
Polly, d. Sam[ue]ll, d. Dec. 9, 1810   4
Rebekah, d. [Jabez & Damarus], b. Feb. 2, 1787   3
Rosell, d. Lucius & Rebecca, b. Mar. 12, 1831   38
Sally, d. [Hosea & Mary], b. May 23, 1789   3
Sally, Mrs., d. Apr. 21, 1820   29
Samuel, s. [Samuel & Polly], b. Aug. 31, 178[ ]   3
Sarah, Mrs., d. July 28, 1827   29
Sephrona, d. [Samuel & Polly], b. July 21, 1802   3
Thomas White, s. [Samuel & Polly], b. July 30, 1789   3
Thomas White, s. [Samuel & Polly], b. July 31, 1789   3
Thomas White, Jr., s. Thomas W. & Sophia, b. Feb. 7, 1816   29
Wyllys, s. [Hosea & Mary], b. Nov. 10, 1791   3
CHAPPEL, Cyrus, d. Apr. 2, 1807   4
Edward, d. Feb. 26, 1826   29
Samuel, d. Nov. 10, 1818   29
CHARTER, Abitha Sophrona, d. [Anson & Lydia], b. Dec. 31, 1806   3
Charles, s. [George & Clorinda], b. Dec. 8, 1791   3
Charlotte, d. [John, Jr. & Sarah], b. Apr. 4, 1790   4
Charlotte, d. July 25, 1815   4
Charlotte, d. July 25, 1815   29
Daniel, s. [John, Jr. & Sarah], b. Apr. 29, 1782   4
Daniel, s. John, Jr., d. May 30, 1801   4
Eunice, d. [John, Jr. & Sarah], b. May 15, 1797   4
George, s. [George & Clorinda], b. Sept. 26, 1775   3
George, d. Dec. 24, 1821   29
George Ransom, s. Allen & Dorcas, b. Nov. 18, 1815   29
Hannah, d. [Anson & Lydia], b. May 15, 1805   3
Harriet, d. Roswell & Alice, b. Jan. 1, 1811   29
John, Jr., m. Sarah BEYSELL, Nov. 7, 1777   4
John, 3rd, s. [John, Jr. & Sarah], b. Apr. 22, 178[ ]   4

Page

CHARTER, (cont.)

John, d. Nov. 3, 1807   4
John, d. Mar. 7, 1826   29
Lemuel, s. [John, Jr. & Sarah], b. May 7, 1786   4
Levi, s. [George & Clorinda], b. Dec. 25, 1785   3
Levi, d. Sept. 11, 1810   4
Lydia, d. [Anson & Lydia], b. Apr. 7, 1802   3
Mary, d. [John, Jr. & Sarah], b. Apr. 15, 1792   4
Mary, Mrs., d. Dec. 14, 1801   4
Nathan, s. [John, Jr. & Sarah], b. Apr. 2, 1784   4
Nathaniel, s. [George & Clorinda], b. May 19, 1780   3
Polly, d. [George & Clorinda], b. Sept. 28, 1778   3
Rebecca, d. [John, Jr. & Sarah], b. Apr. 19, 1795   4
Roswel, s. [George & Clorinda], b. Sept. 29, 1787   3
Samuel, s. [Anson & Lydia], b. July 30, 1798   3
Sanford, s. [Anson & Lydia], b. Feb. 25, 1800   3
Sarah, d. [John, Jr. & Sarah], b. Apr. 16, 1788   4
Sarah, Mrs., d. Dec. 15, 1815   29
Wyllys, s. Allen & Dorcas, b. Oct. 16, 1802   29
Zebulon, [s. George & Clorinda], b. Oct. 23, 1789   3
Zebulon, d. May 12, 1810   4

CHUBBUCK, CHUBUCK, Aaron, s. [Nathaniel & Chloe], b. Aug. 4, 1791   3
Anna, d. Eben[eze]r, Jr. & Lucina, b. July 12, 1788   3
Chloe, d. [Nathaniel & Chloe], b. Dec. 8, 1803   3
Daniel Ostrander, s. [Nathaniel & Chloe], b. May 17, 1805   3
Hannah, d. [Nathaniel & Chloe], b. Feb. 16, 1793   3
Jacob, s. [Nathaniel & Chloe], b. Mar. 5, 179[ ]   3
James, s. [Nathaniel & Chloe], b. Apr. 5, 1801   3
John, s. [Nathaniel & Chloe], b. Feb. 22, 179[ ]   3
Nathaniel, s. Nath[anie]ll & Chloe, b. Sept. 5, 1789   3
Patience, m. John **SHURTLIFF**, May 24, 1781   18
Sheldon, s. [Nathaniel & Chloe], b. June 3, 1799   3
Sheldon, s. Nath[anie]ll, d. Feb. 22, 1805   4

CLARK, Aaron, see under Aren
Anna, d. [Wicome & Ruth], b. June 10, 1785   4
Aren*, s. [Samuel & Rebeckah], b. Feb. 5, 1787 (*Oren or Aaron?)   3
Chester Davis, s. [Samuel & Rebeckah], b. Aug. 17, 1788   3
Daniel, m. Rebekah **DAVIS**, May 18, 1780   4
Daniel*, s. [Daniel* & Rebeckah], b. Jan. 1, 1781 (*Samuel?)   3
Daniel, d. Aug. 3, 1815   4
Ebenezer, s. Daniel & Rebeckah, b. May 1, 1792   3
Eunice, d. [Samuel* & Rebeckah], b. July 22, 1782 (*Daniel?)   3
Jemima Wolcott, d. [Wicome & Ruth], b. July 3, 1793   4
Jonathan, s. Daniel & Rebekah, b. Jan 8, 1795   3
Levina, d. [Wicome & Ruth], b. Aug. 4, 1779   4
Louisa, m. Nathan **BEEBE**, Oct. 10, 1803   2
Marten Eldridge, s. [Wicome & Ruth], b. July 21, 1791   4
Marven, s. [Samuel* & Rebeckah], b. Aug. 13, 1785 (*Daniel?)   3

Page

CLARK, (cont.)

Olive, d. [Wicome & Ruth], b. Mar. 27, 1775   4

Oren*, s. [Samuel & Rebeckah], b. Feb. 5, 1787 (*Perhaps "Aren"?)   3

Orra, Mrs., d. Mar. 6, 1817   4

Polly, d. [Wicome & Ruth], b. Aug. 16, 1789   4

Rebeckah, d. [Samuel* & Rebeckah], b. Feb. 22, 1784 (*Daniel?)   3

Richard Osborn, s. [Wicome & Ruth], b. Dec. 28, 1798   4

Ruth, d. [Wicome & Ruth], b. Apr. 27, 1781   4

Sally(?), d. [Samuel* & Rebeckah], b. July 7, 1790 (*Daniel?)   3

Samuel*, s. [Samuel* & Rebeckah], b. Jan. 1, 1781 (*Daniel?)   3

Samuel, d. Feb. 7, 1824   29

Sarah Elisabeth, d. Warren H. & Maria J., b. June 22, 1841   38

Tamsien, d. [Wicome & Ruth], b. Dec. 18, 1774   4

Tamsien, m. William SEXTON, Dec. 31, 1809   18

Wicome, m. Ruth CRANE, Nov. 18, 1773   4

Wicome, s. [Wicome & Ruth], b. Feb. 28, 1787   4

Wicome, d. Feb. 25, 1795   4

Wicome, 2d, s. [Wicome & Ruth], b. Mar. 15, 1797   4

William, s. [Wicome & Ruth], b. Sept. 16, 1777   4

Zeruiah, d. [Wicome & Ruth], b. July 10, 1783   4

COLLINS, Anson, s. [Rufus & Esther], b. Jan. 15, 1789   3

Caroline Matilda, d. [Thomas & Hannah], b. Apr. 10, 1802   4

Charlotte, d. [Rufus & Submit], b. Nov. 23, 1803   4

Chester, s. [Rufus], b. July 13, 1785   3

Chester, m. [   ] PIERCE, [   ], 1808   4

Claris[s]a, d. [Rufus], b. Apr. 11, 1781   3

Clarissa Ann, d. [Thomas & Hannah], b. Apr. 11, 1804   4

Esther, d. [Rufus & Esther], b. Oct. 3, 1792   3

George P., s. [Rufus], b. June 30, 1778   3

George P., m. Lydia READ, Feb. 5, 1809   4

Guy, s. Jabesh & Laura*, b. Dec. 3, 1829 *Louisa   46

Horace P., s. Jabesh & Louisa, b. July 2, 1812   46

Irwin, s. Jabesh & Laura*, b. July 17, 1827 *Louisa   46

Jabez, s. [Rufus], b. Sept. 18, 1782   3

Jabesh, m. Loisa PORTER, Mar. 4, 1812   4

Jane, d. Jabesh & Louisa, b. July 22, 1822   46

Jemima, d. [Rufus], b. Feb. 26, 1777   3

John Harris, s. George P. & Lydia, b. May 29, 1810   4

Joseph, s. [Rufus], b. Sept. 5, 1779   3

Joseph, s. [Rufus & Submit], b. Apr. 15, 1800   4

Julia, d. Jabesh & Loisa, b. Sept. 10, 1813   29

Lemuel Albert, s. Jabesh & Loisa, b. Feb. 4, 1816   29

Loisa, d. Jabesh & Loisa, b. Mar. 4, 1820   29

Lorenzo Post, s. Thomas & Hannah, b. Oct. 16, 1808   4

Louisa, Mrs., d. Dec. 18, 1829   29

Mary, d. George P. & Lydia, b. July 8, 1812   4

Maryett, d. Jabesh & Laura*, b. Jan. 26, 1825 *Louisa   46

Nancy, d. [Rufus & Submit], b. Aug. 7, 1798   4

Page

COLLINS, (cont.)

P_____ Warner, s. Thomas & Hannah, b. [   ]   4
Philura, d. Rufus & Submit, b. Sept. 28, 1796   3
Rufus, m. Submit **ALLEN**, May [ ], 1795   4
Rufus, Dea., d. July 20, 1808   4
Sophia Maria, d. [Thomas & Hannah], b. Aug. 12, 1806   4
Thomas, s. [Rufus], b. Aug. 24, 177[ ]   3
Thomas, m. Hannah **WARNER**, Nov. 14, 1799   4
Wyllys Parsons, s. [Thomas & Hannah], b. July 30, 1800   4
CONVERSE, Patty, m. Hosea **CHAPMAN**, Dec. 22, 1803   4
COOK, Achsah, d. [Elisha & Hulda], b. June 1, 1795   3
Clary, d. [Elisha & Huldah], b. Feb. 4, 1792   3
Electa, d. [Elisha & Huldah], b. Dec. 29, 1798   3
Elisha, m. Huldah **PRATT**, Mar. 17, 1791   4
Elisha Pratt, s. [Elisha & Huldah], b. Aug. 9, 1802   3
COOPER, Anson Hall, s. Sylvanus & Polly, b. Dec. 22, 1809   4
Charles, s. [Sylvanus & Polly], b. July 23, 1803   3
Rosanna, d. [Sylvanus & Polly], b. Apr. 3, 1801   3
Sylvanus, m. Polly **GILES**, Dec. 8, 1799   4
William Giles, s. [Sylvanus & Polly], b. May 22, 1806   3
COVEL, Ebenezer, s. [Isaac & Ruth], b. June 9, 1782   3
Isaac, s. [Isaac & Ruth], b. Apr. 17, 1780   3
Nathaniel, s. [Isaac & Ruth], b. Nov. 9, 1787   3
Sally, d. [Isaac & Ruth], b. Apr. 9, 1785   3
CRANE, Hannah, d. [William & Hannah], b. Nov. 2, 1803   4
Rebecca, d. William & Hannah, b. Aug. 28, 1802   4
Ruth, m. Wicome **CLARK**, Nov. 18, 1773   4
William, m. Hannah **HAMILTON**, Mar. 14, 1801   4
CROSBY, Nancy, Mrs., d. Aug. 27, 1818   29
CROSS, George, s. [John & Mary], b. Nov. 9, 1779   3
Mehetable, d. [John & Mary], b. Nov. 29, 1777   3
CUSHMAN, Eunice, d. Elverton* & Abigail, b. Apr. 25, 1790 (*Written
"Werton")   3
DAMON, Aaron, Jr., s. [Aaron & Hearty], b. Oct. 25, 1785   5
Aaron, m. Agnes **GRISWOLD**, July 11, 1804   5
Aaron, Jr., d. Nov. 5, 1813   5
Aaron, d. Nov. 18, 1816   28
Daniel, s. [Aaron & Hearty], b. Apr. 19, 1798   5
David, s. [Aaron & Hearty], b. May 31, 1794   5
David, m. Eunice **PITKIN**, Nov. 18, 1819   5
David, d. Aug. 11, 1827   28
Ebenezer, s. [Aaron & Hearty], b. Mar. 21, 1787   5
Edmund, s. [Aaron & Heart], b. Aug. 21, 1800   5
Eunice, d. David & Eunice, b. June 14, 1822   28
Hearty, w. Aaron, d. Aug. 28, 1801   5
Jonathan, s. [Nathan & Thankful], b. Dec. 23, 1790   5
Jonathan, d. Jan. 30, 1810   5
Judith, d. [Aaron & Hearty], b. Mar. 11, 1792   5

Page

DAMON, (cont.)
    Nathan, m. Thankful **LUMBAR**, b. Mar. 17, 1785   5
    Nathan, s. [Nathan & Thankful], b. Nov. 16, 1788   5
    Nathan, d. Jan. 7, 1831   5
    Orin, s. [Nathan & Thankful], b. Apr. 17, 1787   28
    Orin, d. Sept. [ ], 1791   5
    Roxa, d. July 6, 1816   5
    Roxa, d. [Aaron & Hearty], b. May 31, 1790   5
    Roxa, d. July 6, 1816   28
    Sarah, Mrs. (?), d. Oct. 28, 1802   5
DARBY, DARBE, Hannah, d. Jesse & Lydia, b. Dec. [ ], 1764   5
    Hannah, m. Lemuel **WARNER**, June 2, 1789   20
DARTMOUTH, Cyrus, d. Sept. 2, 1818   28
    James, d. Feb. 6, 1818   28
DAVIS, Dan H., s. Daniel & Mary, b. May 16, 1790   5
    Daniel, d. May 17, 1815   5
    Lydia, m. Josiah **DEWEY**, Apr. 20, 1780   5
    Mary, Mrs., d. Dec. 9, 1802   5
    Rebekah, m. Daniel **CLARK**, May 18, 1780   4
DAVISON, Abner Pember, s. Abner P. & Hannah, b. Sept. 10, 1812   5
    Clarissa, d. Abner P. & Hannah, b. Apr. 6, 1817   5
    Hannah, d. Abner P. & Hannah, b. Feb. 21, 1821   5
    Jane, d. Abner P., d. Mar. 4, 1826   28
    Sarah Jane, d. Abner P. & Hannah, b. June 8, 1823   28
    Stephen Pember, s. Abner P. & Hannah, b. May 21, 181[1?]   5
DAY, Ariel, m. Eunice **RUSSELL**, Jan. 26, 1791   5
    -----, wid., d. Jan. 28, 1802   5
[DEAN], DEAINES, DEINS, Thomas, d. Apr. 14, 1816   5
    Thomas, d. Apr. 24, 1816   28
    ----, Mrs., d. May 7, 1834   28
DEWEY, Betsey, m. Nathaniel **NEWELL**, Jr., Dec. 18, 1794   14
    Fanny, d. [Joseph & Lydia], b. Nov. 25, 1788   5
    Josiah, m. Lydia **DAVIS**, Apr. 20, 1780   5
    Josiah, s. [Joseph & Lydia], b. Feb. 15, 1786   5
    Lydia, d. [Joseph & Lydia], b. June 7, 1783   5
    Mary, d. [Joseph & Lydia], b. Feb. 14, 1791   5
    Sarah, m. Asahel **SHURTLIFF**, Nov. 8, 1781   18
DIMMICK, DIMMIK, Ellis, s. Amasa & Matilda, b. Sept. 30, 1806   5
    Ellis, d. July 20, 1808   5
    Frances Aresby, d. July 15(?), 1808   5
    Harvey, d. Oct. 14, 1827   28
DOANE, Narsissa, d. June 5, 1807   5
DORCHESTER, Eunice, m. John **HALL**, Jan. 21, 1771   9
DORMAN, DORMON, Amos, Jr., m. Nancy **PORTER**, Dec. 16, 1802   5
    Amos, Sr., d. Sept. 9, 1811   5
    Amos, Jr., d. Nov. 10, 1812   5
    Amoret, d. Orlin C. & Juliana, b. Nov. 2, 1831   28
    Dolan, s. John P. & Amelia, b. Jan. 7, 1841   28

FROST, (cont)

Lucy, d. Josiah & Nancy, b. Oct. 22, 1823   7
Moses Bourne, s. Josiah, Jr. & Nancy, b. June 13, 1813   7
Sally, d. Josiah & Nancy, b. July 22, 1817   7
Thankful, d. [Josiah, Jr. & Nancy], b. Apr. 11, 1811   7
FULLER, Albert B., s. Horace D. & Mariah R., b. Aug. 8, 1840   7
Amanda, d. Lydia, b. Oct. 16, 1802   7
Betsey, Mrs., d. May 10, 1838   7
Jacob, d. Dec. 6, 1799   7
James A., d. May 11, 1837   7
Jerusha, d. young, b. July 30, 1737   7
Jerusha, m. Joseph **PINNEY**, July 16, 1761   15
Lydia had s. Milton, b. Mar. 29, 1791   7
Lydia had d. Rosina, b. Feb. 13, 1800   7
Lydia had d. Amanda, b. Oct. 16, 1802   7
Lydia, wid., d. June 2, 1814   7
Maria R., Mrs., d. Jan. 3, 1841   7
Mary Melissa, d. John & Sarah, b. Feb. 3, 1810   7
Milton, s. Lydia, b. Mar. 29, 1791   7
Orran D., d. Apr. 20, 1842   7
Phila, m. Justus **McKINNEY**, Oct. 31, 1805   13
Rosina, d. Lydia, b. Feb. 13, 1800   7
GAGE, Aaron Alvin, s. Aaron & Annis, B., b. Oct. 2, 1841   8
Orlanda Burt, s. Aaron & Annis B., b. Nov. 2, 1843   8
GIBBS, Oliver, d. June 7, 1829   8
GIFFORD, Amanda, d. Eli & Abi, b. May 9, 1810   8
Betsey, d. May 31, 1801   8
Edith, Mrs., d. Nov. 15, 1829   8
Eli, m. Abi **BOOTH**, Jan. 24, 1804   8
Eli, s. Eli & Abi, b. Dec. 2, 1818   8
Eli, d. Oct. 21, 1826   8
Julius, s. Eli & Abi, b. Aug. 8, 1813   8
Lester Fitch, s. Eli & Abi, b. Aug. 20, 1808   8
Louisa, d. Eli & Abi, b. Nov. 8, 1805   8
Martha, m. Nathaniel **WARNER**, June 24, 1796   20
Ziba, d. June 11, 1819   8
GILES, Polly, m. Sylvanus **COOPER**, Dec. 8, 1799   4
GILLIGAN, John, s. [Matthew & Desire], b. Nov. 28, 1793   8
Matthew, m. Desire **KING**, Aug. 11, 1791   8
Matthew, d. Nov. 26, 1805   8
Philomela, d. [Matthew & Desire], b. Jan. 18, 1792   8
Thomas, m. Lydia **JENNINGS**, May 7, 1789   8
GOLD, Rozzamon, m. James **LOVETT**, Nov. 22, 1779   12
GOODALE, [see under **GOODELL**]
GOODELL, GOODALE, Betsey, d. Titus & Deborah, b. May 24(?), 1801   8
Edwin, s. Thomas & Naomi, b. Mar. 24, 1809   8
Eliza, d. Thomas & Naomi, b. Apr. 1, 1805   8
Ellen Louisa, d. Francis & Sophia Louisa, b. May 8, 1847   48

Page

GOODELL, GOODALE, (cont.)

Emma, d. Titus & Deborah, b. Sept. 26, 1806 — 8

Francis, s. Thomas & Naomi, b. May 29, 1813 — 8

Julia, d. Thomas & Naomi, b. Jan. 2, 1811 — 8

Mary, d. Titus & Deborah, b. May 25, 1804 — 8

Mira, d. Thomas & Naomi, b. June 9, 1803 — 8

Naomi, Mrs., d. Feb. 28, 1826 — 8

Philo Dwight, s. Titus & Deborah, b. Sept. 28, 1808 — 8

Rhoda, m. Reuben **PORTER**, Mar. 30. 1786 — 15

Rufus Grant, s. Thomas & Naomi, b. Nov. 30, 1819 — 8

Sally, d. Thomas & Naomi, b. Oct. 15, 1815 — 8

Thomas, m. Naomi **PIERCE**, Oct. 8, 1802 — 8

Thomas, d. Mar. 3, 1826 — 8

Titus, m. Deborah **PIERCE**, May 15, 1800 — 8

William Whitney, s. Francis & Sophia Louisa, b. Jan. 20, 184[5?] — 48

GOODRICH, Eunice, d. John H. & Mary, b. Mar. 30, 1795 — 8

John H., m. Mary **READ**, Sept. 26, 1793 — 8

Thomas, d. Mar. 16, 1802 — 8

GRANT, Keturah, Mrs., d. Mar. 9, 1826 — 8

Mary, Mrs., d. May 27, 1811 — 8

Phebe, Mrs., d. Apr. 7, 1828 — 8

Philena, b. Dec. 28, 1797; m. Silvester **NASH**, eldest s. of Ebenezer, Jr. & Paris, Sept. 23, 1824; d. Feb. 3, 1830, at St. Albans, Vt. — 38

Philenda, b. Dec. 28, 1797; m. Silvester **NASH**, eldest s. of Ebenezer, Jr. & Paris, Sept. 23, 1824; d. Feb. 3, 1830, at St. Albans, Vt. — 42

GREEN, Anna, d. [Daniel & Hannah], b. Jan. 11, 1777 — 8

Betsey, d. [Daniel & Hannah], b. Apr. 16, 1784 — 8

Betsey, m. George **PEASE**, June 10, 1802 — 15

Daniel, s. [Daniel & Hannah], b. July 21, 1769 — 8

Daniel, d. Aug. 15, 1813 — 8

David, s. [Daniel & Hannah], b. Oct. 4, 1779 — 8

Docia, d. Daniel, Jr. & Docia, b. July 18, 1796 — 8

Hannah, [d. Daniel & Hannah], b. Apr. 8, 1782 — 8

James, s. [Daniel & Hannah], b. May 15, 1794 — 8

John, s. [Daniel & Hannah], b. July 6, 1771 — 8

Sally, d. [Daniel & Hannah], b. Jan. 11, 1789 — 8

GRISWOLD, Agnes, m. Aaron **DAMON**, July 11, 1804 — 5

Harriet Sophia, d. Herman C. & Mary A., b. Mar. 30, 1832 — 48

Mary Jane, d. Herman C. & Mary A., b. Aug. 22, 1836 — 48

GROVER, Betsey Lucinda, d. Phinehas, Jr. & Phebe, b. Apr. 28, 1821 — 8

Daniel, s. [Phenehas & Louisa], b. Sept. 3, 1802 — 8

Edmund, d. Dec. 8, 1814 — 8

Elijah, d. Aug. 17, 1805 — 8

Jemima, Mrs., d. Sept. 5, 1828 — 8

Louisa, d. [Phenehas & Louisa], b. June 26, 1794 — 8

Lucinda, d. [Phenehas & Louisa], b. Sept. 18, 1800 — 8

Mary, Mrs., d. July 17, 1835 — 8

Phen[e]has, s. [Phenehas & Louisa], b. May 10, 1797 — 8

Page

GROVER, (cont.)

Phinehas, d. Aug. 17, 1827	8
HALL, Arthur, s. John & Sophia, b. May 7, 1829	24
Edward, s. John & Sophia, b. Aug. 10, 1809	24
Elethea Kingsley, d. Seth & Hannah, b. Nov. 6, 1822	37
Eliza, d. John & Sophia, b. Feb. 16, 1817	24
Eunice, d. [John & Eunice], b. Apr. 23, 1773	9
Eunice, m. Levi **WELLS,** Jr., Feb. 3, 1791	20
Francis, s. John & Sophia, b. Oct. 27, 1822	24
Frederic, s. John & Sophia, b. Sept. 5, 1827	24
John, m. Eunice **DORCHESTER,** Jan. 21, 1771	9
John, s. [John & Eunice], b. Feb. 26, 1783	9
John, d. May 26, 1796	9
John, m. Sophia **KINGSBURY,** June 5, 1808	9
John, s. John & Sophia, b. Aug. 22, 1813	24
John, d. Oct. 2, 1847	33
Junius, s. John & Sophia, b. June 8, 1811	24
Levi Wells, s. John & Sophia, b. Dec. 25, 1819	24
Maria, d. John & Sophia, b. Feb. 15, 1821	24
Miranda, d. [John & Eunice], b. Apr. 26, 1775	9
Miranda, d. Oct. 17, 1778	9
Miranda, 2d, d. [John & Eunice], b. Sept. 19, 1780	9
Miranda, m. Deodate **BROCKWAY,** Oct. 29, 1799	2
Sophia, d. John & Sophia, b. July 4, 1815	24
Sophia, Mrs., d. May 19, 1829	33
William Maxwell, s. John & Sophia, b. Oct. 7, 1824	24
HAMILTON, Abigail, d. [Daniel & Molly], b. June 5, 1801	33
Anna, d. Theodore & Anna, b. Mar. 15, 1796	33
Arnold, s. [Benjamin & Jerusha], b. Sept. 8, 1799	24
Arnold, s. Benj[ami]n, d. Oct. 5, 1803	33
Arnold, s. Benjamin & Cynthia, b. June 26, 1821	24
Benjamin, m. Jerusha **BLODGET,** Nov. 17, 1790	9
Benjamin, s. [Benjamin & Jerusha], b. Apr. 2, 1794	24
Benjamin,Jr., m. Cynthia **BLODGET,** Oct. 7, 1817	9
Benjamin, d. May 27, 1834	37
Blodget, s. [Benjamin & Jerusha], b. Mar. 2, 1802	24
Blodget, s. Benj[ami]n, d. Oct. 28, 1803	33
Daniel, Jr., s. [Daniel & Molly], b. May 12, 1811	33
Ebenezer B., s. [Benjamin & Jerusha], b. Sept. 14, 1804	24
Elam, s. [Daniel & Molly], b. Sept. 7, 1803	33
Eli, s. [Daniel & Molly], b. Nov. 29, 1798	33
Elizabeth, d. Theodore & Anna, b. Dec. 16, 1818	33
Eunice, d. Theodore & Anna, b. Sept. 24, 1799	33
Hannah, m. William **CRANE,** Mar. 14, 1801	4
Havilah, s. Benjamin, Jr. & Cynthia, b. Nov. 27, 1818	24
Huldah, d. [Paul & Lydia], b. May 26, 1790	9
Huldah, d. Theodore & Anna, b. Sept. 26, 1810	33
Jemima, d. [Benjamin & Jerusha], b. Nov. 14, 1810	24

Page

HAMILTON, (cont.)

Jerusha, d. [Benjamin & Jerusha], b. Jan. 12, 1792	24
John, s. [Daniel & Molly], b. July 5, 1819	33
Joseph, s. [Paul & Lydia], b. Apr. 26, 1792	9
Lovice, d. Theodore & Anna, b. Dec. 14, 1806	33
Lydia, d. [Paul & Lydia], b. Mar. 25, 1781	9
Lydia, d. [Daniel & Molly], b. June 16, 1816	33
Martha, d. [Paul & Lydia], b. Sept. 8, 1782	9
Mary, d. Theodore & Anna, b. Dec. 14, 1814	33
Olive, d. [Daniel & Molly], b. Apr. 4, 1806	33
Patty, d. [Daniel & Molly], b. Dec. 30, 1813	33
Paul, d. Oct. 17, 1824	33
Polly, Mrs., d. Oct. 1, 1824	33
Rachel, d. Theodore & Anna, b. Mar. 30, 1808	33
Rachel, d. Sept. 21, 1828	33
Rebecca, d. [Benjamin & Jerusha], b. Mar. 14, 1797	24
Rebecca, d. Benjamin, d. Nov. 4, 1798	33
Richard S., s. [Benjamin & Jerusha], b. June 19, 1807	24
Sally, d. [Daniel & Molly], b. Aug. 26, 1808	33
Sarah, d. [Paul & Lydia], b. June 16, 1787	9
HAMMOND, George Griswold, s. Elijah & Esther, b. June 28, 1819	33
James, m. Ruth **PARKER**, Dec. 3, 1807	9
Martha Strong, d. Elijah & Esther, b. Mar. 18, 1821	33
Polly*, w. James, d. Sept. 8, 1807 (*Perhaps Sally?)	9
Sanford Parker, s. James & Ruth, b. Sept. 9, 1808	24
HARE, Anne, d. [Stephen], b. July 21, 1783	24
Hannah, d. [Stephen], b. July 31, 1785	24
Samuel M., s. [Stephen], b. Nov. 13, 1794	24
Sophia, d. [Stephen], b. Nov. 17, 1799	24
Stephen, b. Sept. 12, 1755	24
Stephen Arnold, s. Stephen & Anne, b. Aug. 17, 1788	9
Stephen Arnold, s. [Stephen], b. Aug. 17, 1788	24
Sullivan, s. [Stephen], b. Sept. 7, 1792	24
HEATH, Daniel, s. [Simeon & Joanna], b. Feb. 14, 1795	9
Elijah, s. [Simeon & Joanna], b. May 24, 1797	9
HILLS, HILL, Anson Fitch, s. [Leonard & Mary], b. Oct. 13, 1808	24
Betsey, d. Zilpah, b. Jan. 25, 1809	9
Charlotte, m. Cha[u]nc[e]y **FOSTER**, [ ], 1787	7
Emila, d. [Leonard & Mary], b. Mar. 12, 1811	24
Grace, m. Reuben **BRADLEY**, Apr. 14, 1785	2
Grace, Mrs., d. Apr. 28, 1807	9
Laura, d. [Leonard & Mary], b. Jan. 25, 1806	9
Leonard, m. Mary **LADD**, June 8, 1797	9
Leonard Mariner, s. [Leonard & Mary], b. Jan. 9, 1803	9
Lucretia, m. Warham **FOSTER**, July 15, 1781	7
Mary, d. [Leonard & Mary], b. June 25, 1800	9
Nancy, m. George **HOLDEN**, Dec. 18, 1794	9
Samuel, s. Leonard & Mary, b. Feb. 19, 1798	9

Page

HITCHCOCK, Chloe, m. Jacob READ, Dec. 24, 1800   16
HOLABORD, Lois, m. William MORGAN, Sept. 20, 1795   13
HOLDEN, [see also HOLTON], Asenath, d. [George & Nancy], b. Jan. 25,
     1800   24
    George, m. Nancy HILL, Dec. 18, 1794   9
    George, s. [George & Nancy], b. May 22, 1798   24
    George, Jr., s. George, d. May 2, 1799   9
    George, 2d, s. [George & Nancy], b. Nov. 14, 1801   24
    Nancy, w. George, d. Oct. 21, 1812   9
    Phebe, d. [George & Nancy], b. Jan. 1, 1803   24
    Stephen, s. [George & Nancy], b. Feb. 4, 1806   24
HOLTON, [see also HOLDEN], Abigail, d. [John & Abigail], b. July 8,
     1794   24
    Abigail, d. John, d. Dec. 13, 1794   9
    Abigail Wolcott, d. [John & Abigail], b. May 17, 1800   24
    Albert, s. Joseph & Mary, b. Oct. 19, 1807   24
    Betsey, d. [John & Abigail], b. Feb. 12, 1796   24
    Betsey, d. Sept. 15, 1822   33
    Charlot[t]e, d. [Timothy & Mary], b. July 31, 1783   9
    Charlotte, m. Eliphalet KILLAM, Oct. 16, 1803   11
    Clarissa, d. James & Sally, b. Oct. 19, 1814   33
    Clarissa, Mrs., d. Aug. 5, 1818   33
    Damaras, d. Timothy & Damarus, b. Feb. 11, 1768   9
    Damarus, m. Jabez CHAPMAN, Dec. 15, 1785   4
    Damaris Howe, d. [John & Abigail], b. Oct. 21, 1802   24
    Damaris Howe, d. [John], d. May 1, 1803   9
    Damaris Howe, 2d, d. [John & Abigail], b. Sept. 25, 1810   24
    Edward Carlos, s. [John & Abigail], b. Jan. 31, 1816   24
    Israel Putnam, s. James & Sally, b. Apr. 4, 1822   33
    James, s. [Timothy & Mary], b. Jan. 10, 1789   9
    James, d. June 20, 1823   33
    John, s. [Timothy & Damarus], b. Mar. 23, 1770   9
    John, d. Dec. 5, 1820   33
    John Howe, s. [John & Abigail], b. Apr. 7, 1804   24
    Joseph, s. [Timothy & Mary], b. July 6, 1779   9
    Joseph, m. Mary FISK, July 9, 1807   9
    Margaret, d. Joseph, b. Feb. 4, 1800   24
    Martha Maria, d. [Joseph & Mary], b. June 23, 1809   24
    Mary, Mrs., d. Dec. 12, 1812   9
    Mary, d. James & Sally, b. Jan. 14, 1817   33
    Polly, d. [Timothy & Mary], b. Aug. 7, 1781   9
    Polly, d. [Timothy & Mary], b. Nov. 26, 1787   9
    Polly, d. June 18, 1788   9
    Roger Wolcott, s. [John & Abigail], b. Nov. 5, 1812   24
    Salle, d. [Timothy & Mary], b. Oct. 13, 1777   9
    Samuel, s. James & Sally, b. Nov. 5, 1819   33
    Sophia, d. [John & Abigail], b. Aug. 19, 1792   24
    Tamer, d. [Timothy & Damarus], b. Feb. 25, 1772   9

Page

JOHNSON, (cont.)

Sarah Ann, d. Azel, b. Sept. 4, 1820 — 10

JONES, Anne Hare, d. [Daniel & Betsey], b. Sept. 28, 1788 — 10

Daniel, m. Betsey WHEELER, Oct. 31, 1787 — 10

Daniel, m. Marcy BEEBY, June 2, 1806 — 10

Daniel Lovell, s. [Daniel & Betsey], b. Oct. 28, 1790 — 10

Ezra Taylor, s. Daniel & Marcy, b. May 11, 1808 — 10

Hannah, d. [Daniel & Betsey], b. Sept. 21, 1793 — 10

KEITH, Mary, d. James. b. Aug. 29, 1773 — 11

KELLOGG, Olive, m. David MAKER, Nov. 21, 1782 — 13

[KENNEDY], KENEDY, Bill, s. [Thomas & Sarah], b. July 11, 1775 — 11

Bill, d. Nov. 18, 1776 — 11

Bill, 2d, s. [Thomas & Sarah], b. Apr. 11, 1777 — 11

Hannah, d. [Thomas & Sarah], b. June 4, 1781 — 11

Martha, d. [Thomas & Sarah], b. July 27, 1783 — 11

Martha, m. Elijah ALGIER, Jan. 1, 1807 — 1

Sarah, d. [Thomas & Sarah], b. Dec. 7, 1779 — 11

Sarah, 2d, d. May 9, 1816 — 11

Thomas, s. [Thomas & Sarah], b. Nov. 10, 1786 — 11

Thomas, Jr., d. Apr. 10, 1822 — 11

Thomas, d. Aug. 9, 1834 — 11

KENT, Jerusha, m. John McKNIGHT, May 27, 1799 — 13

KIBBE, KIBBEE, Deborah, m. James McKINNEY, Feb. [ ], 1811 — 13

Edward Hopkins, s. Lyman S. & Lydia, b. Apr. 3, 1817 — 11

KILLAM, Charlotte, d. July 11, 1816 — 11

Eliphalet, m. Charlotte HOLTON, Oct. 16, 1803 — 11

James Maddison, s. [Eliphalet & Charlotte], b. Apr. 29, 1809 — 11

Mary Charlotte, d. Eliphalet & Charlotte, b. July 6, 1811 — 11

Timothy Holton, s. [Eliphalet & Charlotte], b. Dec. 19, 1805 — 11

William Holton, s. [Eliphalet & Charlotte], b. Apr. 13, 1804 — 11

KIMBALL, Amy C., Mrs., d. May 22, 1827 — 11

Asenath, d. Daniel & Mariam, b. Sept. 27, 1795 — 11

Carlos Clinton, s. Daniel, Jr. & Roxana, b. Apr. 24, 1828 — 42

Dan[ie]ll Norton, s. Dan[ie]ll, Jr. & Roxana, b. July 4, 1821 — 11

Elizabeth McCray, d. Daniel, Jr. & Roxana, b. Dec. 20, 1830 — 42

Mary Eveline, d. Josiah & Amy, b. Sept. 14, 1821 — 11

Miriam, Mrs., d. Dec. 23, 1823 — 11

Roxana Roan*, d. Dan[ie]ll, Jr. & Roxana, b. Nov. 4, 1818 (*Bacon?) — 11

KING, Azubah, d. [Samuel & Azubah], b. Feb. 17, 1768 — 11

Clarissa, Mrs., d. May 31, 1821 — 11

Clarissa, Mrs., d. May 31, 1831* (*Entry crossed out) — 11

Clarissa Maria, d. Jeremiah & Esther, b. Dec. 1, 1827 — 42

Desire, d. [Samuel & Azuba], b. Nov. 24, 1771 — 11

Desire, m. Matthew GILLIGAN, Aug. 11, 1791 — 8

Elizabeth Jane, d. Jeremiah & Esther, b. May 30, 1832 — 42

Emery, d. Feb. 17, 1830 — 11

Hannah, d. [Samuel & Azubah], b. Jan. 7, 1770 — 11

Jabez, s. [Samuel & Azubah], b. Apr 26, 1785 — 11

Page

LITTLE, Anna, d. [Russell & Charlotte], b. Nov. 26, 1789   12
 Charlotte, d. [Russell & Charlotte], b. Mar. 6, 1785   12
 Deodate, d. July 14, 1815   12
 Jerusha, d. [Russell & Charlotte], b. Sept. 9, 1782   12
 Russell, m. Charlotte PINNEY, June 2, 1782   12
 Russell, s. [Russell & Charlotte], b. Apr. 26, 1795   12
LOOMIS, Lyman H., s. Zacheus & Hannah, b. June 21, 1815   12
 Sally, m. Elisha S. PEMBER, May 2, 1793   15
LOVETT, Alanson, s. [James & Rozzamon], b. Mar. 10, 1793   12
 Alanson, m. Huldah NEWTON, May 17, 1819   12
 Augustus, s. Alanson & Huldah, b. Sept. 28, 1819   12
 Betsey, d. [James & Rozamon], b. Feb. 15, 1802   12
 Erastus, s. [James & Rozzamon], b. Dec. 18, 1786   12
 Eunice, d. [James & Rozzamon], b. Jan. 28, 1791   12
 Hannah, d. [James & Rozzamon], b. Feb. 11, 1789   12
 James, m. Rozzamon GOLD, Nov. 22, 1779   12
 James, d. Mar. 12, 1832   12
 James Lyman, s. [James & Rozamon], b. Dec. 24, 1799   12
 Jerusha, d. Feb. 3, 1816   12
 John Gold, s. [James & Rozzamon], b. Oct. 30, 1780   12
 Louisa, d. [James & Rozzamon], b. Mar. 5, 1784   12
 Persey, d. Alanson & Huldah, b. Sept. 8, 1821   12
 Polly, d. [James & Rozamon], b. Aug. 24, 1797   12
 Richman Crandall, s. [James & Rozamon], b. Oct. 18, 1804   12
 Rosamond, d. Roxa, b. June 3, 1811   12
 Roxa had d. Rosamond, b. June 3, 1811   12
 Roxa had d. Laura Chapman, b. June 3, 1814   12
 Roxalania, d. [James & Rozzamon], b. Feb. 10, 1782   12
 Roxelanea, d. Nov. 2, 1801* (*Perhaps 1831?)   12
 Sally, d. [James & Rozamon], b. Apr. 16, 1795   12
LUCE, Reuben, m. Rhoda PARSONS, Feb. 9, 1795   12
 ------, s. Reuben & Rhoda, b. Nov. 3, 1795   12
LUMBAR, Thankful, m. Nathan DAMON, Mar. 17, 1785   5
MACK,Rachel, d. Daniel & Hopestill, b. Aug. 21, 1807   27
MAKER, David, m. Olive KELLOGG, Nov. 21, 1782   13
 David, s. [David & Olive], b. July 23, 1784   13
 Justin, s. [David & Olive], b. Sept. 5, 1786   13
 Sally, d. [David & Olive], b. Sept. 28, 1788   13
 Sally, d. David & Olive, b. Oct. 22, 1790   13
MANLY, Lorin, d. Dec. 16, 1831   27
MARTIN, John, d. Sept. 3, 1832   40
 Marilda Porter, d. Meltiah & Marilda, b. Apr. 29, 1813   27
 Meletiah, d. Sept. 24, 1821   27
 Peleg, d. Jan. 18, 1830   27
 Sarah Ann, d. John & Sarah, b. Mar. 19, 1820   35
 Treat, d. Apr. 30, 1831   27
 Zelinda, d. Peleg, d. Apr. 13, 1811   13
MATHER, Jemima, m. Allyn HYDE, May 30, 1805   9

McKINNEY, (cont.)
McKINSTRY, Abigail, d. May 15, 1814   27
McKNIGHT, Alanson Abbe, s. Horace & Asenath, b. Mar. 25, 1821   27

NASH, (cont.)

Frances Burdett, [child of Ebenezer, Jr. & Susannah, b.] Nov.
  16, 1812   38
Frances Burdett, [child of Ebenezer, Jr. & Susannah], b. Nov.
  16, 1812   42
Harlin, [s. of Ebenezer, Jr. & Susannah, b.] Nov. 8, 1799; d. [ ],
  1828, in Mexico   38
Harlin, [s. of Ebenezer, Jr. & Susannah, b.] Nov. 8, 1799; d. [ ],
  1828, in Mexico   42
Harlin, [s. Silvester & Philenda, b.] Aug. 29, 1828, in St. Albans;
  d. Feb. 27, 1829   42
James Clark, [s. Ebenezer, Jr. & Susannah, b.] Feb. 11, 1818;
  d. June 18, 1843   38
James Clark, [s. Ebenezer, Jr. & Susannah], b. Feb. 11, 1818;
  d. June 18, 1843   42
Laura, [d. Ebenezer, Jr. & Susannah, b.] Sept. 30, 1797   38
Laura, [d. Ebenezer, Jr. & Susannah, b.] Sept. 30, 1797   42
Mary An[n], [d. Ebenezer, Jr. & Susannah, b.] June 23, 1807   38
Mary Ann, [d. Ebenezer, Jr. & Susannah], b. June 23, 1807   42
Matilda, [d. Ebenezer, Jr. & Susannah], b. Nov. 10, 1791;
  d. Feb. 8, 1792   38
Matilda, [d. Ebenezer, Jr. & Susannah], b. Nov. 10, 1791;
  d. Feb. 8, 1792   42
Matilda, 2d, [d. Ebenezer, Jr. & Susannah], b. May 8, 1793;
  d. May 6, 1796   38
Matilda, 2d, [d. Ebenezer, Jr. & Susannah], b. May 8, 1793;
  d. May 8, 1796   42
Nancy Miranda, [child of Ebenezer, Jr. & Susannah], b. Feb. 8, 1815   38
Nancy Miranda, [d. Ebenezer, Jr. & Susannah, b.] Feb. 8, 1815   42
Norman, s. [Ebenezer & Susana], b. Nov. 17, 1791   14
Patty, d. [Ebenezer & Susana], b. Dec. 30, 1775   14
Philenda Grant, [d. Silvester & Philenda, b.] Jan. 8, 1830;
  d. Aug. 20, 1834   42
Polly, d. [Aaron], b. Aug. 13, 1812   14
Polly, d. Aaron, d. Jan. 25, 1814   14
Prudence, d. [Ebenezer & Susana], b. Dec. 28, 1773   14
Rodolphus Kibbe, s. Stedman & Sophia, b. Dec. 24, 1812   34
Samuel, s. [Ebenezer & Susana], b. Jan. 13, 1780   14
Sarah Kellogg, [d. Ebenezer, Jr. & Susannah, b.] Apr. 8, 1805   38
Sarah Kellogg, [d. Ebenezer, Jr. & Susannah], b. Apr. 8, 1805   42
Sedgwick, s. [Aaron], b. May 30, 1814   14
Sophia, d. Stedman & Sophia, b. Aug. 18, 1819   34
Stedman, s. [Ebenezer & Susana], b. Feb. 4, 1786   14
Stedman, Jr., s. Stedman & Sophia, b. Dec. 16, 1814   34
Susan Inkeep, twin with William Meade, [d. Silvester & Philenda]
  b. Dec. 31, 1826, in St. Albans, Vt.   42
Susan[n]a, d. [Ebenezer & Susana], b. Oct. 9, 1781   14
Susanna, Mrs., d. Feb. 18, 1834   14

NASH, (cont.)

Sylvester, s. [Ebenezer & Susana], b. Dec. 11, 1771 — 14

Silvester, [s. Ebenezer, Jr. & Susannah], b. May 8, 1795 — 38

Silvester, [s. Ebenezer, Jr. & Susannah, b.] May 8, 1795 — 42

Silvester, eldest s. Ebenezer, Jr. & Paris, m. Philena **GRANT**, Sept. 23, 1824 — 38

Silvester, eldest s. Ebenezer, Jr. & Paris, m. Philenda **GRANT**, Sept. 23, 1824 — 42

Silvester, eldest s. of Ebenezer, Jr. & Paris, m. 2d w. Elizabeth Bosworth **SMITH**, of Bristol, R. I., July 6, 1832 — 38

Silvester, eldest s. of Ebenezer, Jr. & Paris, m. 2d w. Elizabeth Bosworth **SMITH**, of Bristol, R. I., July 6, 1832 — 42

Silvester Smith, [s. Silvester & Elisabeth Bosworth], b. Jan. 1, 1835, in E. Greenwich, R. I. — 42

William Barlow, [s. Ebenezer, Jr. & Susannah, b.] Mar. 6, 1810 — 38

William Barlow, [s. Ebenezer, Jr. & Susannah], b. Mar. 6, 1810 — 42

William Meade, twin with Susan Inkeep, [s. Silvester & Philenda], b. Dec. 31, 1829, in St. Albans, Vt., d. Sept. 27, 1829 — 42

Zanus, [twin with Aaron], s. [Ebenezer & Susana], b. Oct. 20, 1783 — 14

NEWCOMB, Hannah, d. Oct. 8, 1804 — 14

NEWELL, Abigail, 2d, d. Aug. 31, 1807 — 14

Abigail, d. Jan. 17, 1810 — 14

Adonijah, d. June 16, 1834 — 14

Alvah, s. [John & Deborah], b. Dec. 26, 1792 — 14

Amherst, s. [Nathaniel, Jr. & Betsey], b. Apr. 28, 1804 — 14

Betsey, d. [Nathaniel, Jr. & Betsey], b. Feb. 8, 1796 — 14

Carlos Lyman, s. Alvah & Laura, b. Feb. 4, 1827 — 34

Clarissa, d. [John & Deborah], b. May 6, 1797 — 14

Deborah, Mrs., d. Feb. 17, 1830 — 14

Ezekiel, s. [John & Deborah], b. Feb. 18, 1795 — 14

Hannah Abbott, d. [Nathaniel, Jr. & Betsey], b. [ ] — 14

Horrace, s. [Nathaniel, Jr. & Betsey], b. Mar. 2, 1798 — 14

Huldah, Mrs., d. Oct. 6, 1821 — 14

John, m. Deborah **WEBSTER**, Feb. 11, 1790 — 14

John, Dea., d. Feb. 11, 1836 — 14

John Alvah, s. Alvah & Laura, b. July 5, 1825 — 34

John L., d. Nov. 15, 1830 — 14

John Lyman, s. John & Deborah, b. Jan. 5, 1791 — 14

Laura, d. [John & Deborah], b. June 30, 1799 — 14

Laura, d. John, d. Mar. 23, 1806 — 14

Laura Sophronia, d. Alvah & Laura, b. Oct. 5, 1823 — 34

Martha, m. Nathaniel **WARNER**, Oct. 6, 1815 — 20

Martha, [twin with Mary], d. Alvah & Laura, b. Aug. 8, 1830 — 34

Mary, [twin with Martha], d. Alvah & Laura, b. Aug. 8, 1830 — 34

Marry Orrilla, d. Ezekiel & Orrilla, b. Feb. 11, 1833 — 34

Miranda, d. [Nathaniel, Jr. & Betsey], b. Feb. 26, 1800 — 14

Nathaniel, Jr., m. Betsey **DEWEY**, Dec. 18, 1794 — 14

Nathaniel, s. [Nathaniel, Jr. & Betsey], b. Dec. 6, 1806 — 14

NEWELL, (cont.)
Nath[anie]ll, d. Nov. 13, 1807	14
Orrin Dimmick, s. Ezekiel & Orrilla, b. Sept. 5, 1828	34
Sally, d. [John & Deborah], b. Jan. 17, 1804	14
Samuel, s. Alvah & Laura, b. May 30, 1828	34
Warren D., s. [Nathaniel, Jr. & Betsey], b. Mar. 11, 1802	14
NEWTON, Alven, s. [Moses & Zerbiah], b. Feb. 25, 1790	14
Chloe, d. [Moses & Zerviah], b. July 7, 1786	14
Elizabeth, d. John, Jr. & Sarah, b. Oct. 24, 1817	34
Hannah, d. [John & Ruth], b. Feb. 17, 1785	14
Huldah, d. [John & Ruth], b. May 27, 1787	14
Huldah, m. Alanson **LOVETT**, May 17, 1819	12
Jabez, s. [John & Ruth], b. Mar. 19, 1791	14
Jabez, s. John, Jr. & Sarah, b. May 17, 1821	34
John, s. [John & Ruth], b. Mar. 23, 1783	14
John, d. Nov. 30, 1831	14
John Clark, s. John, Jr. & Sarah, b. June 8, 1819	34
Jotham, s. [John & Ruth], b. Sept. 6, 1793	14
Moses, s. [Moses & Zerviah], b. Nov. 15, 1794	14
Moses, m. Mary **SEAVER**(?), Feb. 2, 1795	14
Moses, d. July 15, 1798	14
Moses, d. Nov. 2, 1803	14
Orin, s. [Moses & Zerbiah], b. Mar. 10, 1792	14
Persis, d. Moses, d. Feb. 12, 1801	14
Ruth, d. Mar. 6, 1813	14
Sarah, m. Ebenezer **DURFY**, June 1, 1786	5
William, s. [Moses & Zerviah], b. Apr. 10, 1788	14
William, s. Moses, d. Jan. 11, 1802	14
PARKER, Anna, d. Seth & Anna, b. Mar. 7, 1817	22
Betsey, d. [John & Elisabeth], b. Nov. 27, 1796	15
Bitsey Belinda, d. Ephraim & Bitsey, b. Sept. 20, 1819	22
Desey*, m. Leveritt **BUCKLAND**, Oct. 2, 1813 (*Doxey?)	2
Doxey, see under Desey	
Edatha, d. [John & Elisabeth], b. Aug. 6, 1786	15
Elizabeth Fidelia, d. Seth & Anna, b. Oct. 23, 1813	22
Ephraim, s. [John & Elisabeth], b. June 11, 1790	15
Ephraim, m. Betsey **MILLARD**, Dec. 30, 1812	15
Ephraim, s. Ephraim & Betsey, b. Jan. 12, 1822	22
Eunice, d. Ephraim & Lucy, b. May 24, 1757	15
James E., s. Juliana, b. Dec. 29, 1838	43
John, m. Elisabeth **SQUIRE**, Nov. 6, 1783	15
John, s. [John & Elisabeth], b. Dec. 26, 1787	15
John, d. Feb. 14, 1832	22
John Benjamin, s. Seth & Anna, b. Sept. 30, 1814	22
Juliana, d. Ephraim & Betsey, b. Oct. 30, 1813	22
Juliana, d. Ephraim, d. June 23, 1815	22
Juliana, d. Epraim & Betsey, b. Feb. 28, 1816	22
Juliana had s. James E. **PARKER**, b. Dec. 29, 1838	43

PARKER, (cont.)

Mary, d. [John & Elisabeth], b. July 5, 1784   15

Roxey, see under Desey

Ruth, m. James **HAMMOND,** Dec. 3, 1807   9

Seth, s. [John & Elisabeth], b. Mar. 25, 1793   15

Seth, m. Anna **CHAPMAN,** Dec. 29, 1812   15

Seth, s. Seth & Anna, b. Nov. 29, 1815   22

PARSONS, Harvey, d. Feb. 23, 1826   22

Joseph, Jr., d. Jan. 11, 1811   15

Rhoda, m. Reuben **LUCE,** Feb. 9, 1795   12

PEARSON, Jerusha, Wid., d. Jan. 19, 1814   22

Samuel, d. Dec. 13, 1790   15

PEASE, Bethshebe, d. [Thomas & Mercy], b. Sept. 5, 1789   15

Cragan(?)*, s. [George & Betsey], b. Dec. 23, 1806 (*Oragan?)   22

George, m. Betsey **GREEN,** June 10, 1802   15

George, Jr., s. [George & Betsey], b. Feb. 11, 1803   22

Jonathan, d. Feb. 25, 1825   22

Joseph, s. [Jonathan & Mary], b. Aug. 28, 1783   15

Joseph, d. Nov. 7, 1803   15

Joseph, s. [George & Betsey], b. Nov. 27, 1804   22

Levi, s. [Jonathan & Mary], b. June 30, 1785   15

Marcy, wid., d. Oct. 7, 1827   22

Mary, d. Nov. 2, 1803   15

Oragan*, s. [George & Betsey], b. Dec. 23, 1806 (*Cragan?)   22

Sally Calista, d. Rufus & Basheba, b. June 30, 1829   25

Sarah, d. [Jonathan & Mary], b. Jan. 12, 1782   15

Thomas, d. Aug. 2, 1815   22

Willys, s. [Thomas & Mercy], b. Feb. 27, 1788   15

PEMBER, Andrew, d. Jan. 26, 1810   15

Anna, d. [Elisha S. & Sally], b. Apr. 14, 1802   22

Austin, s. [Elisha S. & Sally], b. Oct. 20, 1799   22

Austin, d. Feb. 21, 1826   22

Carlos, s. Justus & Louisa, b. Sept. 5, 1837   43

David Sprague, s. [Elisha S. & Sally], b. Mar. 2, 1795   22

Elijah, d. Mar. 15, 1812   15

Elisha, 2d, s. Elisha & Sally, b. Sept. 29, 1807   22

Elisha S., m. Sally **LOOMIS,** May 2, 1793   15

Elisha S., d. Mar. 12, 1812   15

Hannah, Mrs., d. Apr. 5, 1798   15

Horace W., s. David S. & Martha, b. Feb. 27, 1822   25

Justus, s. [Elisha S. & Sally], b. June 18, 1804   22

Justus, d. Oct. 23, 1845   22

Perley, s. [Elisha S. & Sally], b. Apr. 26, 1797   22

Sarah Ann, d. David S. & Martha, b. Oct. 11, 1825   25

PHILLIPS, Alonzo Dwight, s. [Hubbard & Hannah], b. May 9, 1805   15

Gideon, d. Nov. 6, 1833   22

Hubbard, m. Hannah **FOSTER,** June 28, 1803   15

Mar Foster, s. [Hubbard & Hannah], b. Dec. 13, 1803; d. May 25, 1804

Page

PINNEY, (cont.)

William, s. [Benjamin & Susanna], b. Oct. 20, 1806   22

Zeruiah, Mrs., d. Nov. 27, 1814   15

PITKIN, Ann, m. John CHAPMAN, Jan. 21, 1819   4

Charles Hyde, s. Joseph & Louisa, b. Mar. 23, 1828   43

Chester Hyde, s. Joseph, d. Sept. 2, 1829   22

Eunice, m. David DAMON, Nov. 18, 1819   5

Harriet B., d*. Timothy & Mary, b. Oct. 14, 1822 (*Written "son")   22

Harris, s. Timothy, d. Dec. 28, 1824   22

Jerusha, Mrs., d. Feb. 18, 1819   22

Joseph Wells, s. Joseph & Louisa, b. May 16, 1824   43

Joseph Wells, s. Joseph, d. Nov. 28, 1824   22

Joseph Wells, 2d, s. Joseph & Louisa, b. Aug. 31, 1825   43

Mary Ann, d. Timothy & Mary, b. Sept. 24, 1817* (*Entry crossed out)   22

Mary Ann, d. Timothy & Mary, b. Sept. 28, 1819   22

Mary Ann, d. Timothy, d. Sept. 23, 1830   22

Timothy, m. Mary CHAPMAN, May 15, 1816   15

POLWINE, Rachel, m. Gurdon PINNEY, Sept. 6, 1791   15

PORTER, Achsah, d. [Joseph L.], b. Aug. 26, 1785   15

Betsey, d. [Jonathan & Marcy], b. Aug. 13, 1795   22

David, s. [Reuben & Ruth], b. Sept. 6, 1780   15

Dolly, d. [Jonathan & Marcy], b. May 16, 1801   22

Dolly, d. June 30, 1823   22

Elisabeth, Mrs., d. Feb. 16, 1793   15

Eunice, d. [Reuben & Ruth], b. Nov. 26, 1778   15

Guy, s. [Jonathan & Marcy], b. June 27, 1803   22

Horace, s. [Jonathan & Marcy], b. May 7, 1799   22

Horace Philo, s. Philo & Claris[s]a B., b. Feb. 6, 1839   43

Jerusha, d. [Jonathan & Marcy], b. May 5, 1797   22

Jonathan, Jr., s. [Joseph L.], b. Oct. 2, 1783   15

Jonathan, m. Mercy FOOT, July 7, 1785   15

Jonathan, d. Mar. 25, 1825   22

Joseph L., m. Deborah ROGERS, Apr. 2, 1783   15

Louisa, d. [Jonathan & Mercy], b. Nov. 24, 1788   15

Lo[u]isa, m. Jabesh COLLINS, Mar. 4, 1812   4

Louisa Clarissa, d. Philo & Clarissa B., b. Aug. 24, 1842   43

Lovel, s. [Joseph L. & Deborah], b. Nov. 11, 1791   15

Nancy, m. Amos DORMAN, Jr., Dec. 16, 1802   5

Philo, s. [Jonathan & Marcy], b. June 27, 1806   22

Reldy, d. [Jonathan & Mercy], b. May 21, 1790   15

Reuben, m. Ruth KINGSBURY, Feb. 8, 1776   15

Reuben, m. Rhoda GODDELL, Mar. 30, 1786   15

Reuben, s. [Reuben & Rhoda], b. Jan. 7, 1787   15

Rhoda, d. [Reuben & Rhoda], b. Mar. 12, 1789   15

Rhoda, d. Apr. 25, 1796   15

Ruth, d. Reuben & Ruth, b. Dec. 14, 1776   15

Ruth, Mrs., d. Mar. 26, 1783   15

Page

RUSSELL, (cont.)
Rachel, d. [Jonathan & Thankful], b. Apr. 22, 1779   16
Ruth, d. Nathan & Mercy, b. Apr. 7, 1780   16
Sophia, d. [Jonathan & Thankful], b. June 3, 1789   16
Stephen Otis, s. [Wyllys & Emelia], b. Dec. 13, 1793   16
Stephen Otis, m. Mary McCRAY, Mar. 28, 1816   16
Thankful, d. [Jonathan & Thankful], b. Feb. 16, 1794   16
William Henry, s. Stephen O. & Mary, b. Oct. 25, 1818   16
Wyllys, s. Eben[eze]r & Hannah, b. Jan. 9, 1770   16
Wyllys, m. Emelia WOLCOTT, July 16, 1793   16
Wyllys, d. Mar. 12, 1851   16
RYAN, Betsey, m. Josiah A. KINGSBURY, Jan. 27, 1813   11
ST. CLAIR, Betsey, d. [Matthew & Hannah], b. Aug. 21, 1808   32
Hannah, d. [Matthew & Hannah], b. May 22, 1803   32
Hiram, s. [Matthew & Hannah], b. Aug. 2, 1821   32
Joel, s. [Matthew & Hannah], b. June 26, 1812   32
Marble, s. [Matthew & Hannah], b. June 29, 1817   32
Matthew, s. [Matthew & Hannah], b. July 16, 1806   32
Norman, s. [Matthew & Hannah], b. July 24, 1810   32
Orril, d. [Matthew & Hannah], b. May 2, 1814   32
Sally, d. [Matthew & Hannah], b. Feb. 2, 1820   32
Solomon, s. [Matthew & Hannah], b. Feb. 2, 1818   32
William, s. [Matthew & Hannah], b. Feb. 13, 1805   32
SANGER, SANGOR, Aruthur, s. [Daniel & Allis], b. July 5, 1791   17
Arthur, s. [Daniel & Allis], b. Apr. 9, 1793   17
Cilynda, d. [Daniel & Allis], b. Aug. 15, 1789   17
Chester, s. [Daniel & Allis], b. Dec. 1, 1795   17
Daniel, Jr., d. Aug. 13, 1813   18
SAWIN, SAWING, Abijah. m. Polly TWING, Apr. 13, 1808   18
Chester Crocker, s. Abijah & Polly, b. Feb. 4, 18[ ]   17
Elam, s. Abijah & Polly, b. Feb. 4, 1809   17
Horrace, s. Abijah & Polly, b. July 18, 181[ ]   17
SCRIPTURE, Marvin Kyes, s. Marvin & Lucy Julia, b. Sept. 19, 1840   41
SEARLE John, d. Sept. 4, 1810   18
SEAVER, Mary(?), m. Moses NEWTON, Feb. 2, 1795   14
SESSIONS, Betsey, d. [Samuel & Abigail], b. Nov. 10, 1791   17
Edward, s. [Samuel & Abigail], b. Oct. 29, 1786   17
Erastus, s. [Samuel & Abigail], b. May 7, 1789   17
George, s. [Samuel & Abigail], b. Oct. 3, 1770   17
Hannah, d. [Samuel & Abigail], b. Aug. 22, 1778   17
Nabby Ruggles, d. [Samuel & Abigail], b. June 18, 1774   17
Nancy, d. [Samuel & Abigail], b. May 5, 1776   17
Pircy, d. [Samuel & Abigail], b. Mar. 19, 1781   17
Samuel, s. [Samuel & Abigail], b. Aug. 30, 1783   17
SEXTON, Alfred, [s. Charles & Mary], b. Aug. 26, 1815   18
Charles Bartlett, s. [Charles & Mary], b. Oct. 26, 1809   18
Docia, d. [William & Docia], b. May 23, 1798   17
Docia, d. [William & Docia], b. Nov. 29, 1803   17

Page

SMITH, (cont.)

Betsey, d. Ebenezer & Hepzibah, b. June 29, 1803	17
Charles, s. John & Susan, b. Sept. 14, 1821	18
Chester, s. [Graves & Roxalania], b. Dec. 4, 1791	17
Chester, 2d, s. Joshua W. & Persis, b. Jan. 23, 1819	18
Chester, d. Sept. 14, 1828	32
Clarissa, d. [Graves & Roxalania], b. May 12, 1785	17
Cynthia, d. [Graves & Roxalania], b. July 29, 1800	17
David, s. [Moses & Hannah], b. Apr. 13, 1782	17
David, m. Sarah **BATTIN**, [ ], 1805	18
David L., s. David & Sarah, b. June 17, 1812	32
Edward Holton, s. Joseph & Almira, b. Mar. 28, 1825	41
Elisabeth, d. Mar. 5, 1799	18
Elisabeth Bosworth, of Bristol, R. I., b. Sept. 20, 1798;	
m. as 2d w. [Silvester **NASH**, eldest s. Ebenezer, Jr. & Paris],	
July 6, 1832; d. Jan. 3, 1835, at East Greenwich, R. I.	42
Elizabeth Bosworth, of Bristol, R. I., b. Sept. 20, 1798, m. as	
2d w. [Silvester **NASH**, eldest s. Ebenezer, Jr. & Paris], July 6,	
1832; d. Jan. 3, 1835, at East Greenwich, R. I.	38
Emily, d. Ebenezer & Hepzibah, b. Dec. 13, 1805	17
Esther, d. David & Sarah, b. Nov. 12, 1809	32
Eunice, d. [Moses & Hannah], b. Feb. 16, 1791	17
George, s. Gordon & Lydia, b. July 25, 1828	41
George Washington, s. Thomas & Diana, b. Dec. 26, 1804	18
Graves, s. Richard & Susanna, b. Mar. 18, 1759	17
Graves, m. Roxalania **McKINNEY**, Dec. 20, 1781	18
Graves, d. Dec. 16, 1828	32
Hannah, d. [Moses & Hannah], b. Sept. 1, 1777	17
Hannah, m. Walter **HYDE**, Jan. 10, 1804	9
Hannah, d. David & Sarah, b. Apr. 15, 1811	32
Hannah, d. David d. Aug. 23, 1811	32
Hannah, Mrs., d. Sept. 7, 1827	32
Harriot, d. Asa & Sally, b. July 27, 1806	17
Harriot H., d. David & Sarah, b. July 14, 1817	32
Harriet H., d. David, d. July 1, 1818	32
Henry, s. Gorden & Lydia, b. Mar. 23, 1824	41
Henry B., s. David & Sarah, b. May 8, 1815	32
Henry Weston, s. Joshua W. & Persis, b. Jan. 23, 1827	41
Hepzibah, d. Apr. 22, 1807	18
Hiram M., s. David & Sarah, b. Apr. 7, 1819	32
James, s. [Graves & Roxalania], b. June 12, 1796	17
James, d. Aug. 18, 1816	18
James Leach, s. Joseph & Almira, b. Nov. 28, 1823	41
John, d. Apr. 22, 1804	18
John, s. John & Susan, b. May 14, 1820	18
John Pratt, s. [Peter & Polly], b. Apr. 13, 1780	17
Joseph W., s. Joseph & Almira, b. Sept. 16, 1828	41
Joshua W., d. Sept. 22, 1839	32

Page

SMITH, (cont.)

Judith, d. Thomas & Diana, b. Feb. 17, 1811	18
Lorin, s. Joseph & Almira, b. June 27, 1833	41
Maria, d. Thomas & Diana, b. Nov. 29, 1806	18
Maria, d. Joseph & Almira, b. Jan. 8, 1821	32
Maria, d. Joseph & Almira, b. Jan. 8, 1821	41
Mariet, d. Chester & Betsey, b. Sept. 5, 1819	18
Martha, d. [Moses & Hannah], b. Mar. 25, 1780	17
Mary, d. [Graves & Roxalania], b. Sept. 16, 1794	17
Moses, s. [Moses & Hannah], b. Nov. 24, 1793	17
Moses, d. July 13, 1817	32
Nancy, d. [Graves & Roxalania], b. Nov. 4, 1782	17
Nancy, d. Sept. 2, 1818	32
Norris, s. Ebenezer & Hepzibah, b. June 22, 1801	17
Peter Turner, s. [Peter & Polly], b. Feb. 12, 1798	17
Philo, s. Joseph & Almira, b. Apr. 10, 1830	41
Roxana, d. [Graves & Roxalania], b. Oct. 16, 1788	17
Sally, d. David & Sarah, b. Dec. 8, 1806	32
Samuel, s. [Moses & Hannah], b. Oct. 16, 1786	17
Samuel, s. Moses, d. June 2, 1804	18
Samuel, s. David & Sarah, b. May 6, 1808	32
Samuel, s. David, d. Jan. 16, 1809	32
Samuel, s. Joseph & Almira, b. Apr. 7, 1836	41
Sarah, d. [Moses & Hannah], b. Aug. 28, 1784	17
Sarah, d. Joseph & Almira, b. Sept. 16, 1826	41
Silvester, b. Jan. 1, 1835, at East Greenwich, R. I.	42
Silvester, [ ]	38
SNELLINGS, Penelope, m. Joseph **ALLEN**, Jr., Oct. [ ], 1810	1
SNOW, Daane*, d. Nov. 22, 1828 (*Arnold Copy has "Duane")	32
Dudley(?)*, d. Nov. 22, 1828 (Written "Daane")	32
Elisabeth, m. Walter **BUCKLAND**, July 11, 1790 (**KROW?**)	2
Nathaniel, d. Dec. 23, 1821	32
Pattiee Parmelia, d. Dudley & Mary, b. May 18, 1821	32
SPEAR, David, d. Feb. 3, 1813	18
Esther, m. William **MAY**, Jan. 19, 1787	13
Mary, d. Apr. 21, 1803	18
William, Jr., d. July 22, 1802	18
SPKESMAN(?), Conrad, d. Mar. 24, 1801	18
SQUIRE, Charles Watson, s. Nathaniel & Hannah, b. Aug. 15, 1832	41
Elisabeth, m. John **PARKER**, Nov. 6, 1783	15
STANLEY, STANLY, Emily, d. Roswell & Rebecca, b. May 2, 1819	17
John, s. Roswell & Rebecca, b. July 1, 1810	17
John, s. Roswell, d. June 24, 1811	18
Roswell, m. Rebecca **BURNSS**, Dec. 21, 1800	18
Sanford, s. [Roswell & Rebecca], b. Oct. 25, 1801	17
Sidney, s. [Roswell & Rebecca], b. May 6, 1805	17
STEBBINS, Eliza, d. John & Tacy, b. Nov. 12, 1813	18
Harriot, d. John & Tacy, b. Apr. 17, 1820	18

Page

TAYLOR, (cont.)

Sarah, Mrs., d. May 24, 1801* (*Arnold Copy has 1811) 19

Stephen, s. [John & Hannah], b. Apr. 10, 1784 19

William, s. [John & Hannah], b. Nov. 5, 1786 19

William, d. Sept. 2, 1810 19

William, s. William & Maria, b. Jan. 1, 1818 30

TEW, Sarah, wid., d. Mar. 23, 1807 19

THACHER, John, s. [Thomas, Jr. & Jane], b. Mar. 12, 1806 19

Laura, d. [Thomas, Jr. & Jane], b. Nov. 14, 1800 19

Lucy, d. [Thomas, Jr. & Jane], b. June 19, 1799 19

Polly, d. [Thomas, Jr. & Jane], b. Nov. 14, 1802 19

Thomas, Jr., m. Jane **LEWIS**, Jan. 19, 1798 19

Thomas Jefferson, s. [Thomas, Jr. & Jane], b. June 12, 1804 19

-----, wid., d. Mar. 23, 1812 19

THOMPSON, THOMSON, Calvin, s. [Asahel & Mary], b. Mar. 25, 1798 30

Eleanor, d. [Asahel & Mary], b. May 18, 1802 30

Elisabeth, d. Feb. 7, 1803 19

Ellen, d. Samuel, 2d, & Mary, b. Aug. 20, 1834 44

Emily, d. Samuel, 2d, & Mary, b. Dec. 20, 1818 30

Harvey, s. [Asahel & Mary], b. May 7, 1804 30

Jane, d. Samuel, 2d, & Mary, b. Sept. 19, 1823 44

Joseph Abbot, s. Samuel, 2d, & Mary, b. Apr. 29, 1827 44

Laura, d. Samuel, 2d, & Mary, b. July 17, 1829 44

Leonard, s. [Asahel & Mary], b. Mar. 23, 1800 30

Lory, [child of Asahel & Mary], b. June 31, 1812 30

Luther, s. [Asahel & Mary], b. Jan. 28, 1796 30

Lydia, Mrs., d. June 16, 1832 30

Mary, w. Asahel, d. Mar. 3, 1813 19

Mary, d. Samuel, 2d, & Mary, b. Apr. 18, 1816 30

Mary Ann, d. William C. & Miranda, b. Apr. 23, 1815 19

Mehitable, Mrs., d. Dec. 8, 1845 30

Melissa, d. Harvey & Dorcas, b. Aug. 19, 1825 44

Nancy, d. [Asahel & Mary], b. May 2, 1806 30

Nancy, d. Asahel, d. May 14, 1806 19

Nancy, 2d, d. [Asahel & Mary], b. July 31, 1808 30

Phila E., s. Samuel, 2d, & Mary, b. Jan. 26, 1811 30

Roxalania, m. Asa **WILLEY**, May 10, 1807 20

Ruth, d. Harvey* & Dorcas, b. Apr. 22, 1823 (*Henry?) 44

Samuel, 3rd, s. Samuel, 2d, & Mary, b. Aug. 18, 1813 30

Samuel, d. June 20, 1815 19

Sylidia, d. [Asahel & Mary], b. June 1, 1810 30

Sibel, d. [Asahel & Mary], b. Feb. 27, 1790 19

Sibil, d. Mar. 26, 1813 19

Thankful, d. [Asahel & Mary], b. Sept. 7, 1791 19

William Clark, s. [Asahel & Mary], b. Nov. 28, 1793 19

THRALL, Celinda, see under Sallinda

Clarissa, d. Reuben & Sallinda, b. Nov. 3, 1804 30

Clark, s. [Oliver & Dolly], b. Oct. 30, 1803 19

Page

WELLS, WILLS, (cont.)
Emma, d. [Asa & Chloe], b. Sept. 22, 1817   39
Eunice, Mrs., d. Nov. 12, 1827   23
Gideon, d. Feb. 10, 1806   20
Levi, Jr., m. Eunice **HALL**, Feb. 3, 1791   20
Levi, d. Dec. 18, 1803   20
Levi, s. Asa & Chloe, b. Jan. 28, 1806   20
Levi, d. Apr. 9, 1828   23
Louisa, d. [Asa & Chloe], b. Sept. 8, 1800   20
Lucian, s. Asa & Chloe, b. Oct. 8, 1810   20
Matthew Hyde, s. Asa & Chloe, b. June 16, 1808   20
Rowena, d. [Asa & Chloe], b. Mar. 7, 1802   20
WEST, Laura, m. Joseph **ABBOTT,** Jr., Mar. 12, [ ] 1
WHEELER, Betsey, m. Daniel **JONES,** Oct. 31, 1787   10
WHITE, Benjamin, d. June 1, 1823   23
Benoni H., s. William & Zilpah, b. Oct. 14, 1788   23
Editha had d. Laura **WHITE,** b. June 7, 1824   23
Laura, d. [William & Zilpah], b. May 25, 1804   23
Laura, d. Editha, b. June 7, 1824   23
Nathan, d. Apr. 26, 1805   20
Sophia, d. [William & Zilpah], b. Apr. 4, 1802   23
William, Jr., s. W[illia]m, d. Oct. 18, 1802   20
WHITING, Elisabeth, b. June 20, 1825, in Virginia   42
WHITNEY, Almira, d. [George & Mariam], b. Sept. 3, 1796 20
David, s. [George & Miriam], b. Feb. 18, 1799   20
George Lovel, s. [George & Mariam], b. Jan. 27, 1804   20
Joseph, d. Jan. 27, 1819   23
Mariam, d. [George & Miriam], b. May 17, 1801   20
WHITON, Abigail, d. Flavel & Mary, b. Sept. 28, 1827 39
Betsey, d. Nov. 10, 1828   23
Esther, d. Flavel & Eunice, b. Oct. 7, 1817   23
Esther, Mrs., d. Nov. 14, 1817   23
Flavel, m. Mary **McKNIGHT,** May 12, 1819   20
Flavel, [twin with Flaveline], s. Flavel & Mary, b. Nov. 6, 1832 39
Flaveline, [twin with Flavel], d. Flavel & Mary, b. Nov. 6, 1832 39
Flavia Rodelia, d. Flavel & Mary, b. Nov. 25, 1825   23
Jane Rosetta, d. Flavel & Mary, b. Apr. 2, 1822   23
Mary, d. Flavel & Mary, b. May 13, 1820   23
WILLEY, Asa, m. Roxalania **THOMSON,** May 10, 1807   20
George Thomson, s. Asa & Roxalania, b. Apr. [ ], 1810   20
George Thomson, s. Asa, d. Oct. 26, 1810   20
Junius Marshal, s. Asa & Roxalany, b. May 27, 1821   23
-----, Mrs., d. June 3, 1817   23
WOLCOTT, Amelia, d. Royes* & Dorcas, b. Feb. 2, 1778 (*Arnold Copy
has "Roger")   20
Emelia, m. Wyllys **RUSSELL,** July 16, 1793   16
Jemima, m. James **STEEL,** Nov. 19, 1782   18
WOOD, Elisabeth, m. Allon **SMITH,** July 23, 1789   18

ELLINGTON MARRIAGE RECORDS
PART II
1820 - 1853

165

Page

ANDREWS, Aurelia, of Tolland, m. Ebenezer DOANE, of Vernon, Aug. 28,
   1848   95
  George, of Tolland, m. Amelia CONVERSE, of Ellington, July 5,
   1824   12-12a
ARNOLD, Willard A., of Grafton, Mass., m. Susan BEASLY, of Ellington,
   Jan. 28, 1834   39
ATWOOD, Lodelia, of Somers, m. Peleg MORGAN, Nov. 28, 1839   57
AVERY, Daniel, of Stafford, m. Mary PEASE, of Ellington, Jan. 3, 1843, at
   Ellington   68
  Franklin M., m. Elisabeth L. WARREN, of Vernon, July 4, 1847   88
BADGE, Sally, of Lebanon, m. Ishmael I. JACKSON, of Tolland, Mar.
   19, 1834   40
BAILEY, Polly, of West Springfield, Mass., m. Eliphalet WOODWORTH,
   of Columbia, Conn., May 8, 1824   12-12a
  Randall S., of East Windsor, m. Tamsien BLOOD, of Ellington, May 1,
   1833   35
BAKER, Eliza M., m. William B. WHITTLE, b. of Tolland, Feb. 28, 1846   80
  Israel, Sr., of Vernon, m. An[n] ROYCE, of Tolland, Nov. 21, 1847   90
  Orren, m. Elisabeth W. TALCOTT, Oct. 14, 1844   74
  Sevalla S., of Ellington, m. Samuel P. CHARTER, of Enfield, Oct.
   10, 1847   89
  William, of Ellington, m. Naomi CONGDEN, of Mendon, Mass., Oct.
   15, 1837   51
BALCH, Daniel, of East Windsor, m. Rachel DAVIS, of Mansfield, Sept.
   5, 1830   27
BANCROFT, David Owen, of East Windsor, m. Lovisy HAMILTON, of
   Ellington, Nov. 1, 1826   17
  Lucinda, of East Windsor, m. Leonard BEMENT, of East Hartford,
   Mar. 18, 1849   96
BARBER, Edward W., of South Windsor, m. Sarah D. BEASLEY, of
   Ellington, May 5, 1847   88
  Ralph, of Vernon, m. Maria ISHAM, of Ellington, Oct. 22, 1834   43
BARKER, Ira, of Wilbraham, Mass., m. Eliza L. SWEATMAN, of
   Ellington, Mar. 3, 1830   25
BARNABYE, Ann, of Ellington, m. Alanson HORTON, of East Windsor,
   Apr. 18, 1830   25
BARNES, Asa, of Morristown, N. J., m. Harriet L. CHARTER, of
   Ellington, Oct. 2, 1842   68
BARTHOLDS, William M., m. Harriet RIDER, of Rockville, Apr. 12, 1846   81
BATTEN, Mary I., of Ellington, m. Levi C. COOLEY, of Somers, Oct. 1,
   1843   71
BEASLY, Abagail, m. Lorenzo RISLEY, b. of Ellington, Apr. 25, 1852   105
  Elisabeth, m. Elah C. STACY, b. of Ellington, May 23, 1839   56
  Emaline A., of Ellington, m. E[ ] HANOVER, Major, of Stafford,
   Aug. 29, 1852, in Ellington   105
  Harriet, of Ellington, m. Henry CLARK, of East Windsor, May
   7, 1845   77
  John, Jr., of Ellington, m. Laura An[n] CLARK, of South

Page

BEASLY, (cont.)

Windsor, May 5, 1847   88

Sarah D., of Ellington, m. Edward W. **BARBER**, of South Windsor, May 5, 1847   88

Susan, of Ellington, m. Willard A. **ARNOLD**, of Grafton, Mass., Jan. 28, 1834   39

BEEBE, Martin, m. Anna **PEMBER**, of Ellington, Apr. 15, 1823   9

BELKNAP, Leveritt, of East Windsor, m. Maria **HAMILTON**, of Ellington, Mar. 19, 1835   43

BEMENT, Leonard, of East Hartford, m. Lucinda **BANCROFT**, of East Windsor, Mar. 18, 1849   96

BENTON, Rachel F., of Glastonbury, m. William H. **PERKINS**, Sept. 4, 1835   44

BIDWELL, Weslley(?), of Manchester, m. Lucretia M. **HARRIS**, of Rockville in Vernon, Nov. 8, 1845   79

BILLINGS, Abigail, of Ellington, m. Owen **SNOW**, Feb. 13, 1822   5

Asa H., of Springfield, m. Sarah G. **EATON**, of Longmeadow, June 14, 1846   83

Hiram, m. Parmeccy **TAYLOR**, Feb. 28, 1825   14

Solomon, Jr., of Somers, m. Nabby **STEELE**, of Ellington, Nov. 27, 1822   7

BINGHAM, Eliphalet, of Vernon, m. Catherine **CHAFFEE**, of Tolland, Feb. 16, 1831   29

Ithamer, m. Anne W. **CHAFFEE**, b. of Ellington, July 21, 1833   37

Melinda, m. Philo **McCRAY**, b. of Ellington, Mar. 24, 1834   40

Orra, m. Horace **GARDNER**, b. of Ellington, Nov. 16, 1823   10

BIRGE, Edwin, of East Windsor, m. Esther **WHITAN**, of Ellington, Oct. 2, 1841   64

BISSELL, BISSEL, George S., of Vernon, m. Mary A. **HASKENS**, of Manchester, Mar. 15, 1846   80

Joseph W., of Mary An[n] **HYDE**, b. of Ellington, Jan. 25, 1838   53

BLACKMAN, Charles C., of Pittsfield, Mass., m. Martha J. **McCRAY**, of Ellington, May 6, 1846   82

BLAKE, Louisa, of Manchester, m. Lewis **SIMON**, of Hartford, Sept. 5, 1843   70

BLINN, Elizabeth W., m. Simeon **BLOOD**, b. of Ellington, June 4, 1834   41

BLISS, Henry A., of East Windsor, Broad Brook, m. Catharine A. **GRANT**, of Ellington, Nov. 16, 1847   90

Samuel M., of Wilbraham, Mass., m. Lora **WARNER**, of Ellington, Sept. 30, 1830   27

BLODGET, BLADGET, Jannet, of Ellington, m. Nelson R. **OSBORN**, of East Windsor, Jan. 20, 1836   45

Julia, of Ellington, m. Cyrus **DUNHAM**, of Hebron, Oct. 22, 1823   10

BLOOD, Simeon, m. Elizabeth W. **BLINN**, b. of Ellington, June 4, 1834   41

Tamsien, of Ellington, m. Randall S. **BAILEY**, of East Windsor, May 1, 1833   35

BOAKER, Louis, m. Mina **SCHULZ**, Sept. 17, 1853   105

BONNEY, Lopister, of Hartford, m. Eliza **M'CRAY**, of Ellington, May

Page

BONNEY, (cont.)

29, 1833   36

BOSWORTH, Elijah, of Roxbury, m. Tirzah **DRAKE**, of Ellington, Feb.

20, 1827   19

BRADLEY, Austin, m. Laura **WOODWORTH**, May 9, 1830   26

Elijah, of Stafford, m. Lorenza **TAYLER**, of Ellington, Apr. 3, 1834   41

Elisha K., m. Grace An[n] **GREEN**, of Stafford, Dec. 2, 1841   64

Huldah, m. John Lewis **NEWELL**, June 9, 1821   3

Leonard, of Enfield, m. Roxana **THRALL**, of Ellington, Jan. 30, 1822   4

BRAINARD, W[illia]m H., of Somers, m. Matilda **KIBBEE**, of Ellington,

Apr. 22, 1846   82

BRAMAN, BRUMON, Eliza L., m. Charles W. D. **WRIGHT**, b. of

Ludlow, Mass., Mar. 6, 1842   65

Joseph, m. Amanda **BURBANKS**, b. of Ellington, May 27, 1830   26

Uzziel, m. Orela **KNOABTON**, b. of East Hampton, Mass., June

15, 1832   33-33a

Warren, of Rockville, m. Caroline M. **CLARK**, of Ellington, Nov.

28, 1850   101

BRINK, Abagail T., Mrs., m. Benjamin L. **BRINK**, b. of Ellington,

Sept. 8, 1850   100

Benjamin L., m. Mrs. Abagail T. **BRINK**, b. of Ellington, Sept.

8, 1850   100

BROCKWAY, Edwin, m. Sophronia **WARNER**, b. of Ellington, Sept. 19,

1831   30

BROWN, Constant, of Peterham, Mass., m. Hannah **WARNER**, of

Ellington, Oct. 3, 1825   15-16

David, m. Artemosia B. **BURNHAM**, of Rockville, May 1,

1848   94

Hannah W., of Ellington, m. Walter R. **KIBBE**, of Somers, May 27,

1841   62

Jonas, of Plainfield, Mass., m. Ann **WARNER**, of Ellington, Sept.

26, 1822   6

Ona M., of Ellington, m. Abnour **LEWIS**, of Bristol, May 7, 1835   44

BROWNING, Joseph D., of Brimfield, Mass., m. Submit **McCRAY**, of

Ellington, Oct. 31, 1833   38

BRUCE, William C., of Vernon, m. Abzina **CRANDALL**, of Middlefield,

N. Y., Feb. 9, 1845   76

BUCK, Charles D., of New Orleans, m. Sophronia **SMITH**, of Ellington,

Sept. 18, 1844   73

BUCKLAND, Docia, of Ellington, m. Joel **CLARK**, of East Windsor,

Dec. 6, 1821   4

Fanny, m. Wareham T. **SIMONS**, Oct. 13, 1833   38

Hulda, of Ellington, m. Alexander Hamilton **LORD**, of East

Windsor, Aug. 25, 1833   37

Jonathan, m. Maria An[n] **SNOW**, Nov. 30, 1848   96

Louisa, m. John M. **DRESSER**, Dec. 12, 1830   28

Margaret E., of Ellington, m. Edward **MOSELY**, of Hampton, May

16, 1843   69

Page

CHAPMAN, (cont.)

Aug. 11, 1852 — 105

Charity, of Ellington, m. Cyrus **DONE**, of Coventry, Sept. 21, 1838 — 54

Chester, m. Abigail **LOOMIS**, of Ellington, Mar. 21, 1832 — 32

Chester, m. Elisabeth **BULL**, b. of Ellington, Dec. 28, 1840 — 61

Damaris, m. Thomas W. **CHAPMAN**, Jr., b. of Ellington, Dec. 17, 1840 — 60

Elisabeth, of Ellington, m. Calvin G. **PARSONS**, of East Windsor, May 24, 1849 — 97

Emeline, of Ellington, m. Marcus **SHAW**, of Wilbraham, Mass., Apr. 20, 1842 — 66

Gurdon T., of Ellington, m. Charlotte M. **DART**, of Springfield, Mass., Jan. 19, 1845 — 76

Jabez, m. Charity **McKNIGHT**, b. of Ellington, Nov. 5, 1822 — 6

James, m. Agnes **HARRISON**, Nov. 19, 1820 — 1

Julia, m. William L. **RANSOM**, b. of Ellington, May 21, 1833 — 36

Lucius, m. Rebecca **WILLEY**, of Ellington, Apr. 28, 1830 — 25

Lydia, of Ellington, m. Pliny **CHAPIN**, of Springfield, Mass., May 4, 1821 — 2

Mary W., of Ellington, m. Asahel H. **PERRIN**, of Vernon, Apr. 22, 1842 — 66

Melissa, m. Thomas J. **WHITING**, b. of Ellington, Nov. 17, 1833 — 39

Olivia P., m. Henry **M'KNIGHT**, b. of Ellington, Dec. 24, 1851 — 104

Reuben, of Tolland, m. Eunice **McKINNEY**, of Ellington, Aug. 7, 1833 — 37

Roxa A., of Ellington, m. Seth E. **SACKET**, of Springfield, Mass., Jan. 19, 1845 — 76

Sarah T., of Vernon, m. Eli **READ**, of Ludlow, Mass., Sept. 9, 1850 — 100

Simon, Dea., of Tolland, m. wid. Mary **SPEAR**, of Ellington, June 23, 1825 — 15-15a

Simon C., of Tolland, m. Jerusha **McKNIGHT**, of Ellington, Nov. 4, 1830 — 27

Susan, of Ellington, m. Salathiel [ ], Apr. 1, 1822 — 5

Thomas W., Jr., m. Damaris **CHAPMAN**, b. of Ellington, Dec. 17, 1840 — 60

[CHAPPELL], CHAPPEL, Edward, Jr., of Ellington, m. Violet **WILLIAMS**, of Belcher, Mass., May 11, 1823 — 9

Sally, of Ellington, m. Charles **MOC**(?), of Wilbraham, Nov. 28, 1826 — 18

CHARTER, Aaron, Jr., m. Abigail **WARNER**, Oct. 8, 1835 — 44

An[n] Louisa, of Ellington, m. Addison L. **TRACY**, of Vernon, Rockville, Apr. 5, 1848 — 94

Eunice, of Ellington, m. Rufus **JOHNSON**, of Tolland, Sept. 18, 1820 — 1

Harriet L., of Ellington, m. Asa **BARNES**, of Morristown, N. J., Oct. 2, 1842 — 68

Martha R., of Ellington, m. D. E. **ALLEN**, of East Windsor, Jan. 1, 1851 — 102

Mary, of Ellington, m. Albert **ABORNS**(?), of Tolland, Nov. 27, 1844 — 74

Mary L., of Ellington, m. John S. **FIELD**, of Somers, Apr. 20, 1842 — 65

Nathan W., m. Clarissa M. **NEWELL**, b. of Ellington, Apr. 20, 1843 — 69

Page

CHARTER, (cont.)

Oliver W., m. Sophronia E. **DIMMICK,** b. of Ellington, Nov. 25, 1847   91-2

Samuel, of Ellington, m. Ruth **WEBSTER,** of Tolland, Jan. 22, 1823   8

Samuel P., of Enfield, m. Sevalla S. **BAKER,** of Ellington, Oct. 10, 1847   89

Silvester, m. Sophronia **PAGE,** b. of Enfield, Jan. 1, 1851   102

Sophronia, m. Samuel Milo **DARBY,** b. of Ellington, June 17, 1834   42

CHASE, Anson B., m. Lydia **HUNTLY,** of Ellington, July 4, 1822   5

Joseph, of Tolland, m. Eliza Ann **McKINNEY,** of Ellington, Dec. 18, 1833   29

Lucinda, of Ellington, m. Joel **MARIAM,** June 19, 1823   9

CLAPP, Increase, Mr., of East Windsor, m. Sarah **MORRIS,** of South Wilbraham, Mass., Apr. 19, 1837   50

CLARK, CLARKE, Bradley, of Windsor, m. Jannett **WILLIAMS,** of Windsor, Mar. 17, 1839   56

Caroline M., of Ellington, m. Warren **BRUMON,** of Rockville, Nov. 28, 1850   101

Henry, of East Windsor, m. Harriet **BEASLEY,** of Ellington, May 7, 1845   77

Joel, of East Windsor, m. Docia **BUCKLAND,** of Ellington, Dec. 6, 1821   4

John N., of East Windsor, m. Eleza S. **SNOW,** of Ellington, May 2, 1848   94

Jonathan P., of Somers, m. Clarinda E. **SLATER,** of Ellington, Feb. 5, 1851   102

Laura An[n], of South Windsor, m. John **BEASLEY,** Jr., of Ellington, May 5, 1847   88

Mary A., of N. Mansfield, m. Nathaniel C. **TALMADGE,** of Rockville, Mar. 29, 1846   81

Norman, of East Windsor, m. Emily **LOOMIS,** of Ellington, Jan. 2, 1828   21

Oliver, of [ ], m. Evelina Abagail **SNOW**(?), of Ellington, May 28, 1851   104

Perez, m. Polly **KETH,** b. of Northhampton, Mass., Oct. 7, 1827   20

Sally, Mrs., m. Elisha **BUCKLEY,** Oct. 20, 1824   13

Sally, of Ellington, m. Stephen A. **HASE,** Apr. 9, 1840   58

COBB, Elisabeth, m. John **HARGADIN,** b. of Vernon, Sept. 6, 1846, in Ellington   84

Roxana, of Vernon, m. Edmund **JOSLIN,** of Tolland, Apr. 4, 1847   87

COGSDELL, Mary, m. Austin **NEFF,** Dec. 25, 1832   35

[COGSWELL], COGGSWELL, William F., of Tolland, m. Maria **McKINNEY,** of Ellington, Nov. 20, 1828   22

COLBURN, Jonas, of Stafford, m. Dorcas **NEFF,** of Ellington, July 1, 1840   59

COLEMAN, Timothy, of Coventry, m. Philena **THRALL,** of Ellington, Feb. 17, 1825   14

COLLINS, Jane, of Ellington, m. Franklin **MILLER,** Nov. 28, 1844   74

Louisa, of Ellington, m. Carlos* E. **KIBBEE,** Apr. 8, 1849   *("Charles")   96

Page

DAMON, (cont.)
William m. Ann DAMON, Mar. 7, 1831, b. of Ellington 29
DANIELS, Richard, m. Phebe OCRY, b. of Hartford, Conn., Feb. 10, 1839 55
DART, DARTT, Charlotte M., of Springfield, Mass., m. Gurdon T.
CHAPMAN, of Ellington, Jan. 19, 1845 76
Waite H., m. Calista WILLIS, b. of Somers, May 4, 1851 103
Wolcott, of Manchester, m. Sophia WALDOW, of Ellington, Feb. 9,
1826 15-16
DAVIS, John, of Stafford, m. Amelia ALLEN, of Ellington, Mar. 4, 1850 99
Lester, m. Saphronia LEE, of Stafford, Nov. 28, 1834 43
Rachel, of Mansfield, m. Daniel BALCH, of East Windsor, Sept.
5, 1830 27
DAVIDSON, Clarissa, of Ellington, m. David S. ALLEN, of East Windsor,
Jan. 1, 1838 52
DAVISON, Hannah, of Ellington, m. James WHIDDEN, of East Windsor,
Jan. 7, 1845 75
DAY, Nancy, of Somers, m. Reuben THRALL, of Ellington, Apr. 27, 1837 50
DELANO, William A., m. Sophia HALL, Oct. 21, 1839 57
DERBY, DARBY, Samuel Milo, m. Sophronia CHARTER, b. of Ellington,
June 17, 1834 42
William C., of Enfield, m. Cornelia V. D. CHAFFEE, of Ellington,
Jan. 9, 1850 98
DIBBLE, Loiza, m. Lewis FRENCH(?), b. of Granby, Nov. 7, 1847 90
DICKINSON, Ransom, of Weathersfield, m. Lucy H. SMITH, of Ellington,
May 23, 1830 26
[DIMOCK], DIMMICK, Armessia, m. Lyman MARTIN, b. of Stafford,
Dec. 22, 1844 75
Dan, m. Alithea WOODWORTH, May 10, 1832 33-33a
Elijah, of Peru, Ill., m. Mary A. PHILLIPS, of Ellington, June 7, 1842 66
Harriot, of Ellington, m. Lorain DIMMICK, of Stafford, May 23, 1831 30
Harvey, m. Harriet NEWELL, b. of Ellington, Feb. 4, 1824 12-12a
Lois, of Ellington, m. George WATTS, of Chalorsville, Ohio,
July 1, 1821 3
Lorain, of Stafford, m. Harriot DIMMICK, of Ellington, May 23, 1831 30
Nancy, of Ellington, m. Erastus FOOT, of Mantua, Ohio, June
28, 1821 3
Sophronia E., m. Oliver W. CHARTER, b. of Ellington, Nov. 25, 1847 91-2
DOANE, DONE, Cyrus, of Coventry, m. Charity CHAPMAN, of Ellington,
Sept. 21, 1838 54
Desire, m. George L. CARPENTER, July 6, 1851 103
Ebenezer, of Vernon, m. Aurelia ANDREWS, of Tolland, Aug. 28,
1848 95
William, m. Abiah SPENCER, b. of Somers, Jan. 23, 1842, at
Ellington 64
DORCHESTER(?), Susannah, m. Arnold ISHAM, June 21, 1829 24
DORMAN, Artonsia, of Ellington, m. Calvin CHAPMAN, of Tolland, Apr.
14, 1831 29

Page

DORMAN, (cont.)

John, m. Amelia **SMITH,** b. of Ellingtin, Apr. 22, 1832   33-33a

DOW*, Mary An[n], of Ellington, m. Frederick M. **WALKER,** of Enfield,
May 18, 1843 *("DAN"?)   69

DRAKE, Tirzah, of Ellington, m. Elijah **BOSWORTH,** of Roxbury, Feb.
20, 1827   19

DRESSER, John M., m. Louisa **BUCKLAND,** Dec. 12, 1830   28

DUNHAM, Chauncey J., m. Jane S. **FENTON,** of Vernon, July 3, 1845   77

Cyrus, of Hebron, m. Julia **BLADGET,** of Ellington, Oct. 22, 1823   10

Julia An[n], m. Benjamin **HAMILTON,** b. of Ellington, Dec. 17, 1837   52

DWYER, Philo, of Vernon, m. Juliette **MARTIN,** of Ellington, Oct. 21,
1847   90

DYER, Mary Jane, of Tolland, m. Chauncey **FIELD,** of Somers, Nov. 25,
1841   63

Sarah M., of Somers, m. Thomas S. **WASHBURN,** of Rockville, June
22, 1851   104

EARL, William P.,of Hartford, m. Elisabeth **PINNEY,** of Ellington, Apr.
13, 1836   46

EATON, Alonzo L., of Stafford, m. Mary L. **STONE,** of Rockville, July
28, 1844, in Ellington   72

Isaac H., of Tolland, m. Ethelynda **TAYLOR,** of Ellington, Nov.
30, 1820   2

Jane L., of Stafford, m. William **RICHARDSON,** of Somers, Oct. 6,
1846   85

John C., m. Ulrica **FRINK,** Dec. 12, 1830   28

Mary, of Ellington, m. Moses **ALLEN,** of Vernon, Apr. 12, 1848   92-3

Oliver, m. Clarissa **McKINNEY,** of Ellington, Dec. 18, 1845   79

Phebe, of Ellington, m. Timothy **CARPENTER,** Mar. 5, 1848   92-3

Sarah G., of Longmeadow, m. Asa H. **BILLINGS,** of Springfield,
June 14, 1846   83

Solomon, of Tolland, m. Pheba **GLEASON,** of Ellington, Aug. 10,
1828   22

EDMUNDS, Malissa I., of Vernon, Rockville Society, m. Jonas S.
PARKER, Mar. 28, 1847   87

EDSON, Emily, of Stafford, m. Austin **NEFF,** of Ellington, Jan. 26, 1841   61

EDWARDS, Almira, m. Austin **GROVES,** Aug. 22, 1824   13

Joseph, of Ellington, m. Submit **HOWARD,** of Somers, Oct. 27, 1823   10

ELLIS, Benjamin, of Longmeadow, Mass., m. Emeline **KIMBALL,** of
Somers, Conn., Mar. 5, 1835   43

ELY, Angeline R., m. Edward C. **HOLTON,** Apr. 12, 1850   99

Lora, of Ellington, m. John B. **McCRAY,** May 17, 1843   69

Oscar, m. Rebecca **PRATT,** b. of Ellington, Aug. 28, 1844   73

FALLS(?), Thurlene, of Butternuts, N. Y., m. Mary **McNALL,** of Ellington,
Oct. 8, 1844   73

FARMER, Cornelia, of Ellington, m. Benjamin S. **HURLBERT,** of
Amherst, Mass., June 11, 1846   83

Sarah, m. Justus **PEMBER,** b. of Ellington, Sept. 22, 1841   63

FARNHAM, Asa, m. Betsey **POTTAGE,** Mar. 27, 1825   15-15a

Page

FARNSWORTH, Elisabeth, of Stafford, m. Henry I. KENEE, of
    Manchester, Apr. 12, 1848   92-3
FENTON, Jane S., of Vernon, m. Chauncey J. DUNHAM, July 3, 1845   77
FIELD, Chauncey, of Somers, m. Mary Jane DYER, of Tolland, Nov. 25,
    1841   63
    John S., of Somers, m. Mary L. CHARTER, of Ellington, Apr. 20,
    1842   65
FIRMIN(?), Horace, of Wilbraham, Mass., m. Orpha J. WOOD, of Somers,
    Nov. 29, 1838   55
FISH, Charles E., of Tolland, m. Ann E. PERRIN, of Vernon, Sept. 28,
    1845   78
FLETCHER, John, m. Armessia D. HARWOOD, b. of Stafford, May 21,
    1848   95
FLINT, Ariel, of Quincy, Ill., m. Persis PINNEY, of Ellington, June
    6, 1832   33-33a
FOOT, Erastus, of Mantua, Ohio, m. Nancy DIMMICK, of Ellington, June
    28, 1821   3
FOSTER, Abagail A., of Ellington, m. Jonathan E. HALE, of Somers,
    Jan. 16, 1845   76
    Augusta, of Ellington, m. Henry MANNING, of Lebanon, Nov. 14,
    1850   101
    Charlotte, of Ellington, m. Daniel B. WATERMAN, of Hartford,
    Mar. 28, 1836   46
    Miranda, of Ellington, m. Fuller RANSAN, of Vernon, Mar. 18, 1847 87
    Phila, of Ellington, m. Lemuel WARNER, Jr., July 9, 1820, by
    Asa Willey, J. P.   1
FOWLER, Anson, of Lebanon, m. Roxana PEASE, of Ellington, Jan. 13,
    1850   98
    Sarah M., of Ellington, m. William S. WELLS, of Pittsfield, Mass.,
    Oct. 15, 1846   85
FOX, Daniel D., of Bolton, m. Minerva ALLEN, of Ellington, Nov. 16,
    1831   30
FRANKLIN, Henry, m. Sally ALLEN, Oct. 22, 1837   51
FRENCH(?), Lewis, m. Loiza DIBBLE, b. of Granby, Nov. 7, 1847   90
FRINK, Ulrica, m. John C. EATON, Dec. 12, 1830   28
FULLER, Dorcas, of Ellington, m. Harvey THOMPSON, Mar. 26, 1822   5
    Gorham, m. Jemima HAMILTON, b. of Ellington, Mar. 31, 1850   99
    Hannah H., of Ellington, m. Nelson H. RICH, of Chicopee, Mass.,
    Nov. 12, 1850   101
    Harriet E., of Ellington, m. W[illia]m A. OSBORNE, of Pittsfield,
    Mass., May 10. 1846   82
    Jane T., of Ellington, m. William E. ROLLO, of Springfield, Mass.,
    Oct. 26, 1845   78
    Joseph, m. Betsey WALLACE, of Ellington, June 27, 1822   5
    Lucinda, of Stafford, m. Gustavus CUSHMAN, of Somers, Oct. 26,
    1845   78
    Persis L., of Vernon, m. Henry R. SMITH, of East Windsor, May

Page

FULLER, (cont.)

3, 1840   58

GABRIEL, Anthony, of Ellington, m. Laura **HALL,** of Longmeadow, Mass.,

Nov. 29, 1838   55

GAGER, William A., m. Laura E. **NILES,** b. of Ellington, Nov. 23, 1845   79

GARDNER, Horace, m. Orra **BINGHAM,** b. of Ellington, Nov. 16, 1823   10

Nicholas G., m. Reliance **WILLIAMS,** of Ellington, Apr. 23, 1837   49

[GAYLORD], GALORD, Caroline, of Weathersfield, m. Newman A.

HUNTLEY, of Ellington, June 15, 1839   57

GIFFORD, Amanda, m. Austin **McKINNEY,** b. of Ellington, Oct. 18, 1832   34-34a

Louisa, m. Justus **PEMBER,** b. of Ellington, Apr. 23, 1833   35

GLAZIER, Sylvester, of Vernon, m. Manissa **McKINNEY,** of Ellington,

June 27, 1827   20

GLEASON, Pheba, of Ellington, m. Solomon **EATON,** of Tolland, Aug.

10, 1828   22

GOODELL, Francis, of Ellington, m. Sophia L. **BURPEE,** of Somers,

Nov. 23, 1843   71

Sally, of Ellington, m. Lotrop **PEASE,** of Vernon, Apr. 1, 1841   62

GOWDY, Franklin, of East Windsor, m. Martha **JOHNSON,** of Ellington,

Apr. 15, 1846   81

GRANT, Catharine A., of Ellington, m. Henry A. **BLISS,** of East Windsor,

Broad Brook, Nov. 16, 1847   90

Harriet S., of Ellington, m. Lyman W. **CRANE,** of Windsor, Nov. 2,

1846   86

Luther, of East Windsor, m. Huldah **HAMILTON,** of Ellington, Sept.

20, 1827   20

Sanford, Esq., of Vernon, m. Mary M. **KINNEY,** of Ellington, Mar.

21, 1837   49

Sidney, of New York, m. Mary Ann **McKENNEY,** of Ellington, Mar.

27, 1827   19

GRAY, Emily H., of Stafford, m. Elijah **NEFF,** of Ellington, Nov. 24,

1846   86

Gilbert, of Bolton, m. Harriet **NEFF,** of Ellington, July 4, 1838   53

Nancy E., of Rockville, m. Andrew **CAMPBELL,** of Stafford, Nov. 24,

1846   86

Persis, of Enfield, m. John **PARKER,** Sept. 19, 1844   73

William, of Manchester, m. Eliza **THOMPSON,** of Ellington, June

28, 1842   67

GREEN, Grace An[n], of Stafford, m. Elisha K. **BRADLEY,** Dec. 2, 1841   64

Laura An[n], of Ellington, m. Lorin **TRASK,** of Stafford, June 25,

1848   95

GRIFFIN, Maria, m. Moses **ALLEN,** b. of Ellington, Apr. 28, 1850   99

GRIGGS, Daniel, Jr., of Tolland, m. Harriet B. **HASBACK,** of Ellington,

Dec. 13, 1840   60

GROVES, Austin, m. Almira **EDWARDS,** Aug. 22, 1824   13

HALE, Jonathan E., of Somers, m. Abagail A. **FOSTER,** of Ellington, Jan.

16, 1845   76

HALL, Emeline, m. Calvin N. **KIBBE,** b. of Springfield, Sept. 3, 1845   77

HALL, (cont.)
Laura, of Longmeadow, Mass., m. Anthony **GABRIEL,** of Ellington,
Nov. 29, 1838   55
Sophia, m. William A. **DELANO,** Oct. 21, 1839   57
HAMILTON, Abigail, of Ellington, m. Lewis **HAYES,** of East Windsor,
Nov. 23, 1826   18
Benjamin, of Ellington, m. Julia An[n] **DUNHAM,** of Ellington,
Dec. 17, 1837   52
Daniel, m. Mrs. Clarissa **MAXON,** b. of Ellington, Apr. 22, 1849   97
Havillah, of East Windsor, m. Betsey M. **ALLEN,** of Ellington,
June 1, 1843   70
Huldah, of Ellington, m. Luther **GRANT,** of East Windsor, Sept.
20, 1827   20
Jemima, m. Gorham **FULLER,** b. of Ellington, Mar. 31, 1850   99
John, m. Sarepta **ABBE,** of Ellington, May 2, 1844   72
Lovisy, of Ellington, m. David Owen **BANCROFT,** of East Windsor,
Nov. 1, 1826   17
Maria, of Ellington, m. Leveritt **BELKNAP,** of East Windsor,
Mar. 19, 1835   43
Marsha, of Hartford, m. Eli **PARKISS,** of Ellington, Sept. 20, 1840   59
Martha, of Ellington, m. James R. **PARSONS,** of Ludlow, Mass., Apr.
19, 1837   50
Olive, m. Robert M. **ROGERS,** b. of Ellington, Dec. 6, 1831   31
Sarah, of Ellington, m. Israel **SILLSWERTH,** of Hanibal, New York,
Oct. 1, 1834   42
[HANNIFORD], HANNAFORD, John, of Hartford, m. Louisa F. **MEECH,**
of Ellington, June 12, 1843   70
HANOVER, E[ ], Major, of Stafford, m. Emaline A. **BEASLEY,** of
Ellington, Aug. 29, 1852, in Ellington   105
Melina, Mrs., of Somers, m. John T. **OLCOTT,** of Vernon,
[Apr. 8], 1849   96-7
HARGADIN, John, m. Elisabeth **COBB,** b. of Vernon, Sept. 6, 1846, in
Ellington   84
HARR[E]NDON, Horace, m. Nancy **THOMPSON,** Dec. 9, 1824   14
HARRIS, Lucretia M. of Rockville, in Vernon, m. Weslley(?) **BIDWELL,**
of Manchester, Nov. 8, 1845   79
HARRISON, Agnes, m. James **CHAPMAN,** Nov. 19, 1820   1
Wadsworth, m. Betsey **SMITH,** b. of Ellington, Oct. 21, 1827   20
HARWOOD, Armessia D., m. John **FLETCHER,** b. of Stafford, May 21,
1848   95
Hannah A., of Stafford, m. Anson S. **LULL,** May 30, 1848   94
HARVEY, Abial, of Enfield, m. Elisabeth **CHAFFEE,** of Somers, Feb.
24, 1850   98
HASBACK, Harriet B., of Ellington, m. Daniel **GRIGGS,** Jr., of Tolland,
Dec. 13, 1840   60
HASKELL, Joseph, m. Thankfull **DAMON,** July 23, 1820   1
HASKENS, Mary A., of Manchester, m. George S. **BISSEL,** of Vernon,

Page

HASKENS, (cont.)

Mar. 15, 1846

HAYES, HASE, Betsey M., of Ellington, m. David ALLEN, June 18, 1829   23

Julia An[n], of Ellington, m. William TALBOT, of Granby, Apr.
13, 1836   46

Lewis, of East Windsor, m. Abigail HAMILTON, of Ellington, Nov.
23, 1826   18

Stephen A., m. Sally CLARK, of Ellington, Apr. 9, 1840   58

HENDRICK, Pearson, of East Hampton, m. Polly MOSELEY, of Westfield,
Mass., Nov. 16, 1826   18

HENRY, Lemuel, m. Lousia PARKISS, Nov. 24, 1831   31

HIBBARD, Roxana R., of Tolland, m. Nelson E. PINNEY, of Ellington,
May [ ], 1845   77

HITCHCOK, Harriet, of Bloomfield, m. Joseph S. PHELPS, of Somers,
Nov. 22, 1837   52

HOLMES, Lovina, of Stafford, m. Henry A. KINGSBURY, of Ellington,
July 7, 1847   89

HOLTON, HOLTEN, Abigail W., of Ellington, m. Marvin CONE, of
Manchester, Oct. 14, 1829   24

Damaris H., of Ellington, m. Caleb HOPKINS, of Springfield, Mass.,
Sept. 4, 1834   42

Edward C., m. Angeline R. ELY, Apr. 12, 1850   99

Israel P., m. Jerusha M'KINSTRY, of Ellington, Apr. 19, 1849   97

Roger W., m. Mary SMITH, b. of Ellington, June 18, 1834   41

Sarah, of Ellington, m. Wyllys THRALL, Mar. 27, 1825   15-15a

HOPKINS, Caleb, of Springfield, Mass., m. Damaris H. HOLTON, of
Ellington, Sept. 4, 1834   42

Joseph B., of Springfield, m. Mary Amelia RUSSELL, of Ellington,   7
Sept. 19, 1832   34-34a

HORTON, HORTEN, Alanson, of East Windsor, m. Ann BARNABYE, of
Ellington, Apr. 19, 1830   25

Lucius C., of Vernon, Rockville, m. Jane A. CARPENTER, of
Tolland, Apr. 18, 1847   88

HOUSE, Abigail, of Hartford, m. Giles REMINGTON, Dec. 14, 1831,
at Ellington   31

HOWARD, Submit, of Somers, m. Joseph EDWARDS, of Ellington, Oct.
27, 1823   10

HOYT, Josiah B., of Enfield, Conn., m. Elisabeth WILLIAMS, of Windsor,
July 3, 1847   88

HUBBARD, Henry, of Hartford, m. Delia PEASE, of Ellington, Aug. 12,
1832   34-34a

HUGHES, John A., of New Haven, m. Rebecca L. BULL, of Ellington,
Mar. 20, 1842   65

HUMPHREY, Eunice P., m. Joseph McCLARY, Nov. 28, 1833   39

George, of Hartford, m. Mary Ann MARTIN, of Ellington, Nov.
11, 1832   34-34a

George, of Hartford, m. Emily MARTIN, of Ellington, June 20, 1838   54

HUNT, Charles V. N., of Louisville, Kentucky, m. Betsey SMITH, of

Page

HUNT, (cont.)
    Ellington, Oct. 21, 1851   104
    Laura P., of Vernon, m. Addison L. **TRACY,** Jan. 14, 1845, at
        Ellington   75
HUNTLEY, HUNTLY, Lydia, of Ellington, m. Anson B. **CHASE,** July 4,
    1822   5
    Newman A., of Ellington, m. Caroline **GALORD,** of Westersfield, June
        15, 1839   57
HURLBURT, HULBERT, HURLBERT, Benjamin S., of Amherst, Mass.,
    m. Cornelia **FARMER,** of Ellington June 11, 1846   83
    Gaius P. m. Laura* M. **SPENCER,** b. of Somers, Jan. 13, 1850
        *("Lucy" first written)   98
    Lor[e]nzo, of Somers, m. Maria **SMITH,** of Ellington, Nov. 25, 1841   64
HYDE, Mary An[n], m. Joseph W. **BISSELL,** b. of Ellington, Jan. 25, 1838   53
    Nancy, of Ellington, m. Nathaniel **SQUIRE,** of Ashford, June 21, 1829   23
    Oliver M., m. Mary **THOMSON,** b. of Ellington, Nov. 9, 1837   52
    Sarah, m. William **SMITH,** Aug. 21, 1842   67
    Tirza, m. Moses **ALLEN,** b. of Ellington, Mar. 19, 1827   19
    Uriah R., m. Martha **THRALL,** of Ellington, Sept. 29, 1825   15-16
INMAN, Dewey, of Somers, m. Eleanor **THOMPSON,** of Ellington, Aug.
    29, 1824   13
IRWIN, Mary An[n], of Ellington, m. Henry **SWIFT,** of Rockville,
    Jan. 26, 1851   102
ISHAM, Arnold, m. Susannah **DORCHESTER**(?), June 21, 1829   24
    Maria, of Ellington, m. Ralph **BARBER,** of Vernon, Oct. 22, 1834   43
JACKSON, Ishmael I., of Tolland, m. Sally **BADGE,** of Lebanon, Mar.
    19, 1834   40
JAMES, Harriet J., of Meriden, m. Ely F. **PARKISS,** of Ellington,
    Jan. 2, 1845   75
JOHNSON, Betsey, m. Timothy **CARPENTER,** b. of Ellington, Dec. 8,
    1823   11-11a
    Elizabeth, of Ellington, m. William H. **VINTON,** of Monson, Mass.,
        May 8, 1839   56
    Emeline, of Ellington, m. S[   ] **STREETER,** of Keene, N. H.,
        May 19, 1836   47
    Julian, m. Asa R. **MANLEY,** May 2, 1827   20
    Loranza M., of Ellington, m. Aaron **PEASE,** of Chatham, Dec. 23,
        1831   32
    Martha, of Ellington, m. Franklin **GOWDY,** of East Windsor, Apr.
        15, 1846   81
    Mary, of Stafford, m. Henry **PINNEY,** of Ellington, Oct. 19, 1848   96
    Rufus, of Tolland, m. Eunice **CHARTER,** of Ellington, Sept. 18, 1820   1
JOSLIN, Edmund, of Tolland, m. Roxana **COBB,** of Vernon, Apr. 4, 1847   87
JUDSON, Samuel H., of Southbridge, Mass., m. Mary **McCRAY,** of
    Ellington, June 10, 1834   41
KEENEY, Albert, m. Jane R. **WHITON,** b. of Ellington, Apr. 15, 1841   62
[KEITH], KETH, Polly, m. Perez **CLARK,** b. of Northampton, Mass.,
    Oct. 7, 1827   20

KENEE, Henry L., of Manchester, m. Elisabeth **FARNSWORTH**, of
    Stafford, Apr. 12, 1848   92-3
[KIBBY], **KIBBE, KIBBEE**, Calvin N., m. Emeline **HALL**, b. of
    Springfield, Sept. 3, 1845   77
    Carlos* E., m. Louisa **COLLINS**, of Ellington, Apr. 8, 1849
        ("Charles)   96
    Haney A., of Ellington, m. Roland **SELEW**, of Glastonbury, Dec.
        27, 1838   55
    Helen C., m. Nelson **WARNER**, b. of Ellington, Mar. 23, 1851   103
    Julius, m. Ellen **WARNER**, b. of Ellington, Jan. 21, 1851   102
    Matilda, of Ellington, m. W[illia]m H. **BRAINARD**, of Somers,
        Apr. 22, 1846   82
    Walter R., of Somers, m. Hannah W. **BROWN**, of Ellington, May 27,
        1841   62
KIMBALL, Daniel N., m. Jane **THOMPSON**, b. of Ellington, Jan. 20, 1848   91-2
    Elijah P., of Springfield, Mass., m. Mary T. **RUSSELL**, of Ellington,
        Oct. 27, 1836   48
    Emeline, of Somers, Conn., m. Benjamin **ELLIS**, of Longmeadow,
        Mass., Mar. 5, 1835   43
    Josiah, m. Eunice **DAMON**, b. of Ellington, Sept. 18, 1828   22
    Roxana Roman, of Ellington, m. Henry **McCRAY**, Dec. 17, 1846   87
KING, George T., m. Lucy A. **WHEELER**, of West Springfield, Mass.,
    Mar. 10, 1846   80
    Jane, of Ellington, m. Asaph **McKINNEY**, of Vernon, Apr. 28, 1840   58
    Jeremiah, m. Esther **WARD**, b. of Ellington, Nov. 15, 1821   4
    John M. B., of Vernon, m. Emeline **SMITH**, of Ellington, Dec. 3, 1828   23
    Oliver H., Esq., of Vernon, m. Eunice **PINNEY**, of Ellington,
        Nov. 24, 1824   14
KINGSBURY, Henry A., of Ellington, m. Lovina **HOLMES**, of Stafford,
    July 7, 1847   89
KINNEY, Mary M., of Ellington, m. Sanford **GRANT**, Esq., of Vernon,
    Mar. 21, 1837   49
KNOABTON, Orela, m. Uzziel **BRAMAN**, b. of East Hampton, Mass., June
    15, 1832   33-33a
LANGDON, John W., of Wilbraham, Mass., m. Louisa L. **M'CRAY**, of
    Ellington, Nov. 18, 1840   60
LAWRENCE, Henry H., of Middlebury, Vt., m. Martha Ann **THRALL**,
    Oct. 2, 1850   100
LEE, Nelson, of Hebron, m. Sophia **NEFF**, of Vernon, Nov. 28, 1847   90
    Saphronia, of Stafford, m. Lester **DAVIS**, Nov. 28, 1834   43
LEONARD, George L., of Thompson, Ohio, m. Julia **ALLEN**, of Ellington,
    Sept. 17, 1848   95
LEWIS, Abnour, of Bristol, m. Ona M. **BROWN**, of Ellington, May 7, 1835   44
    Mary M., m. Henry A. **SWEET**, b. of Tolland, Sept. 2, 1838   54
LIEPS(?), Catharine, m. John **ZIMERMAN**, b. of Ellington, Feb. 24, 1850   98
LINCOLN, Sarah B., of Ellington, m. Ralph **SCRIPTURE**, of Vernon, Mar.
    31, 1841, in Ellington   61

LIVELY(?), Amos, of Havanna, Alabama, m. Mary B. SEXTON, of
    Ellington, Sept. 22, 1836   48
LOOMIS, Abigail, of Ellington, m. Chester CHAPMAN, Mar. 21, 1832   32
    Congdon P., of Enfield, m. Esther NEWTON, of Enfield, Apr. 8, 1838   53
    Emily, of Ellington, m. Norman CLARKE, of East Windsor, Jan. 2,
        1828   21
    Harriet, of Somers, Conn., m. Watson CROCKER, of Granville, Mass.,
        Dec. 18, 1842   68
LORD, Alexander Hamilton, of East Windsor, m. Hulda BUCKLAND, of
    Ellington, Aug. 25, 1833   37
    Lavinia, of Ellington, m. Andrew MACLEAN(?), of Lower Sanduskey,
        Ohio, Nov. 2, 1840   60
    Sidney F., of East Windsor, m. Margaret M. WARNER, of Enfield,
        Apr. 10, 1842   65
LOVELL, Jane, of Ellington, m. Amanda(?) POND, of Bristol, Apr. 23,
    1851   103
LOVETT, Persis M., of Ellington, m. Experience STEARNS, of
    Manchester, June 30, 1846   83
LULL, Anson S., m. Hannah A. HARWOOD, of Stafford, May 30, 1848   94
LYMAN, Wadsworth P., of Northamton, Mass., m. Roby An[n] MARTIN,
    of Ellington, Sept. 6, 1846, in Ellington   84
LYON, Asa P., of Springfield, m. Emeline TAYLOR, of Ellington, Aug.
    13, 1828   21
McCLARY, Joseph, m. Eunice, P. HUMPHREY, Nov. 28, 1833   39
McCRAY, Asenath, of Ellington, m. Eleazer S. PITKIN, of East Hartford,
    Nov. 13, 1822   7
    Chloe, of Ellington, m. Abraham ALLEN, of East Windsor, Oct. 23,
        1822   6
    Eliza, of Ellington, m. Lopister BONNEY, of Hartford, May 29, 1833   36
    Fanny E., m. Henry G. RANSOM, b. of Ellington, May 12, 1848   92-3
    Guilford, m. Harriet WARNER, b. of Ellington, May 13, 1821   3
    Henry, m. Roxana Roman KIMBALL, of Ellington, Dec. 17, 1846   87
    John R., m. Lora ELY, of Ellington, May 17,1843   69
    Louisa L., of Ellington, m. John W. LANGDON, of Wilbraham, Mass.,
        Nov. 18, 1840   60
    Margaret, of Ellington, m. Joseph WORK, of Wilbraham, Jan. 9, 1823   7
    Maria, of Ellington, m. Lorin STACY, of Wilbraham, Mass., Oct. 29,
        1835   45
    Martha J., of Ellington, m. Charles C. BLACKMAN, of Pittsfield,
        Mass., May 6, 1846   82
    Mary, of Ellington, m. Samuel H. JUDSON, of Southbridge,
        Mass., June 10, 1834   41
    Philo, m. Melinda BINGHAM, b. of Ellington, Mar. 24, 1834   40
    Submit, of Ellington, m. Joseph D. BROWNING, of Brimfield,
        Oct. 31, 1833   38
McGREGORY, Mary, of Ellington, m. Jeremiah WATROUS, of E.
    Longmeadow, May 6, 1846   82

Page

McKENNEY, McKINNEY, Asaph, of Vernon, m. Jane KING, of Ellington,
Apr. 28, 1840 58

Austin, m. Amanda GIFFORD, b. of Ellington, Oct. 18, 1832 .... 34-34a

Clarissa, of Ellington, m. Oliver EATON, Dec. 18, 1845 79

Eliza Ann, of Ellington, m. Joseph CHASE, of Tolland, Dec. 18, 1833 39

Eunice, of Ellington, m. Reuben CHAPMAN, of Tolland, Aug. 7, 1833 37

Jane, of Ellington, m. Joseph M. MORRISSON, of West Springfield,
Mass., Feb. 6, 1848 91-2

Julia A., m. Elijah C. NYE, Nov. 30, 1843 72

Manissa, of Ellington, m. Sylvester GLAZIER, of Vernon, June 27,
1827 20

Maria, of Ellington, m. William F. COGGSWELL, of Tolland, Nov.
20, 1828 22

Mary Ann, of Ellington, m. Sidney GRANT, of New York, Mar. 27,
1827 19

Miranda, of Ellington, m. Nelson PINNEY, Dec. 27, 1827 21

M'KINSTRY, Jerusha, of Ellington, m. Israel P. HOLTEN, Apr. 19, 1849 97

McKNIGHT, Charity, m. Jabez CHAPMAN, b. of Ellington, Nov. 5, 1822 6

Henry, m. Olivia P. CHAPMAN, b. of Ellington, Dec. 24, 1851 104

James D., m. Mary F. THOMPSON, b. of Ellington, Oct. 10, 1850 101

Jerusha, of Ellington, m. Simon C. CHAPMAN, of Tolland, Nov. 4,
1830 27

Sarah, of Ellington, m. Christopher H. TERRY, of Enfield, May
9, 1833 36

McLEAN, MACLEAN, Andrew, of Lower Sanduskey, Ohio, m. Lavinia
LORD, of Ellington, Nov. 2, 1840 60

Otis, of Vernon, m. Clarissa MUNSEL, of Ellington, July 16, 1822 6

McNALL, Mary, of Ellington, m. Thurlene FALLS(?), of Butternuts,
N. Y., Oct. 8, 1844 73

MANLEY, Asa B., m. Julian JOHNSON, May 2, 1827 20

Chloe, of Ellington, m. Edward PAGE, Jan. 1, 1823 7

Deletia H., m. Anson NEFF, June 3, 1838, in Ellington 53

Eliza, m. Lemuel RUSSELL, b. of Ellington, Nov. 17, 1844 74

MANNING, Henry, of Lebanon, m. Augusta FOSTER, of Ellington, Nov.
14, 1850 101

MARIAM, Joel, m. Lucinda CHASE, of Ellington, June 19, 1823 9

MARTIN, Betsey, of Ellington, m. John STREETER, of Somers, Dec. 1,
1831 31

Emily, of Ellington, m. George HUMPHREY, of Hartford, June 20,
1838 54

Joseph, m. Cynthia SMITH, of Ellington, Sept. 24, 1823 10

Juliette, of Ellington, m. Philo DWYER, of Vernon, Oct. 21, 1847 90

Louisa M., of Ellington, m. Jonathan H. MOORE, of Worcester,
Mass., Mar. 28, 1839 56

Lyman, m. Armessia DIMMICK, b. of Stafford, Dec. 22, 1844 75

Mary Ann, of Ellington, m. George HUMPHREY, of Hartford,
Nov. 11, 1832 .... 34-34a

Matilda, of Ellington, m. Horace WARNER, Oct. 1, 1826 17

Page

MARTIN, (cont.)
Roby An[n], of Ellington, m. Wadsworth P. **LYMAN,** of Northamton,
Mass., Sept. 6, 1846, in Ellington 84
MAXON, Clarissa, Mrs., m. Daniel **HAMILTON,** b. of Ellington, Apr.
22, 1849 97
MAYNARD, William C., m. Betsey **ST. CLAIR,** b. of Ellington, Aug.
3, 1831 30
MEACHAM, Henry, of Somers, m. Emily **SLAFTER,** of Ellington, Jan. 4,
1847, in Ellington 86
MEECH, Louisa F., of Ellington, m. John **HANNAFORD,** of Hartford, June
12, 1843 70
[MERTON], MERTEN, Frederick, of East Windsor, m. Clarissa B.
PARKER, of South Coventry, Oct. 18, 1847 89
MILLER, Franklin, m. Jane **COLLINS,** of Ellington, Nov. 28, 1844 74
MOC(?), Charles, of Wilbraham, m. Sally **CHAPPEL,** of Ellington, Nov.
28, 1826 18
MOODY, Emeline, of Ellington, m. Alfred A. **PRISBEY,** of Willington,
Apr. 9, 1848 92-3
Harriet P., m. E. C. V. **PINNEY,** b. of Ellington, June 8, 1851 104
MOORE, Asenath, of Ellington, m. Ames **PEASE,** of Somers, May 24,
1849 97
Clark B., of Willington, m. Amelia M. **CHAPMAN,** of Ellington,
Oct. 12, 1843 71
Jonathan H., of Worcester, Mass., m. Louisa M. **MARTIN,** of
Ellington, Mar. 28, 1839 56
Martha G., of Hartford, m. Marshall V. **TIBBILS,** June 7, 1846 83
Mary, m. Andrew **PINNEY,** b. of Ellington, Jan. 23, 1833 35
MORGAN, Peleg, m. Lodelia **ATWOOD,** of Somers, Nov. 28, 1839 57
MORRIS, Sarah, of South Wilbraham, Mass., m. Increase **CLAPP,** of
East Windsor, Apr. 19, 1837 50
MORRISON, MORRISSON, Jacob, colored, of Somers, m. Harriet
PARKISS, colored, of Ellington, Sept. 29, 1833 37
Joseph M., of West Springfield, Mass., m. Jane **M'KINNEY,** of
Ellington, Feb. 6, 1848 91-2
MOSELEY, MOSELY, Edward, of Hampton, m. Margaret E.
BUCKLAND, of Ellington, May 16, 1843 69
Polly, of Westfield, Mass., m. Pearson **HENDRICK,** of East Hampton,
Nov. 16, 1826 18
William, Jr., of Wilbraham, Mass., m. Eunice P. **DAMON,** of
Ellington, May 19, 1842 66
MUMFORD, Martha An[n], of Springfield, Mass., m. Otis **PHILLIPS,**
of Somers, May 25, 1848 94
MUNSELL, MUNSEL, Clarissa, of Ellington, m. Otis **McLEAN,** of
Vernon, July 16, 1822 6
Sabra, of East Windsor, m. John **SCRIPTURE,** of Willington,
Nov. 23, 1825 15-16
NEFF, Anson, m. Deletia H. **MANLEY,** June 3, 1838, in Ellington 53
Asa, m. Candace **CUNNINGHAM,** July 5, 1835 44

Page

NEFF, (cont.)

Austin, m. Mary **COGSDELL**, Dec. 25, 1832   35

Austin, of Ellington, m. Emily **EDSON**, of Stafford, Jan. 26, 1841   61

Dorcas, of Ellington, m. Jonas **COLBURN**, of Stafford, July 1, 1840   59

Elijah, of Ellington, m. Emily H. **GRAY**, of Stafford, Nov. 24, 1846   86

Harriet, of Ellington, m. Gilbert **GRAY**, of Bolton, July 4, 1838   53

Jamima, m. Calvin Otis **PEASE**, Dec. 29, 1839, at Ellington   58

Sophia, of Vernon, m. Nelson **LEE**, of Hebron, Nov. 28, 1847   90

NELSON, Mary A., m. Calvin H. **WHEELER**, Feb. 6, 1842   64

NEWELL, Clarissa M., m. Nathan W. **CHARTER**, b. of Ellington, Apr. 20,
1843   69

Harriet, m. Harvey **DIMMICK**, b. of Ellington, Feb. 4, 1824   12-12a

John Lewis, m. Huldah **BRADLEY**, June 9, 1821   3

Nathaniel, of Ellington, m. Nancy An[n] **ROCKWELL**, of Vernon,
Oct. 12, 1846   85

NEWTON, Esther, m. Congdon P. **LOOMIS**, b. of Enfield, Apr. 8, 1838   53

NILES, Laura E., m. William A. **GAGER**, b. of Ellington, Nov. 23, 1845   79

NORMAN, Mary Jane, of Vernon, m. Francis E. **WHITAKER**, of East
Windsor, Nov. 9, 1846   86

NYE, Elijah C., m. Julia A. **M'KINNEY**, Nov. 30, 1843   72

OCRY, Phebe, m. Richard **DANIELS**, b. of Hartford, Conn., Feb. 10, 1839   55

OLCOTT, Betsey, of Coventry, m. Sidney **PITKIN**, Dec. 10, 1823   11-11a

John T., of Vernon, m. Mrs. Melina **HANOVER**, of Somers, [Apr. 8],
1849   96-7

OSBORN, OSBORNE, Nelson R., of East Windsor, m. Jannet **BLODGET**,
of Ellington, Jan. 20, 1836   45

W[illia]m A., of Pittsfield, Mass., m. Harriet E. **FULLER**, of Ellington,
May 10, 1846   82

PAGE, Edward, m. Chloe **MANLEY**, of Ellington, Jan. 1, 1823   7

Sophronia, m. Silvester **CHARTER**, b. of Enfield, Jan. 1, 1851   102

PARKER, Clarissa B., of South Coventry, m. Frederick **MERTEN**, of East
Windsor, Oct. 18, 1847   89

Ephraim, m. Persis **SMITH**, b. of Ellington, Aug. 29, 1844   73

John, m. Persis **GRAY**, of Enfield, Sept. 19, 1844   73

Jonas S., m. Malissa I. **EDMUNDS**, of Vernon, Rockville Society,
Mar, 28, 1847   87

PARKISS, Alpheus, m. Maria **PARKISS**, b. of Ellington, Feb. [ ], 1846   80

Eli, of Ellington, m. Marsha **HAMILTON**, of Hartford, Sept. 20, 1840   59

Ely F., of Ellington, m. Harriet J. **JAMES**, of Meriden, Jan. 2, 1845   75

Harriet, colored, of Ellington, m. Jacob **MORRISON**, colored, of
Somers, Sept. 29, 1833   37

Louisa, m. Lemuel **HENRY**, Nov. 24, 1831   31

Maria, m. Alpheus **PARKISS**, b. of Ellington, Feb. [ ], 1846   80

PARSONS, Abel, Jr., of Somers, m. Mary **BURDICK**, of Ellington, June
2, 1836   47

Calvin G., of East Windsor, m. Elisabeth **CHAPMAN**, of Ellington,
May 24, 1849   97

Jabez, of Enfield, m. Harriet **ALLEN**, of Ellington, Oct. 17, 1833   38

Page

PARSONS, (cont.)
James R., of Ludlow, Mass., m. Martha HAMILTON, of Ellington,
    Apr. 19, 1837   50
Nathaniel, of Somers, m. Martha PHILLIPS, of Ellington, Jan. 5, 1831   28
PATTON, Robert, of Tolland, m. Mary E. COMSTOCK, of Ellington, Feb.
    6, 1843   68
PAULK, George Martin, of Rockville, m. Abby Holten SMITH, of
    Ellington, Jan. 5, 1848   91-2
PEASE, Aaron, of Chatham, m. Loranza M. JOHNSON, of Ellington,
    Dec. 23, 1831   32
Ames, of Somers, m. Asaneth MOORE, of Ellington, May 24, 1849   97
Calvin Otis, m. Jamima NEFF, Dec. 29, 1839, at Ellington   58
Clarissa, m. Charles SAUNDERS, b. of Ellington, Apr. 1, 1832   32
Delia, of Ellington, m. Henry HUBBARD, of Hartford, Aug. 12, 1832   34-34a
Lotrop, of Vernon, m. Sally GOODELL, of Ellington, Apr. 1, 1841   62
Lovicy, of Enfield, m. Henry L. WRIGHT, of Granville, Jan. 2, 1837,
    in Ellington   49
Mary, of Ellington, m. Daniel AVERY, of Stafford, Jan. 3, 1843,
    at Ellington   68
Polly, m. Asa C. SHELDON, b. of Somers, Aug. 24, 1837   51
Reuben, of Wilbraham, Mass., m. Hannah CRANE, of Ellington, Oct.
    12, 1829   24
Roxana, of Ellington, m. Anson FOWLER, of Lebanon, Jan. 13, 1850   98
Salman, m. Azubah WOODWORTH, b. of Ellington, Dec. 31, 1840   61
Saphronia, of Ellington, m. Dan CHAFFEE, of Hartford, Ct.,
    Oct. 23, 1850   100
Theodore B., of Somers, m. Lydia J. RUSSELL, of Ellington, Apr.
    26, 1846   81
PEMBER, Anna, of Ellington, m. Martin BEEBE, Apr. 15, 1823   9
David S., m. Patty WARNOR, Nov. 19, 1820   1
Justus, m. Louisa GIFFORD, b. of Ellington, Apr. 23, 1833   35
Justus, m. Sarah FARMER, b. of Ellington, Sept. 22, 1841   63
Pamelia, of Ellington, m. Jeramas TAYLER, of East Pennsylvania,
    May 6, 1847   88
PERKINS, William H., m. Rachel F. BENTON, of Glastonbury, Sept. 4,
    1835   44
PERRIN, Ann E., of Vernon, m. Charles E. FISH, of Tolland, Sept. 28,
    1845   78
Asahel H., of Vernon, m. Mary W. CHAPMAN, of Ellington, Apr. 22,
    1842   66
PHELPS, Joseph S., of Somers, m. Harriet HITCHCOK, of Bloomfield,
    Nov. 22, 1837   52
PHILLIPS, Asa, of Somers, m. Esther WADSWORTH, of Ellington, July
    6, 1823   9
Martha, of Ellington, m. Nathaniel PARSONS, of Somers, Jan. 5, 1831   28
Mary A., of Ellington, m. Elijah DIMMICK, of Peru, Ill., June 7, 1842   66
Nathaniel, of Ellington, m. Maria WILLIAMS, of Westfield, July
    30, 1844   72

Page

PHILLIPS, (cont.)

Otis, of Somers, m. Martha An[n] **MUMFORD,** of Springfield, Mass.,
May 25, 1848   94

Permelia, of Somers, m. Darius **CRANE,** of Ellington, Nov. 23, 1845   79

PIERCE, Eli, m. Mary **ALLEN,** b. of Ellington, Nov. 27, 1823   11

Eli, m. Mary **ALLEN,** b. of Ellington, July 27, 1824   11a

Eli, of East Windsor, m. Wealthy **SCOTT,** of Somers, Mar.10, 1825   15-15a

Shepard, of York, State of New York, m. Mary C. **PITKIN,** of
Ellington, Apr. 27, 1826   17

PINNEY, Albert, of Ellington, m. Lavinia A. **TIBBALS,** of Tolland, Jan.
27, 1846   80

Andrew, m. Mary **MOORE,** b. of Ellington, Jan. 23, 1833   35

Benjamin, Jr., m. Caroline **SMITH,** of Ellington, Jan. 18, 1832   32

E. C. V., m. Harriet P. **MOODY,** b. of Ellington, June 8, 1851   104

Elisabeth, of Ellington, m. William P. **EARL,** of Hartford, Apr.
13, 1836   46

Eunice, of Ellington, m. Oliver H. **KING,** Esq., of Vernon, Nov. 24,
1824   14

Henry, of Ellington, m. Mary **JOHNSON,** of Stafford, Oct. 19, 1848   96

Nelson, m. Miranda **McKINNEY,** of Ellington, Dec. 27, 1827   21

Nelson E., of Ellington, m. Roxana R **HIBBARD,** of Tolland, May [ ],
1845   77

Persis, of Ellington, m. Ariel **FLINT,** of Quincy, Ill., June 6, 1832   33-33a

Susan E., m. Elisha N. **WILLIAMS,** Nov. 19, 1840   59

PITKIN, Eleazer S., of East Hartford, m. Asenath **McCRAY,** of Ellington,
Nov. 13, 1822   7

Elisabeth, m. Elisha **SMITH,** b. of Ellington, Sept. 8, 1846, in
Ellington   84

Joseph B., of Tolland, m. Louisa **WELLS,** of Ellington, Aug. 6, 1823   10

Mary An[n], of Ellington, m. W[illia]m P. **TOWNSEND,** of Lockport,
N. Y., June 7, 1842   67

Mary C., of Ellington, m. Shepard **PIERCE,** of York, N. Y., Apr.
27, 1826   17

Sidney, m. Betsey **OLCOTT,** of Coventry, Dec. 10, 1823   11-11a

POND, Amanda(?), of Bristol, m. Jane **LOVELL,** of Ellington, Apr. 23,
1851   103

PORTER, Emily, m. William C. **RUSSELL,** b. of Ellington, Oct. 19, 1843 71

POST, John H., of Hebron, m. Loisa **WEST,** of Ellington, May 12, 1824 12-12a

POTTAGE, Betsey, m. Asa **FARNHAM,** Mar. 27, 1825   15-15a

PRATT, Almon, m. Sarah M. **RICHARDS,** Aug. 28, 1844, both of
Ellington   73

Rebecca, m. Oscar **ELY,** b. of Ellington, Aug. 28, 1844   73

PRISBEY, Alfred A., of Willington, m. Emeline **MOODY,** of Ellington,
Apr. 9, 1848   92-3

RANSOM, RANSAN, Daniel W., of Ellington, m. Prudence **TAYLER,** of
South Glastonbury, Oct. 1, 1846   85

Fuller, of Vernon, m. Miranda **FOSTER,** of Ellington, Mar. 18, 1847   87

Henry G., m. Fanny E. **McCRAY,** b. of Ellington, Mar. 12, 1848   92-3

Page

RANSOM, RANSAN, (cont.)

William L., m. Julia **CHAPMAN**, b. of Ellington, May 21, 1833   36

RATHBONE, RATHBURN, Wealthy, of Vernon, m. William **WOOD**, of
Hartford, June 4, 1837   50

READ, REED, Austin, of Hebron, m. Mary **RICHARDSON**, of Ellington,
Oct. 20, 1824   13

Cordelia, of Rockville, Vernon, m. William **WALTON**, July 18, 1847   89

Eli, of Ludlow, Mass., m. Sarah T. **CHAPMAN**, of Vernon, Sept. 9,
1850   100

REMINGTON, Giles, m. Abigail **HOUSE**, of Hartford, Dec. 14, 1831, at
Ellington   31

RICH, Nelson H., of Chicopee, Mass., m. Hannah H. **FULLER**, of
Ellington, Nov. 12, 1850   101

RICHARDS, Sarah M., m. Almon **PRATT**, b. of Ellington, Aug. 28, 1844   73

RICHARDSON, Daniel, of East Windsor, m. Betsey **BUTTON**, of
Ellington, May 27, 1829   23

Harvey, m. Eliza **SLATER**, b. of Enfield, Apr. 22, 1839   56

Mary, of Ellington, m. Austin **REED**, of Hebron, Oct. 20, 1824   13

William, of Somers, m. Jane L. **EATON**, of Stafford, Oct. 6, 1846   85

RIDER, Harriet, of Rockville, m. William M. **BARTHOLUS**, Apr. 12, 1846   81

Otis F., of Stafford, m. Mrs. Mary An[n] **ANDERSON**, of Ellington,
Nov. 29, 1849   97

Watson, m. Zady **ABBY**, of Rockville in Vernon, July 21, 1844, in
Ellington   72

RISING, Ervin, of Ellington, m. Sarah F. **ALLEN**, of East Windsor, May
23, 1839   57

RISLEY, Lorenzo, m. Abigail **BEASLY**, b. of Ellington, Apr. 25, 1852   105

ROBINSON, Richard, of East Windsor, m. Mary An[n] **CRANDALL**, of
Ellington, Apr. 15, 1841   62

ROCKWELL, Nancy An[n], of Vernon, m. Nathaniel **NEWELL**, of
Ellington, Oct. 12, 1846   85

ROGERS, Mary E., m. William M. **TIRNNY**(?), b. of Ellington, May 19,
1831   29

Robert M., m. Olive **HAMILTON**, b. of Ellington, Dec. 6, 1831   31

ROLLO, William E., of Springfield, Mass., m. Jane T. **FULLER**, of
Ellington, Oct. 26, 1845   78

ROYCE, An[n], of Tolland, m. Israel **BAKER**, Sr., of Vernon, Nov. 21,
1847   90

RUSSELL, Henry P., of Acadia, Missouri, m. Mary **WHITON**, of Ellington,
Feb. 22, 1843   69

Lemuel, m. Lydia **TAYLOR**, b. of Ellington, Apr. 4, 1821   2

Lemuel, m. Eliza **MANLEY**, b. of Ellington, Nov. 17, 1844   74

Lydia J., of Ellington, m. Theodore B. **PEASE**, of Somers,
Apr. 26, 1846   81

Mary Amelia, of Ellington, m. Joseph B. **HOPKINS**, of Springfield,
Sept. 19, 1832   34-34a

Mary T., of Ellington, m. Elijah P. **KIMBALL**, of Springfield,
Mass., Oct. 27, 1836   48

Page

RUSSELL, (cont.)

William C., m. Emily **PORTER**, b. of Ellington, Oct. 19, 1843   71

SACKET, Seth E., of Springfield, Mass., m. Roxa A. **CHAPMAN**, of
Ellington, Jan. 19, 1845   76

SADD, Emily, Mrs., of Ellington, m. Henry **STOUGHTON**, of South
Windsor, Nov. 27, 1851   104

Roswell R., of East Windsor, m. Laura **ALLEN**, of Ellington, May
1, 1833   36

Wells F., of East Windsor, m. Emely **ALLEN**, of Ellington, Sept.
9, 1841   62

ST. CLAIR, Betsey, m. William C. **MAYNARD**, b. of Ellington, Aug. 3,
1831   30

SAUNDERS, Charles, m. Clarissa **PEASE**, b. of Ellington, Apr. 1,
1832   32

SCHULZ, Mina, m. Louis **BOAKER**, Sept. 17, 1853   105

SCOTT, Wealthy, of Somers, m. Eli **PIERCE**, of East Windsor, Mar.
10, 1825   15-15a

SCRIPTURE, John, of Willington, m. Sabra **MUNSELL**, of East Windsor,
Nov. 23, 1825   15-16

Ralph, of Vernon, m. Sarah B. **LINCOLN**, of Ellington, Mar. 31,
1841, in Ellington   61

SELEW, Roland, of Glastonbury, m. Haney A. **KIBBE**, of Ellington,
Dec. 27, 1838   55

SEXTON, Amanda B., of Ellington, m. W[illia]m P. **SPALDING**, of Sault
St. Marie, Michigan, Feb. 22, 1848   91-2

Jonathan C., of Ellington, m. Hannah **CONVERSE**, of Tolland, Feb.
9, 1823   8

Joseph, of Somers, m. Caroline **WARNER**, of Ellington, Nov. 14, 1844   74

Lyman, of Somers, m. Mary Ann **SMITH**, of Ellington, Nov. 16, 1826   17

Mary B., of Ellington, m. Amos **LIVELY**(?), of Havanna, Alabama,
Sept. 22, 1836   48

SHAW, Marcus, of Wilbraham, Mass., m. Emeline **CHAPMAN**, of
Ellington, Apr. 20, 1842   66

SHELDON, Asa C., m. Polly **PEASE**, b. of Somers, Aug. 24, 1837   51

Eunice, H., of Springfield, Mass., m. David **WAKEFIELD**, Jr.,
of Somers, Apr. 28, 1842   66

SILLSWERTH, Israel, of Hanabal, N. Y., m. Sarah **HAMILTON**, of
Ellington, Oct. 1, 1834   42

[SIMMONS], **SIMON**, **SIMONS**, Adaline M., of Enfield, m. Wells
SPENCER, Oct. 15, 1845   78

Lewis, of Hartford, m. Louisa **BLAKE**, of Manchester, Sept. 5, 1843   70

Parsons, m. Clarissa **THRALL**, b. of Ellington, Nov. 24, 1836   48

Wareham T., m. Fanny **BUCKLAND**, Oct. 13, 1833   38

SKINNER, Austin, of East Windsor, m. Harriet **SPEAR**, of Ellington,
Feb. 16, 1823   8

SLAFTER, Emily, of Ellington, m. Henry **MEACHAM**, of Somers, Jan.
4, 1847, in Ellington   86

Lydia, of Ellington, m. Jesse **WYLLYS**, of Tolland, Nov. 6, 1820   2

Page

TRACY, (cont.)
    Addison L., of Vernon, Rockville, m. An[n] Louisa **CHARTER,** of
        Ellington, Apr. 5, 1848   94
    Wallace, of Coventry, m. Elisabeth **WOLCOTT,** of Vernon, Sept. 23,
        1845   78
TRASK, Lorin, of Stafford, m. Laura An[n] **GREEN,** of Ellington, June
    25, 1848   95
VAN HORNE, Elmira J., of East Windsor, m. Lobeah(?) **SMITH,** of
    Vernon, June 10, 1840   58
VINTON, William H., of Monson, Mass., m. Elizabeth **JOHNSON,** of
    Ellington, May 8, 1839   56
WADSWORTH, Chloe, of Ellington, m. Jonathan **CARPENTER,** of
    Ashford, Apr. 13, 1823   8
    Esther, of Ellington, m. Asa **PHILLIPS,** of Somers, July 6, 1823   9
    John, m. Mary **WARNER,** Apr. 24, 1828   21
WAKEFIELD, David, Jr., of Somers, m. Eunice, H. **SHELDON,** of
    Springfield, Mass., Apr. 28, 1842   66
WALDOW, Sophia, of Ellington, m. Wolcott **DARTT,** of Manchester, Feb.
    9, 1826   15-16
WALES, Alvin, of Chicopee Falls, Mass., m. Eliza **WARNER,** of Hartford,
    Aug. 7, 1842   67
WALKER, Frederick M., of Enfield, m. Mary An[n] **DOW*,** May 18, 1843;
    she was of Ellington *("DAN?")   69
WALLACE, Betsey, of Ellington, m. Joseph **FULLER,** June 27, 1822   5
WALTON, Nathaniel P., of Montpelier, Vt., m. Amanda **TANNER,** of
    Ellington, Sept. 26, 1841   63
    William, m. Cordelia **REED,** of Rockville, Vernon, July 18, 1847   89
WARD, Esther, m. Jeremiah **KING,** b. of Ellington, Nov. 15, 1821   4
WARFIELD, Curtis, of Hartford, m. Betsey **COTTON,** of Vernon, Nov. 30,
    1835   45
WARNER, WARNOR, Abigail, m. Aaron **CHARTER,** Jr., Oct. 8, 1835   44
    Ann, of Ellington, m. Jonas **BROWN,** of Plainfield, Mass., Sept.
        26, 1822   6
    Betsey, m. Eleazer **WHITON,** b. of Ellington, Apr. 25, 1827   19
    Caroline, of Ellington, m. Joseph **SEXTON,** of Somers, Nov. 14, 1844   74
    Dan, m. Mary E. **CHAFFEE,** b. of Ellington, Feb. 25, 1834   40
    Eli, of Ellington, m. Minerva C. **STRICKLAND,** of Glastonbury,
        June 23, 1840   59
    Eliza, of Hartford, m. Alvin **WALES,** of Chickopee Falls, Mass.,
        Aug. 7, 1842   67
    Ellen, m. Julius **KIBBEE,** b. of Ellington, Jan. 21, 1851   102
    Hannah, of Ellington, m. Constant **BROWN,** of Peterham,
        Mass., Oct. 3, 1825   15-16
    Harriet, m. Guilford **McCRAY,** b. of Ellington, May 13, 1821   3
    Horace, m. Matilda **MARTIN,** of Ellington, Oct. 1, 1826   17
    Lemuel, Jr., m. Phila **FOSTER,** of Ellington, July 9, 1820, by Asa
        Willey, J. P.   1
    Lora, of Ellington, m. Samuel M. **BLISS,** of Wilbraham, Mass.,